Perspectives in Metropolitan Research VII

Published with the kind support of the Free and Hanseatic City of Hamburg, Ministry of Science, Research, Equalities and Districts

T0335111

The series "Perspectives in Metropolitan Research" is edited by Annette Bögle, Vice President for Research at the HafenCity University

HafenCity Universität Hamburg
Referat für Forschung
Henning–Voscherau–Platz 1
20457 Hamburg
forschung@hcu-hamburg.de

Cover: Johannes Arlt/laif

Editors of this volume: Joachim Thiel, Venetsiya Dimitrova,
Johanna Ruge
Editorial team: Annette Bögle, Venetsiya Dimitrova,
Johannes Dreher, Lennart Fahnenmüller, Gernot Grabher,
Monika Grubbauer, Johanna Ruge, Joachim Thiel
Editorial assistance: Lisa Marie Frank
Copy-editing: Mariangela Palazzi-Williams
Design and Layout: abseiten (Mehmet Alatur | Katrin Bahrs)
Lithography: Bild1Druck
Printed in the European Union

Bibliographic information published by the Deutsche
Nationalbibliothek.
The Deutsche Nationalbibliothek lists this publication in the
Deutsche Nationalbibliografie; detailed bibliographic data are
available on the Internet at http://dnb.d-nb.de

jovis Verlag GmbH
Lützowstraße 33
10785 Berlin

www.jovis.de

jovis books are available worldwide in selected bookstores. Please
contact your nearest bookseller or visit www.jovis.de for information concerning your local distribution.

ISBN 978-3-86859-678-6

Perspectives in Metropolitan Research

Constructing Innovation: How Large-Scale Projects
Drive Novelty in the Construction Industry

Joachim Thiel, Venetsiya Dimitrova, Johanna Ruge (eds.)

Contents

Foto Series II

Synthesis

Contributors

Acknowledgements

This book is the result of a group effort. It builds on the contributions, support, assistance and feedback of the numerous people with whom we collaborated throughout a three-and-a-half-year long process of research and a more than year-long process of writing, editing and finalizing.

First and foremost, we would like to express our deep gratitude to our numerous interview partners, who shared their time, knowledge, and stories with us. Without their perspectives and invaluable insights this project would not have been possible. By letting us hear their memories, they enabled us to look beyond superficial perceptions, and instead get to know intimately six truly outstanding construction projects, each unique in its own way.

We are also grateful to the Ministry of Science, Research, Equalities and Districts of the Free and Hanseatic City of Hamburg for their financial support of the research project "Large-Scale Projects as Drivers of Innovation in the Constuction Industry."

Special thanks are due to our commentators and the photographers, who openly embraced both our view of large-scale projects and our research results, and dedicated their time and personal efforts to our book. Their commentaries and photo series contribute significantly to the collection and add inestimable value by providing additional, enriching perspectives.

Additionally, we highly appreciate the support and guidance of Tim Vogel and Martin Küpper at jovis publishers, copy-editor Mariangela Palazzi-Williams, and our graphic designer Katrin Bahrs from the agency abseiten.

Last, but not least, we would like to thank the large team of colleagues at TUHH and HCU who supported us as principal investigators in the conception of the project, and as research associates and student assistants in the collection, transcription, and analysis of the rich empirical material throughout the duration of the project: Cornelius Herstatt, Sandra-Luisa Moschner, Lilly Altmeyer, Lukas Boy, David Ehrenreich, Matthias Engelmayer, Wajahat Hasan, Lena Hering, Pablo Lapettina, Simon Mayer, Marten Menk, Jantje Morgenstern, Daniel Weber, Linus Weilbacher, and Arne Witte.

The editorial team

Annette Bögle, Venetsiya Dimitrova, Johannes Dreher, Lennart Fahnenmüller, Gernot Grabher, Monika Grubbauer, Johanna Ruge, and Joachim Thiel

April 2021

Introduction

Large-Scale Construction Projects as Drivers of Innovation? Introduction to the Book

Joachim Thiel/Venetsiya Dimitrova/
Johanna Ruge

The conjunction between large-scale construction projects and innovation appears counterintuitive, at least in two respects: for one thing, the recent record of large projects worldwide is anything but a success story (e.g. Flyvbjerg 2011, 2014; Flyvbjerg et al. 2003). According to Flyvbjerg (2011), mega-projects are subject to an "iron law" of chronic underestimation of costs and overestimation of benefits. Big, it seems, is associated with "fragility" (Ansar et al. 2017) rather than with novelty. For another thing, an alleged lack of innovativeness similarly holds for the construction industry in general. Construction firms perform poorly in an inter-industry comparison according to classic innovation indicators such as patents and R&D expenditure (Butzin and Rehfeld 2013; *The Economist* 2017; Reichstein et al. 2005). No wonder, then, that scholarship on innovation tends to ignore the construction business as field of inquiry.

And yet, this is not to say that the design and production of buildings are based purely on the repetitive application of what Groak (1992, p. 6) refers to as "well-tried technical solutions." Throughout its history, the construction industry has regularly introduced new technologies and processes (e.g. Ågren and Wing 2014). More specifically, at present, new technological requirements as well as the digitalization and internationalization of the entire value chain challenge the industry to transform accordingly.

What is more, when looking at the history of construction in greater detail, it seems that specifically large-scale projects have regularly leveraged novel technologies, as well as design and engineering solutions. Crystal Palace, the Eiffel Tower, and St. Pancras Station, to name but a few prominent examples, are regarded as milestones in the implementation of steel structures and prefabrication techniques (Ågren and Wing 2014). And even the Sydney Opera House is less famous as the "great planning disaster" that it in fact was (Hall 1982) than for its innovative concrete shells and the image as one of the architectural icons of the twentieth century (Groák 1992). While this evidence is obvious, there is very little systematic research that tackles how the contribution of large-scale projects to novel technologies, tools and techniques in fact comes about.

A systematic exploration of large-scale projects as innovation vehicles in construction hence requires one to venture into uncharted conceptual terrain. With this book we seek to enter this terrain, and we set out our journey from the nature of construction as a specific project-based industry that is—at least—ambivalent with regard to the industry's innovative capacities (Ekstedt et al. 1999). Building on that, we follow a specific research approach by framing construction projects as "socio-material" systems (e.g., Orlikowski 2010) and looking into these projects in a truly interdisciplinary fashion.

Construction as a Specific Project-Based Industry

The extant literature on construction innovation that has been produced over the past decades in project and construction management research (e.g. Brady and Davies 2014; Dubois and Gadde 2002; Gann and Salter 2000; Harty 2008; Slaughter 2000; Winch 1998), but also in regional studies and economic geography (Butzin and Rehfeld 2013; Rehfeld 2012), essentially revolves around the project-based nature of construction. Two features exemplify this nature: complexity and singularity. That is, every building comprises an assemblage of numerous and diverse components, and the process of assembling is performed by a multiplicity of actors from the construction value chain (Dubois and Gadde 2002). In addition, buildings are one-offs, and they are produced by "temporary organizations" (Lundin and Söderholm 1995) that are established as "quasi-firms" (Eccles 1981) for every single project.

With regard to the generation of innovation, complexity and singularity of construction projects have ambivalent effects. Diverse and changing constellations and tasks create both opportunities (Dubois and Gadde 2002) and pressures (Slaughter 2000) to develop novel solutions. However, the diversity and dynamics of actor constellations imply fragmentation and thereby eventually tend to inhibit the materialization of novelties (Harty 2008). When it comes to the diffusion of innovations, the project nature of construction seems to be a real obstacle, as the transfer of both components (Harty 2008) and knowledge (Gann and Salter 2000) from project to project is difficult.

In addition, construction projects exhibit two features that significantly impact the industry's degree of innovativeness: the first relates to the role of clients, or project owners (e.g., Gann and Salter 2000; Nam and Tatum 1997; Slaughter 2000). Winch (1998) refers to the client in "complex product systems," such as flight simulators, military systems or aircrafts, as benchmark for a client that is supportive of the generation of novelty. The author maintains, however, that construction clients in general are not able to fulfill this role. What is more, the dominant client in the construction business is the public sector, and state bureaucracies have a bad reputation when it comes to their capacity to support novelty (Siebel et al. 2001). However, recent work on UK projects shows that a systematic upgrading of public sector agencies to best practice clients in construction projects can induce far-reaching innovations (Brady and Davies 2014; Davies and Mackenzie 2014).

The second aspect concerns the specific nature of the construction output: the product comprises for each project a singular artifact that, for one, incorporates a complex technical system that is, for another, essentially perceived publicly. The design of buildings leaves a long-lasting mark on the character of public space (Gann and Salter 2000). Innovation in construction therefore essentially embraces technical aspects of buildings as well as design aspects that are judged in public and professional discourses (Grubbauer and Steets 2014). What is more, both features are closely interconnected as design ambition is likely to generate novel tools and techniques in the construction supply chain (Boland Jr. et al. 2007).

Studying Construction Innovation: Socio-Materiality and Interdisciplinarity

While over the last decades research on innovation has shifted from a classic, single-firm centered and product-cycle-driven model of innovation processes (Abernathy and Utterback 1978) to more relational (e.g., Tracey and Clark 2003) or open (e.g., Chesbrough 2003) approaches, the pertinent work still centers upon firms—as clearly discernible entities—that invest in novel products and/or processes in order to obtain competitive advantage in an abstract and anonymous marketplace. As explained above, such analytical clarity holds for the construction industry only to a limited extent.

The approach to studying innovation, on which this book builds, seeks to embrace the aforementioned "exceptionalism" that the construction industry exhibits with regard to how innovations arise and materialize. We see our research as in line with recent scholarly work that has sought to address innovation in the construction business in a more comprehensive and pluralistic fashion (Havenvid Ingemansson et al. 2019; Orstavik et al. 2015). More specifically, our inquiry into construction innovation is both *socio-material* and *interdisciplinary*. For one thing,

hence, we conceive of construction projects as socio-material systems in which organizational ("project") and technical ("building") aspects are genuinely interwoven (Styhre 2017). For another, we have carried out our research in four sub-projects (SPs), each of which represents a particular qualification profile: Urban and Regional Economics (SP 1); Technology and Innovation Management (SP 2); Urban History and Theory (SP 3); Structural Analysis and Design (SP 4). This team constellation does not only cover a broad spectrum of disciplines. Building on team members' recent research experience—geographies of project organizations, user-driven innovation, knowledge practices in architecture, structural analysis—the team structure also mirrors the different features of construction innovation (see Figure 1): the coordination in a temporary *project* (SP 1); the specific role of a concrete *client* (SP 2); the role of the *designers*, both architects and engineers (SP 3); the physical and technical properties as well as materialization processes of the eventual *building* (SP 4).

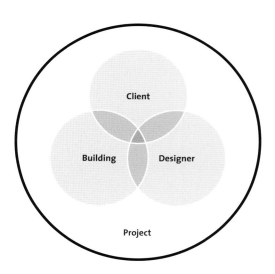

Figure 1: Determinants of Innovation in Construction Projects as Structure of Sub-Projects

The sub-projects were joined together through the cooperative work on six case studies of recent large-scale construction ventures in Germany: two architectural icons (the Elbphilharmonie in Hamburg; the European Central Bank in Frankfurt); two infrastructural complexes (Berlin Central Station; Wehrhahn Underground Line in Düsseldorf); two technically sophisticated bridges (the Gänsebachtal Railroad Bridge in Thuringia; the Kochertal Highway Bridge close to Stuttgart)[1].

1 See a more comprehensive introduction to the cases in the following conceptual and methodological part of the book.

Structure of the Book

This book is the outcome of a collective endeavor, in two senses: it is the result of a three-and-a-half-year interdisciplinary research process that comprised the joint gathering and analysis of a huge amount of particularly qualitative data. The book is also the product of collective writing. Each of the six chapters in the "research results" part of the book has at least two authors, but has also undergone a process of intensive mutual commenting and double-checking across the entire research team.

This "research results" section constitutes the core of the book. Within this core, innovation in construction is examined from six different perspectives. Around this core, we have created a framework in which we introduce the book and our research work (this introduction); outline the conceptual and methodological parameters of both the research project and the book ("studying innovation in construction"); and synthesize the findings.

In the conceptual and methodological part, **Joachim Thiel** introduces the guiding conceptual framework of innovation, which was jointly developed during the research process and that informed the writing of the individual chapters. **Monika Grubbauer** highlights the challenges that arose throughout the research project due to its interdisciplinary approach. She describes the various ways in which the team addressed these challenges, and reflects on the potential of interdisciplinary research with respect to the built environment. **Lennart Fahnenmüller** and **Joachim Thiel** describe the research strategy of the project, emphasizing the process of selecting six cases and conducting in-depth case studies in an interdisciplinary team. In the last chapter of this section, **Venetsiya Dimitrova, Johannes Dreher,** and **Johanna Ruge** present the six selected cases of large-scale construction projects in more detail. They highlight important characteristics of each project with respect to its genesis as well as its outcome.

The book's core contains the results of the research project. It comprises six chapters written by different disciplinary and interdisciplinary teams. The single chapters build on the rich empirical material and draw on an extensive body of academic literature, including construction and project management, economic geography, engineering science, and the sociology of professions. The contributions thus deliver different disciplinary and conceptual perspectives on how large-scale construction projects contribute to the making and diffusion of innovations. To each of the empirical chapters there is a response by an internationally renowned scholar in the respective field, some of whom are also involved as experts in one of the examined projects, reflecting and expanding on the empirical findings and the theoretical contributions.

Joachim Thiel, Venetsiya Dimitrova, and **Johannes Dreher** conceptualize innovation in the construction industry as a change of "cultural frames". For this purpose, they explore in-depth how project participants mobilize discursive, practical, and institutional resources, enact these resources, and translate them back into the discursive, practical, and institutional context. Their main argument is that large-scale construction ventures support the development and implementation, as well as the legitimation of novel ideas, techniques, and practices.

Johannes Dreher, Joachim Thiel, Gernot Grabher, and **Monika Grubbauer** focus on the still little explored spatiality of temporary organizing, investigating how innovation takes place across geographical space, and how proximity and distance facilitate or obstruct the making of novelty. The authors conclude that innovations in large-scale construction projects arise from the interplay between two opposing geographical dynamics: a centrifugal force required for putting together an inter-organizational network, and a centripetal force coming from the construction site as the center of gravity of this network.

In their chapter, **Joachim Thiel** and **Gernot Grabher** challenge the understanding of temporal ambiguities as a problem that needs to be solved, an issue that has long occupied project management research. Instead, they suggest that the significant longevity of large projects allows for embracing temporal properties of both temporary and permanent organizations in a complementary manner. The authors argue that it is precisely through the coexistence of multiple and ambiguous temporalities and their interplay that novelty can arise and materialize.

Lennart Fahnenmüller, Johanna Ruge, and **Annette Bögle** set their focus on the early project stage, analyzing how the way a project is defined impacts on its innovative capacity. The authors consider the role and perspective of structural engineers, analyzing different ways in which they are involved in the very beginning of large-scale projects and how these ways affect engineers' scope of action and eventually the project outcome. The authors conclude that early conscious and interdisciplinary approaches to define the project's aims can spur innovations over the project course.

In their contribution, **Johanna Ruge** and **Annette Bögle** consider the role of materiality for innovation in construction and analyze this topic from the largely unexplored perspective of structural engineers. By analyzing engineers' engagement with different dimensions of materiality and their implications for the realization of ambitious designs, they provide a theoretically and empirically grounded and differentiated understanding of both materiality in construction and the mechanisms behind innovation processes.

Venetsiya Dimitrova, Monika Grubbauer, Johanna Ruge, and **Annette Bögle** conceptualize large-scale construction projects as arenas both for the interactions between architects and engineers and for the negotiations between their distinct professional cultures. By empirically exploring different strategies of maintaining and of dissolving professional cultures, the authors argue that the continuous and coincidental interplay between cognitive dissonance and cognitive convergence serves as a source of innovation.

Two photo series frame the chapters and offer additional perspectives to large-scale projects and innovation in the construction industry. The photo series visually corroborate some of the arguments in the papers presented, drawing particular attention to the material side of construction innovation. In the first photography project, **Michael Zimmermann** depicts the realization of the pedestrian and cycle bridge Passerelle de la Paix in Lyon, which was completed in 2014. The photos reveal the often invisible process of the materialization of innovations. **Hagen Stier's** documentary series shows the recent demolition of the City-Hof building complex in Hamburg, and thus the de-materialization of what was once considered novel. In this way, he draws particular attention to the contexts as well as to the changing valuations and perspectives of large-scale construction projects and innovation.

In the concluding section, **Joachim Thiel, Venetsiya Dimitrova,** and **Johanna Ruge** synthesize the findings and reflect on how the research project and its results aid our understanding of how large-scale construction projects contribute to innovation in the construction sector.

References

Abernathy, W. J. and J. M. Utterback (1978). "Patterns of Industrial Innovation." *Technology Review* 80.7: pp. 40–47.

Ågren, R. and R. D. Wing (2014). "Five Moments in the History of Industrialized Building." *Construction Management and Economics* 32.1-2: pp. 7–15.

Ansar, A., B. Flyvbjerg, A. Budzier, and D. Lunn (2017). "Big is Fragile: An Attempt at Theorizing Scale." B. Flyvbjerg, ed. *The Oxford Handbook of Megaproject Management*. Oxford.

Boland Jr., R. J., K. Lyytinen, and Y. Yoo (2007). "Wakes of Innovation in Project Networks: The Case of Digital 3-D Representations in Architecture, Engineering, and Construction." *Organization Science* 18.4: pp. 631–647.

Brady, T. and A. Davies (2014). "Managing Structural and Dynamic Complexity: A Tale of Two Projects." *Project Management Journal* 45.4: pp. 21–38.

Butzin, A. and D. Rehfeld (2013). "The Balance of Change in Continuity in the German Construction Sector's Development Path." *Zeitschrift für Wirtschaftsgeographie* 57.1-2: pp. 15–26.

Chesbrough, H. (2003). "Open Innovation: Where We've Been and Where We're Going." *Research-Technology Management* 55.4: pp. 20–27.

Davies, A. and I. Mackenzie (2014). "Project Complexity and Systems Integration: Constructing the London 2012 Olympics and Paralympics Games." *International Journal of Project Management* 32.5: pp. 773–790.

Dubois, A. and L.-E. Gadde (2002). "The Construction Industry as a Loosely Coupled System: Implications for Productivity and Innovation." *Construction Management and Economics* 20.7: pp. 621–631.

Eccles, R. G. (1981). "The Quasifirm in the Construction Industry." *Journal of Economic Behavior and Organization* 2.4: pp. 335–357.

Economist (2017). "Least Improved. Efficiency Eludes the Construction Industry." *The Economist*, August 19: pp. 47–48.

Ekstedt, E., R. A. Lundin, A. Söderholm, and H. Wirdenius (1999). *Neo-Industrial Organising. Renewal by Action and Knowledge Formation in a Project-Intensive Economy.* London.

Flyvbjerg, B. (2011). "Over Budget, over Time, over and over Again: Managing Major Projects." P. W. G. Morris, J. K. Pinto, and J. Söderlund, eds. *The Oxford Handbook of Project Management*. Oxford.

Flyvbjerg, B. (2014). "What You Should Know about Megaprojects and Why: An Overview." *Project Management Journal* 45.2: pp. 6–19.

Flyvbjerg, B., N. Bruzelius, and W. Rothengatter (2003). *Megaprojects and Risk: An Anatomy of Ambition.* Cambridge.

Gann, D. M. and A. J. Salter (2000). "Innovation in Project-Based, Service-Enhanced Firms: The Construction of Complex Products and Systems." *Research Policy* 29.7-8: pp. 955–972.

Groák, S. (1992). *The Idea of Building*. New York.

Grubbauer, M. and S. Steets (2014). "The Making of Architects: Knowledge Production and Legitimation in Education, Professional Practice and International Networks." *Architectural Theory Review* 19.1: pp. 4–9.

Hall, P. (1982). *Great Planning Disasters*. California Series in Urban Development. Berkeley.

Harty, C. (2008). "Implementing Innovation in Construction: Contexts, Relative Boundedness and Actor-Network Theory." *Construction Management and Economics* 26.10: pp. 1029–1041.

Havenvid Ingemansson, M., Å. Linné, L. E. Bygballe, and C. Harty (2019). "In Pursuit of a New Understanding of Innovation in the Construction Industry: The Significance of Connectivity." M. Havenvid Ingemansson, Å. Linné, L. E. Bygballe, and C. Harty, eds. *The Connectivity of Innovation in the Construction Industry*. London.

Lundin, R. A. and A. Söderholm (1995). "A Theory of the Temporary Organization." *Scandinavian Journal of Management* 11.4: pp. 437–455.

Nam, C. H. and C. B. Tatum (1997). "Leaders and Champions for Construction Innovation." *Construction Management and Economics* 15.3: pp. 259–270.

Orlikowski, W. J. (2010). "The Sociomateriality of Organisational Life: Considering Technology in Management Research." *Cambridge Journal of Economics* 34.1: pp. 125–141.

Orstavik, F., A. Dainty, and C. Abbott (2015). "Introduction." F. Orstavik, A. Dainty, and C. Abbott, eds. *Construction Innovation*. Chichester

Rehfeld, D. (2012). "Innovationsbiographien in der Bauwirtschaft." A. Butzin, D. Rehfeld, and B. Widmaier, eds. *Innovationsbiographien: Räumliche und sektorale Dynamik* (1 ed., Vol. 1). Baden-Baden.

Reichstein, T., A. J. Salter, and D. M. Gann (2005). "Last among Equals: A Comparison of Innovation in Construction, Services and Manufacturing in the UK." *Construction Management and Economics* 23.6: pp. 631–644.

Siebel, W., O. Ibert, and H.-N. Mayer (2001). "Staatliche Organisation von Innovation: Die Planung des Unplanbaren unter widrigen Umständen durch einen unbegabten Akteur." *Leviathan* 29.4: pp. 526–543.

Slaughter, E. S. (2000). "Implementation of Construction Innovations." *Building Research & Information* 28.1: pp. 2–17.

Styhre, A. (2017). "Thinking about Materiality: The Value of a Construction Management and Engineering View." *Construction Management and Economics* 35.1-2: pp. 35–44.

Tracey, P. and G. L. Clark (2003). "Alliances, Networks and Competitive Strategy: Rethinking Clusters of Innovation." *Growth and Change* 34.1: pp. 1–16.

Winch, G. M. (1998). "Zephyrs of Creative Destruction: Understanding the Management of Innovation in Construction." *Building Research & Information* 26.4: pp. 268–279.

Studying Innovation in Construction

Framing Construction Innovation

Joachim Thiel

What does innovation, the key notion around which this book revolves, actually comprise? While there is a lot of discussion and disagreement in the literature around how innovation comes about (see Bathelt et al. 2017), the basic definition of the term is unequivocal. In a very "simple and technical definition," Cohendet and Simon (2017, p. 33) term innovation "the process of translating an idea into a good or a service that creates value." What is illuminating is the relative clause: "that creates value". It points to the fact that innovation entails more than the mere creation of something new. An invention, such as a new idea, technique or product, is only considered innovative when it comes with a certain degree of acceptance, added value or even economic success. Expressed as a simple equation, it might look like this:

Innovation = Novelty + X

where X represents "exploitation" (Roberts 1988), "success" (Brady and Hobday 2011), or "value creation" (Cohendet and Simon 2017), for example. In addition, the equation also describes a process. The X is no automatic by-product of new ideas, but needs to be actively created through mechanisms of search, selection, implementation, and value capture (e.g., Kreiner 2015).

Neither the simple logic of novelty + X nor the processes of searching, selecting, implementing, and capturing are easily applicable to the construction industry. Given the singular nature of construction, the identification of X in the construction value chain is anything but a simple matter. As a (singular) one-off, every new building is novel by definition. But can it also be qualified as an innovation once it has been built? And, given the complexity of construction projects, buildings do not exhibit novelty as a discrete whole. Projects are complex systems assembled from myriads of components, put together in "an inter-organizational landscape" (Havenvid Ingemansson et al. 2019, p. 5) in which innovations develop in a diffuse and interdependent fashion. An organized process of value creation would be difficult to identify. How, then, should our research capture the X and the process of creating it?

We suggest addressing the two parts of the question separately. When it comes to defining the X we broaden the analytical horizon with regard to how the added value that turns new ideas into innovations is perceived. For this purpose, we build on recent work that addresses innovation as a "pervasive social phenomenon" rather than as a process "restricted to the labs of scientists and engineers, R&D departments in the private economy and ... artist's studios" (Hutter et al. 2015, p. 33). Hutter et al. (2015, p. 37) distinguish three different "observation forms" of innovation: "semantics, pragmatics and grammar." Based on this differentiation, we can describe the X that transforms an invention into an innovation on three different levels. A new idea, practice or artifact would be an innovation (a) when acknowledged in a professional or public discourse (semantics); (b) when proven to be a solution for a problem that comes up in practice (pragmatics); and (c) when it has an impact on the "systems of rules" (p. 37) that constitutes the institutional framework for professional practice (grammar). The three levels are not independent of each other: discourses and rules, for instance, influence practical solutions and vice versa (p. 38). Through the emphasis on rules and discourses we can also capture the soft (e.g., aesthetic) aspects of innovation in construction.

To grasp how novelty turns into an innovation, i.e., how the process underlying the novelty + X-equation unfolds, we turn to what Garud et al. (2016, p. 456) call a "performative view" of innovation processes. Here, we follow an approach to micro-dynamics of innovation that "acknowledges the indeterminacy and openness of an ongoing process, and the futility of trying to control it ... ." This complex and contingent process unfolds in "chains of translations" (Czarniawska and Joerges 1996). In such chains, innovators seek strategically to manipulate relational or temporal settings by establishing and breaking linkages or by mobilizing events from the past, present and future (Garud et al. 2016) in order to promote their own projects and initiatives. Nevertheless, the realization of innovations depends on whether other actors adopt or reject novel initiatives.

Taken together, we open up an analytical space for examining innovation processes in or through construction projects. This space is broad when it comes to the criteria that qualify novelty as innovation; it is, however, narrow and detailed with regard to how the generation and translation of this novelty actually occur. Within this analytical space our research allows for multiple perspectives which are developed in the core part of this book.

References

Bathelt, H., P. Cohendet, S. Henn, and L. Simon (2017). "Innovation and Knowledge Creation: Challenges to the Field." H. Bathelt, P. Cohendet, S. Henn, and L. Simon, eds. *The Elgar Companion to Innovation and Knowledge Creation*. Cheltenham.

Brady, T. and M. Hobday (2011). "Projects and Innovation: Innovation and Projects." P. W. G. Morris, J. K. Pinto, and J. Söderlund, eds. *The Oxford Handbook of Project Management*. Oxford.

Cohendet, P. and L. Simon (2017). "Concepts and Models of Innovation." H. Bathelt, P. Cohendet, S. Henn, and L. Simon, eds. *The Elgar Companion to Innovation and Knowledge Creation*. Cheltenham.

Czarniawska, B. and B. Joerges (1996). "Travels of Ideas." B. Czarniawska and G. Sevón, eds. *Translating Organizational Change*. Berlin.

Garud, R., J. Gehman, A. Kumaraswamy, and P. Tuertscher (2016). "From the Process of Innovation to Innovation as Process." A. Langley and H. Tsoukas, eds. *The SAGE Handbook of Process Organization Studies*. Los Angeles; London; New Delhi; Singapore; Washington DC; Melbourne.

Havenvid Ingemansson, M., Å. Linné, L. E. Bygballe, and C. Harty (2019). "In Pursuit of a New Understanding of Innovation in the Construction Industry: The Significance of Connectivity." M. Havenvid Ingemansson, Å. Linné, L. E. Bygballe, and C. Harty, eds. *The Connectivity of Innovation in the Construction Industry*. London.

Hutter, M., H. Knoblauch, W. Rammert, and A. Windeler (2015). "Innovation Society Today. The Reflexive Creation of Novelty." *Historische Sozialforschung* 40.3: pp. 30–47.

Kreiner, K. (2015). "Built-In Innovation and the Ambiguity of Designing Accessibility." F. Orstavik, A. Dainty, and C. Abbott, eds. *Construction Innovation*. Chichester.

Roberts, E. B. (1988). "What We've Learned: Managing Invention and Innovation." *Research-Technology Management* 31.1: pp. 11–29.

Situating the Research Project at the Intersection of Multi-Disciplinary Debates

Monika Grubbauer

The project team represented different disciplinary approaches, from social science to architecture and engineering research. The overall aim of the collaborative research project was to make productive use of these different perspectives, and to understand construction projects in terms of interdependent organizational, aesthetic, and technical aspects. Thus, each sub-team was meant to focus on different features and dimensions of innovation in large-scale construction projects, namely project, client, designers, materialized building. Yet, integrating these diverse foci also meant bridging differences. The most fundamental difference concerned the understanding of innovation, as it resonated with the disciplinary background of each team. The sub-teams operated within different academic and/or professional discourses; had different levels of familiarity with construction practice; and different types of expertise concerning relevant institutional and regulatory frameworks. Thus, not only did the sub-teams examine different features of innovation, they also had differing perspectives in terms of the three levels of innovation outlined in the preceding section. Or, to put it another way, what constituted innovation in the eyes of one team did not necessarily hold true for the other team.

This interdisciplinary setting proved enormously fruitful because it resulted not only in ongoing conversations between participants but also in the process of learning from each other. As the contributions to this volume illustrate, multi-faceted insights emerged across the sub-projects, case studies, and different collaborative constellations. In this chapter, yet, I wish to highlight some of the challenges we also encountered along the way. First, we had to situate the research project within the different disciplinary debates, also finding a methodology that would be open to all. Second, we had to situate our ongoing work and preliminary outcomes at the intersection of multiple academic communities. And, third, we had to decide on the audience for the outcomes of the project and potential sites for publication. These three challenges are discussed below.

Situating the Research Project within Multiple Disciplinary Perspectives

At the fundamental level, the sub-teams were challenged to define the joint objective of research, i.e., studying "innovation" from the different epistemological perspectives of the respective disciplines. We made productive use of these differences and sought to scrutinize novel solutions in the light of their distinct "value" for the different academic and professional communities involved. Nevertheless, a challenge lay in finding a common language between social sciences and architecture and engineering research in terms of the relevant conceptual approaches. While the social sciences operate with an overall reflection-oriented logic, the built environment disciplines are characterized by their solution-orientation (Grubbauer and Shaw 2018). Conceptual foundations that allowed for bridging the reflection- and solution-oriented perspectives were drawn from a variety of disciplinary contexts, particularly international debates where social science studies of engineering and construction are more prevalent than in Germany (e.g., Harty 2005; Gajendran et al. 2012; Gram-Hanssen and Georg 2018).

The diverse research interests and epistemological perspectives also raised questions concerning the type of case studies that we would focus on and the overall methodology. On the one hand, the case studies had to be promising in terms of providing novel solutions that would potentially advance the relevant field of professional practice; on the other hand, the research process had to be open enough not to predetermine which solutions would be judged as innovative. Thus, we established a methodology that would be open and productive to all sub-teams in terms of insights. As described in more detail in the next chapter, the case studies built on a qualitative research design, with a strong focus on qualitative interviews, complemented by a comprehensive documentary analysis. For the design and engineering researchers, on the one hand, this meant that they had to acquire social science methods of conducting qualitative interviews, working with text-based data, and performing multiple coding-based analyses of the extensive interview data. The social scientists, for their part, were required to learn about some of the design and technical features of the buildings and infrastructures in order to be able to judge the relevance of the case studies and to analyze the data.

Collaborating as a Research Team at the Intersection of Multiple Disciplines

Our work as a team was a learning process, and not only with regard to the above aspects of conceptual and methodological foundations. A second main challenge related to practical issues of our collaborative work. This included the internal discourse in the research project. Here, ongoing translation work was necessary. We regularly presented findings of the sub-projects to the whole team and discussed upcoming papers and presentations together. This interaction was vital and proved invaluable because it forced us to explain to one another how the concepts we used mattered. Clearly, the different abstract theoretical knowledge bases and concepts, upon which the sub-teams drew, were made more accessible when highlighting "the experiential quality of much theory-building" (Leaf 2013, p. vi). At the same time, relevant design and engineering details of the projects also needed to be explained to everyone when the findings from the case studies were discussed. These encounters proved productive by "unsettling" certainties and challenging established conventions around which theories and practices would be relevant.

The practice of collaboration also related to decisions about how to situate the research project in our academic networks, where to discuss the ongoing work for feedback, and which audiences to inform about what we were doing. This proved difficult because construction sits uneasily within the different fields of research. Either construction is placed at the margins of interest, because of the seemingly conservative nature of the industry and/or difficulties in conducting empirical research on site and in the context of a distinct working culture (Sage 2013); or, where construction is the center of interest, it is rarely studied from the angle of our research project. This resulted in ongoing work being presented in very different academic settings, including conferences in organization studies[1] (Grubbauer and Dimitrova 2019; Thiel and Grabher 2018; Thiel et al. 2019), geography[2] (Grabher et al. 2019), and engineering[3] (Ruge et al. 2019). In many cases, the team's contributions stood out due to a perceived transgression of disciplinary boundaries and/or because members of the team ventured into new academic terrains.

Deciding on the Relevant Audiences for the Research Output

Making our final research results accessible to others also constituted a challenge. While we connected our research to various

[1] European Group for Organizational Studies (EGOS)
[2] Nordic Geographers Meeting (NGM)
[3] International Association for Bridge and Structural Engineering (IABSE)

international debates and felt that the results would be highly relevant for an international audience, it proved difficult to find appropriate outlets for our research. International peer-reviewed journals are mostly oriented towards clearly defined disciplinary audiences and often reflect established academic networks and hermetic discourses. While participation in conferences was more easily organized, publications in peer-reviewed journals proved more difficult because they often required adapting our findings to the specific expectations and norms of the respective disciplines. At the time of writing, several papers have, in fact, been published in international peer-reviewed journals or are in the process of submission. Yet, we were not able to identify a journal that would have been suitable as a platform for a special issue along the lines of our research project. In comparison with this volume, which gives a comprehensive overview of the findings, the papers offer more partial insights from the project, with a narrow focus and data from selected case studies (Dreher and Thiel 2021; Grubbauer and Dimitrova 2021; Ruge and Bögle 2019).

Another issue, which made it difficult to decide on a suitable format to present our findings, was whether and how to bridge the gap between theory and practice, i.e., between a purely academic audience and the world of practitioners. The practitioners were particularly important as many had generously supported our research and had contributed their knowledge and experience in extensive and sometimes multiple interviews. During the process, some of these practitioners had also quite legitimately inquired how they might benefit and what opportunities they might gain through our findings. Thus, we took pains to solicit contributions to this volume from commentators not only from the various disciplines but also from practice. In sum, this volume has the ambitious aim not only of advancing disciplinary and interdisciplinary debate, but also of being of value and interest to practitioners and providing in-depth knowledge about the case studies.

Conclusions

This research project enabled us to understand the complexities of innovation in construction in considerable detail and to take into account different disciplinary perspectives. This required constant methodological refinement and ongoing learning and dialog to bridge the different perspectives of social sciences and design and engineering research. The question remains what the more general insights are for research on the construction industry. We analyzed very specific and, in terms of their enormous complexity, one might say extreme cases (Flyvbjerg 2006) of large-scale construction projects. Are interdisciplinary approaches also relevant for research on smaller and more mundane tasks and projects? Yes, certainly. The building industry is one of the main sources of energy and resource consumption. As cities are challenged to conceive of decisive measures that will fundamentally change the trajectory of urban development to more sustainable ways of living, construction is a key target. In order to push for innovation in construction, it is vital to understand not only how different dimensions of innovation, beyond the purely aesthetic or technical, interact.

We also need a clearer and more in-depth understanding of how professionals from the different specializations collaborate in developing novel solutions, how these solutions are accepted within academic and/or professional contexts, and how expectations for professionals differ in respect of audiences and types of intervention. Finally, we hope that our findings contribute to advance the understanding of such questions by highlighting what to learn from large-scale construction projects.

References

Dreher, J. and J. Thiel (2021). "Exceptional Architecture Projects and the Geographies of Innovation in Construction. The Case of the Elbphilharmonie." *European Planning Studies*.

Flyvbjerg, B. (2006). "Five Misunderstandings about Case-Study Research." *Qualitative Inquiry* 12.2: pp. 219–245.

Gajendran, T., G. Brewer, A.R.J. Dainty, et al. (2012). "A Conceptual Approach to Studying the Organisational Culture of Construction Projects." *Australasian Journal of Construction Economics and Building* 12.2: pp. 1–26.

Grabher, G., J. Thiel, and J. Dreher (2019). "Urban Innovation from the Periphery? The Relational Construction of Centre and Periphery in Mega-Project Innovations." Nordic Geographers Meeting, Trondheim.

Gram-Hanssen, K. and S. Georg (2018). "Energy Performance Gaps: Promises, People, Practices." *Building Research & Information* 46.1: pp. 1–9.

Grubbauer, M. and V. Dimitrova (2019). "Organizing the City through Architectural Projects: Non-Standard Solutions, Multi-Sited Cooperation, and Stable Networks in the Construction of the Elbphilharmonie, Hamburg." 35th EGOS Colloquium, Edinburgh.

Grubbauer, M. and V. Dimitrova (2021). "Exceptional Architecture, Learning Processes, and the Contradictory Performativity of Norms and Standards." *European Planning Studies*.

Grubbauer, M. and K. Shaw, eds. (2018). *Across Theory and Practice: Thinking Through Urban Research*. Berlin.

Harty C. (2005). "Innovation in Construction: A Sociology of Technology Approach." *Building Research & Information* 33.6: pp. 512–522.

Leaf M. (2013). "The Practical Skill of Theory." *International Development Planning Review* 35.4: pp. v-ix.

Ruge, J. and A. Bögle (2019). "Models as Agents of Creativity? A Qualitative Description of the Structural Design Process." H. Corres, L. Todisco, and C. Fivet, eds. Proceedings of the *International fib Symposium on Conceptual Design of Structures.* Madrid.

Ruge, J., L. Fahnenmüller, and A. Bögle (2019). "Effects of Problem Formulation on Engineering Innovativeness." Proceedings of the 2019 *IABSE Congress New York City: The Evolving Metropolis.*

Sage D. (2013). "Danger Building Site—Keep Out!?': A Critical Agenda for Geographical Engagement with Contemporary Construction Industries." *Social & Cultural Geography* 14.2: pp. 168–191.

Thiel, J. and G. Grabher (2018). "Beyond the Iron Law? Large-Scale Construction Projects as Drivers of Innovation." 34th EGOS Colloquium, Tallin.

Thiel, J., G. Grabher, J. Dreher, and L. Fahnenmüller (2019). "Strong Owners, Weak Clients? Client Performance and Innovation in Two Iconic Architecture Projects." 35th EGOS Colloquium, Edinburgh.

Case Studies as a Research Strategy: Data and Methods

Lennart Fahnenmüller/Joachim Thiel

The research presented in this book examines large-scale construction projects from various interdisciplinary viewpoints. We address these projects with a well-practiced qualitative method: in-depth case study research. This type of research is advantageous for two reasons. First, it generates context-dependent knowledge (Flyvbjerg 2006), taking into account that large-scale construction projects are unique, built at a specific location at a designated point in time. Second, case study research allows for interdisciplinary cooperation by matching well the requirements of all involved disciplines—urban and regional economics, innovation management, architecture and urban studies, and engineering.

The generation of context-dependent knowledge as one of the key features of case study research is often criticized for not producing generalizable results and only highlighting what is closely connected to the unique conditions of a specific case. For our research project, and for all involved disciplines, this context-dependent knowledge affords rather an opportunity than a problem: understanding, for instance, how the interplay of different stakeholders led to outstanding results in architecture or engineering, or to novel organizational make-ups or modes of client involvement, allows an inductive generation of theoretical statements, but also the development of recommendations for professional practice. While some chapters in this book seek to contribute to more conceptual literature, others "approach the complexities and contradictions of real life" and are more loosely connected to "general propositions and theories" (Flyvbjerg 2006, p. 237). These latter contributions are thereby in line with Flyvbjerg's understanding that "context-dependent knowledge and experience are at the very heart of expert activity" (Flyvbjerg 2006, p. 222). Case study research, by mirroring the complexities of everyday professional activities, can therefore also inform the professional practice that the research looks into—in our case the construction of large-scale projects.

For our research we used a multiple-case design. The trade-off between project resources and the desire to compare various cases, something that is inherent in this design, led to the number of six cases. These were analyzed in-depth—with a grand total of eighty-six interviews. As the involved disciplines have different research foci, specific cases may be more relevant for one discipline than for others. The six cases were therefore sampled strategically and are specifically suited to describe, validate, or reject hypotheses (Flyvbjerg 2006). On the one hand, hence, our sampling treated each case as a "black swan" (Flyvbjerg 2006), i.e., focusing on the unique features of the project. Indeed, when it comes to large-scale construction projects a search for white swan projects with strictly replicable features would be difficult to conceive. On the other hand, however, we sought to integrate structuring aspects that helped to identify cross-case mechanisms related to all cases or to specific sub-groups and thereby enabled us to adopt a comparative perspective. To achieve both aims, we selected projects with outstanding features that were generally accepted as successful, exceptional buildings. Moreover, we decided to take as sample projects some that were recent and completed—leading to a maximum of twelve years after completion date. Finally, we created three sub-groups each of which exemplified a specific innovation theme: two iconic structures for which architectural design is central; two bridge structures that showcase the engineering aspect of large-scale construction projects; and two infrastructural conglomerations (a central railway station and a metro line) that include structural, infrastructural, and design questions and that also exhibit a high degree of system complexity (see Table 1).

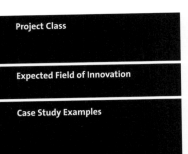

Project Class	Structural Engineering	Infrastructural Engineering	Structural and Infrastructural Engineering combined
Expected Field of Innovation	Architecture (design)	Construction (engineering)	Systems Integration (organization)
Case Study Examples	Elbphilharmonie Hamburg	Gänsebachtal Bridge Buttstädt, Thuringia	Central Station Berlin
	European Central Bank Frankfurt	Kochertal Bridge Geislingen am Kocher	Wehrhahn Line Düsseldorf

Table 1: The Case Studies

Each case is coherent and "stands on its own" (Eisenhardt and Graebner 2007), allowing for an in-depth analysis of the entire large-scale construction project. Additionally, each case offers specific "embedded units" (Yin 2009), i.e., objects of investigation below case-level, that vary with regard to how they meet the interest of involved disciplines. The structure of how to analyze the cases may therefore diverge between the involved research groups without compromising the interdisciplinary approach across all cases.

After sampling was concluded, the processes of data gathering and data analysis involved several phases. Researchers in the project conducted a documentary analysis with related material such as architecture and engineering prizes, articles in architecture and engineering journals, and political documents. This desktop research provided two kinds of information: firstly, key actors in the project were identified and selected as potential interviewees; secondly, the projects were scrutinized for unique or innovative features. Based on this initial empirical material we approached selected interviewees. In a first round, crucial members of core organizations involved in a case were interviewed in order to obtain a comprehensive perspective of the case and of elements that were potentially interesting for a deep-dive into specific innovations. The first wave also served as a generator of additional contacts. For the second wave, we selected up to three specifically interesting (technical, aesthetic, or organizational) components for each project. We probed into these components in more detail by interviewing members of all organizations involved in planning and implementing them. In total, the research team conducted eighty-six interviews with the full range of involved actors: with architects, engineers, project managers and clients, as well as with those with more specific roles, such as political actors or safety authority engineers who were involved only when their function appeared relevant for the case.

The interviews were semi-structured, based on a jointly developed questionnaire that included important aspects related to all involved disciplines. The interview guideline touched on the general involvement of the actor in the project, and their perception of exceptional or novel happenings in the project. In addition, the interviewers sought to obtain more detailed information about the development and implementation of these exceptional instances. In this way, we not only accomplished the interdisciplinary ambition of the project but also managed to successfully generate context-dependent knowledge: firstly, by acquiring exploratory information on the train of construction events that interviewees perceived throughout the project; secondly, by gathering in-depth information on all disciplinary topics whenever the interviewee mentioned these, without compromising the exploratory work by specifically prompting these topics. This second type of information was easy to analyze as technical experts (engineers and architects) were part of the research team. The designated interview length of sixty to ninety minutes also left room for more tailored questions. Specific topics were prepared by the interdisciplinary research team and listed for spontaneous selection during the interview. They either emerged from the study of project-related documents or were "generative, concept-relating" (Strauss and Corbin 1994) for one of the disciplines.

In the interview analysis, we then revisited the interviews relating to each case and searched specifically for patterns and processes of interaction (cf. Strauss and Corbin 1994). Each disciplinary sub-group generated codes for the phenomena that were described by interviewees in conjunction with the group's knowledge base. Codes were then shared and discussed to make them applicable to each discipline. In sum, we built a set of seventy-four codes, which partly met disciplinary needs of urban and regional economics, innovation management, architecture, and engineering that were, however, also applicable across disciplines. The actual coding work was distributed among the researchers. Two researchers coded each interview with half of the entire code set, allowing the use of one or more codes for each segment. Later, we synthesized the codings and made them available for analysis. For use of the interviews in publications, we developed a referencing key, including the number of the case study, the profile of the involved organization, and a serial number (Table 2 – e.g., C1_Own1). Quotations from interviews were then translated into English by the respective chapter authors.

C1	Elbphilharmonie	Own	Owner/Client
C2	European Central Bank	Arc	Architect
C3	Berlin Central Station	Eng	Engineering Consultant
C4	Gänsebachtal Bridge	Proj	Project Management Consultant
C5	Wehrhahn Line	Cont	Main Contractor
C6	Kochertal Bridge	Supp	Supply Chain
		Oth	Other

Table 2: Interview Referencing Key

The generated material was made available to all sub-teams for analysis and interpretation. In this book, we present six specific viewpoints based on which the team has explored this huge reservoir of data. The six chapters that make up the core of this book partly embody disciplinary views drawing on a specialized conceptual apparatus. Others, however, seek to combine different academic perspectives and knowledge bases. In a sense, the book thereby not only examines innovations, but also seeks to enter unknown terrain in its own right.

References

Eisenhardt, K. M. and M. E. Graebner (2007). "Theory Building from Cases: Opportunities and Challenges." *Academy of Management Journal* 50.1: pp. 25–32.

Flyvbjerg, B. (2006). "Five Misunderstandings about Case-Study Research." *Qualitative Inquiry* 12.2: pp. 219–245.

Strauss, A. and J. Corbin (1994). "Grounded Theory Methodology: An Overview." N. K. Denzin and Y. S. Lincoln, eds. *Handbook of Qualitative Research*. Thousand Oaks, CA.

Yin, R. K. (2009). *Case Study Research: Design and Methods* (4th ed). Thousand Oaks, CA.

The Case Studies

Venetsiya Dimitrova/Johannes Dreher/
Johanna Ruge

Over the following pages, the case studies for the research project are presented. From this, we hope that the reader will gain an understanding of the key features of the selected building or structure as well as of the respective planning and realization process. The case study descriptions refer back to the four aspects which constituted the foci of the interdisciplinary research: the project itself, the role of the client, the role of the architectural and structural designers, and, last but not least, the materialized structure as the outcome of the project. Additionally, the presentations provide first insights into the different organizational, architectural, and structural novelties. Furthermore, we aim to highlight the perception of the project in the public as well as the professional discourse, validating its selection as a case study for research on construction innovation.

© Iwan Baan

Hamburg

Elbphilharmonie

The Elbphilharmonie is Hamburg's new architectural icon, conceived as a world-class concert hall within a crystalline structure placed on a 1950s' warehouse like a sculpture on its plinth. Located in the HafenCity district, Hamburg's evolving water-front development and one of the largest inner-city regeneration programs in Europe, the project was expected to underline the city's position as cultural metropolis. Besides the two concert-halls, the building includes a public plaza with a panoramic view of the harbor and the city, a hotel, apartments, garage parking, restaurants, and a souvenir shop. It was designed by the internationally renowned architects and engineers Herzog & de Meuron and Schnetzer Puskas International, respectively, and the star-acoustician Toyota from Nagata Acoustics. The project, which has a gross floor area of around 125,000 square meters, was implemented between 2007 and 2016 by the main contractor Hochtief at the total cost of approximately 870 million euros.

The architectural and structural highlights of the Elbphilharmonie include the integration of the listed warehouse as the base of the building, the development of an innovative acoustic cladding (the so-called "white skin") and of novel spherically curved glass for the façade, as well as the design of a first-class concert hall (that is acoustically decoupled from its surroundings).

The project's planning and realization process is characterized by several specificities. The architects were commissioned without a competition and, after a relatively short planning phase, the Elbphilharmonie was allocated to the main contractor, Hochtief. The project development was marked by multiple disruptions, including a change in the project owners and the responsible managers, alterations to the design, construction difficulties, as well as the restructuring of contractual relations between architects and main contractor—all of which led eventually to a significant increase in cost and substantially delayed completion. The development of the Elbphilharmonie was accompanied by high levels of public interest from the outset. Yet, the initial fascination and enthusiasm that followed the presentation of the first design sketches evolved into more critical media responses as the project progressed. After its completion, the project received several awards, including the Public Architecture Award 2018 and the Nike Award for Symbolism 2019 from the BDA (the Association of German Architects), the structural engineering Building Award 2017, as well as the Ife Award 2018 and the German Innovation Award 2018.

European Central Bank

The European Central Bank Headquarters (ECB) project was initiated based on the Bank's deliberate decision to create an own building for the new European Institution. The high-rise office building located in the city of Frankfurt was designed by the internationally acclaimed architects and engineers of Coop Himmelb(l)au and Bollinger & Grohmann, respectively. Frankfurt's city officials strongly supported the project: keeping the ECB headquarters in the city was central for strengthening Frankfurt's position as a financial center as well as for the revitalization of the Ostend district. The building has a gross floor area of approximately 185,000 square meters and was realized between 1998 and 2014 for a total cost of around 1.2 billion euros.

The architectural and structural highlights of the project include the elaborate refurbishment of the Großmarkthalle, a listed warehouse building, a highly efficient energy concept, the implementation of high safety standards, and the realization of the complex load-bearing structure with its twisted geometry and characteristic hyperbolic paraboloid façade.

The project development process was characterized by an extended phase of careful preparation, planning, and assembly of the project coalition, including a three-step architectural competition and two tendering processes. As a result, the actual construction work started twelve years after the initiation of the project but lasted only four years, less than other similarly complex large-scale undertakings. Moreover, unlike in other large-scale projects, the process of implementing the ECB was characterized by the continuity of objectives supported by the core actors, a constructive approach in solving collaboratively problems as they arose, and the lack of major disruptions.

The project has been the recipient of numerous awards, including the Award for Architecture of the German Architecture Museum (DAM) 2015, a distinction in the German Engineering Award 2016, the Best Tall Building Europe Award 2016, and the German Steel Construction Award 2016.

Frankfurt

© Robert Metsch

© Marcus Bredt

Berlin Central Station

Berlin Central Station is the capital's new main railway station. The project represents an important hub for long-distance and regional railway transport and is part of the so-called "mushroom concept" (*Pilzkonzept*), developed after Germany's reunification and entailing a complete reorganization of Berlin's rail system. Commissioned by the City of Berlin and German Railways (DB), the structure was designed by the renowned architects von Gerkan, Marg and Partners, together with the distinguished engineering firm of Schlaich Bergermann Partner. Since it is also the first completed project in Berlin's new inner-city development area "Europacity," the station is an important commercial site, comprising among others retail and grocery outlets, restaurants, and office space over some 70,000 square meters, across four levels. The costs of the project amounted to 1 billion euros and the development took over eleven years to complete (1995–2006).

The key design principle is a crossover of the structure's main elements: two parallel buildings (*Bügelbauten*) at a north–south orientation, and a 321-meter-long arched glass roof construction at a west–east orientation. A guiding design principle was the vision of column-free and light-flooded spaces, even in the underground, which proved challenging to implement. Architectural and structural novelties were the development of cast-iron columns, the innovative execution of the two north–south buildings using a novel tilting procedure, the combination of tunnel structures and bridges within one station building, as well as the parabolic glass roof, which is curved above the train tracks.

The development of the project was characterized by arguments over budget and the agreed time schedule, which led to significant changes to the original design and a lawsuit between the architects and the DB. After its completion, the project was honored with different awards, including the Station of the Year Award 2007, the Access City Award 2013, the Brunel Award, and the Civil Engineering Award 2006.

Wehrhahn Line

The Wehrhahn Line is Düsseldorf's new underground line, conceived as an addition to the existing subway network. The main characteristic of the project is the successful integration of art into a public transport project, a measure by which the city officials strived to reinforce Düsseldorf's position as a "City of Art." The design of six metro stations was developed by the then relatively unknown architectural office netzwerkarchitekten and the artist Heike Klussmann. Five further artists were chosen for the individual design of the different stations. The City of Düsseldorf commissioned the engineering firms Wendt GmbH and ZPP Engineers for the initial planning phase and the temporary Wehrhahn Engineering Alliance, led by Schüßler Plan for the execution. The project development took fifteen years (2001–2016) and cost approximately 844 million euros.

The design concept is characterized by two key features: the *Continuum*, a bright relief-like network structure made of diamond-shaped pre-fabricated concrete elements across the six stations, and the *Cut*, consisting of individually designed entrances, connecting the underground stations with the city. Furthermore, the entire design is characterized by spaciousness, generous visual links, and the integration of daylight. The main objective was to create an underground line that is not merely functional, but also combines complex engineering and construction solutions with ambitious architectural and artistic concepts. In this sense, the successful implementation of art, as an integral component of the structure rather than as an "add-on," can be regarded as the main innovation.

The ambitious task was achieved via intense collaboration between engineers, architects, and artists throughout the project's duration, facilitated by the project owner from the very beginning. Realized on time and exceeding the budget only within reasonable limits, the project is regarded as an example par excellence of a scandal-free, large-scale urban development intervention.

After its completion, the Wehrhahn Line was celebrated by the public, the media, and the professional community, both in a national and international context. The underground line received the STUVA Award 2015 and the NIKE Award for Atmosphere from the BDA (the Association of German Architects), and was nominated for numerous others, including the World Architecture Award and the Mies van der Rohe Award.

Düsseldorf

© Jörg Hempel, Aachen

© DB AG/Hannes Frank

Gänsebachtal Bridge

The Gänsebachtal Bridge is a semi-integral bridge situated between Erfurt and Leipzig in Thuringia. It carries the new high-speed railway line between Berlin and Nuremberg, which is part of the German Unity Transport Projects (VDE), initiated to improve transportation between the former eastern and western parts of Germany. Commissioned by the client DB Netz AG and the project managers of DB ProjektBau, the bridge was designed by engineers from Schlaich Bergermann Partner and SSF Engineers. The main contractor for construction works was Adam Hörnig. Characteristic of the bridge is its slender design, which harmonizes with the landscape and, in addition, distinguishes it from previously realized high-speed railway bridges, which are often conceived as rather heavy and inelegant. After an initial planning phase in 1995, the project was put on hold and only restarted in 2008. The bridge was completed in 2012 at a total cost of 19.1 million euros.

Most striking is the bridge's innovative slender design, achieved through the use of a semi-integral construction. The Gänsebachtal Bridge constitutes one of the earliest implementations of this structural design for high-speed railway bridges. A semi-integral construction implies that the superstructure of the bridge is monolithically connected to the bridge's columns, resulting in a lean design. In this way, the main objective of the project was realized: to span the Gänsebach valley with a bridge that met all safety requirements of a high-speed railway line while at the same time causing minimal interventions into the landscape. Additionally, maintenance costs were reduced over the long term, as semi-integral bridges have fewer parts requiring upkeep (e.g., bearings and joints) than conventional ones.

The bridge was originally planned in 1995 according to the Framework Planning Scheme, a regulation for railway bridges which predefines spans and cross-sections of new bridges. However, when the project restarted in 2008 the design changed significantly, as the engineers from Schlaich Bergermann Partner, SSF Engineers, and Adam Hörnig proposed the alternative semi-integral construction design as a special offer in the tender procedure, and it was this that was eventually realized.

The Gänsebachtal Bridge won the German Bridge Construction Award 2014 in the category road and railway bridges for its aesthetically convincing structure. Moreover, the bridge is regarded as a successful pilot project for the implementation of the semi-integral construction for high-speed railway bridges all over the world.

Kochertal Bridge

The project comprised the maintenance and reinforcement of the Kochertal Bridge in Geislingen am Kocher, close to Stuttgart, Baden-Württemberg. With 185-meter-high columns, the Kochertal Bridge is the highest concrete bridge in Germany. It is considered an icon of bridge design and construction, and has the status of a listed structure. Built originally in the late 1970s and put into operation in 1979, the bridge carries the A6 highway and is therefore an important east–west infrastructure connection for Germany. Due to damage, identified during bridge inspections, and to the desired expansion of the A6 from four to six lanes, Stuttgart's Regional Council instigated the maintenance and reinforcement of the bridge. Specific to this project is that the planning engineering office commissioned to carry out the maintenance and reinforcement, Leonhardt, Andrä und Partner, had also been responsible for the original design of the bridge. There were two further firms involved: Ingenieurgruppe Bauen as checking engineers, and Leonhard Weiss as main contractor. The project was begun in 2008 and was completed in 2015 with a total cost of 22.4 million euros.

The bridge is the only bridge construction that was not replaced by a new one within the overall extension project for the A6 highway. The successful planning for its maintenance and reinforcement was achieved through extensive investigation and assessment of the bridge's physical condition. The works themselves were also impressive, due to the enormous height of the bridge, its long span, and the fact that all construction took place while the flow of traffic was maintained.

Characteristic of the project development process were the efforts put in by the engineers into the task of maintaining the bridge, which were supported by the client from the beginning even though there was no guarantee of their success.

The project won several engineering awards: the German Bridge Construction Award 2016 (category road and railway bridges), a recognition by the German Engineering Award 2016, and the Ulrich-Finsterwalder Engineering Award 2017—marks of distinction that confirm the high levels of appreciation for the task of maintaining bridges.

Geislingen

© Leonhardt, Andrä und Partner
Beratende Ingenieure VBI AG

Passerelle de la Paix— Materializing Innovation

Michael Zimmermann

This documentary series explores the materialization process of the Passerelle de la Paix, a pedestrian and cycle bridge spanning the Rhône in Lyon, which was completed in 2014. The design of the bridge is the result of a collaboration between Dietmar Feichtinger Architects and Schlaich Bergermann Partner.

The steel-and-wood bridge reminds one of a slender curve and is characterized by a playful and asymmetric form that provides maximum transparency. The bridge has a clear span of 157 meters over the river, extending to 220 meters in total to reach the upper quays on either bank, allowing pedestrians and cyclists to enter the bridge at two different heights on either side of the river. The bridge's three-dimensional steel structure consists of two arches as the bottom chord and a box-girder as the top chord, which are linked and stiffened by triangular steel elements and diagonals. Due to the vertical curvature of the arch, the connecting triangular frames become smaller towards the center, creating in this way the bridge's dynamic and distinctive character. At the apex of the arch, the two decks join together to form the eight meter wide plaza area, from which visitors can enjoy views up and down the river.

The elegant and slender footbridge that touches down lightly on the riverbanks appears effortless in its final form. However, a huge amount of effort was necessary to execute the idea of an open passage. Designed at the limits of feasibility, the material-ization of the bridge is both testimony to engineering at its best and an example of dedicated interdisciplinary cooperation between engineer, architect, client, and contractor.

The aim of this documentary photo series is to capture the materialization process of the Passerelle de la Paix, conserving the ephemeral intermediate construction stages of the bridge. It shows in detail the twenty-four-hour installation of the bridge's superstructure on site. This involved pre-assembling the 160 meter long superstructure, installing a temporary cable support system on its top to stabilize it, lifting the whole structure onto a pontoon, floating the pontoons into the bridge's axis, and finally lowering the superstructure into its position to attach it to the bearing points.

By capturing this process, the photo series sheds light on the various efforts of construction work—the dedication of the construction workers, the necessary temporary equipment, the complex procedures that need to be followed—which are often rendered invisible in the final structure. Thus, the aim is to highlight the work which went into materializing the ambitious and beautiful passageway, as well as to encourage appreciation for the people who make such endeavors possible.

By displaying the different stages of the process, the transition from multiple single structural elements to an integral elegant piece of structural art becomes visible. While the photos do represent the hard and, at times, "dirty" work that is construction, not least the spectacular night views reveal the beauty of how things come together.

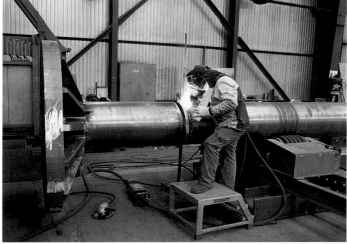

Perspectives in Metropolitan Research

Large-Scale Construction Projects and Innovation: The Research Results

Large-Scale Projects as "Frame Changers" in the Construction Industry?

Joachim Thiel/Venetsiya Dimitrova/
Johannes Dreher

Introduction

Addressing the conjunction between the construction industry and innovation as a counterintuitive undertaking has not only been the starting point for our entire research project, but is also the subject of ample research elsewhere (e.g., Ekstedt et al. 1999). At least according to classic innovation indicators, the industry's record in terms of novelty creation is clearly below average when compared to other sectors (Butzin and Rehfeld 2013; Reichstein et al. 2005). It is therefore no coincidence that relevant research on innovations tends to ignore construction as field of inquiry (Rehfeld 2012). And yet, innovations do occur in construction. However, looking into innovation in construction calls for a specific approach that takes into account the industry's particular features with regard to the generation of novelty—e.g., the project-based nature or the public visibility of the product.

We have therefore broadened our analytical horizon, in particular when it comes to how innovations are perceived and valued. The study of innovation in construction needs to consider a wider context of conceiving innovation than, for instance, is the case in the fields of science or technology development, where the criteria for defining what is new and useful are rather unambiguous and straightforward. For this purpose, we mainly draw on Rammert's (2001) work on the cultural shaping of technologies. The author builds on a "broad anthropological perspective" of seeing "*culture* as a special 'frame'" (Rammert 2001, p. 175, original emphasis) that shapes social practices. This cultural frame comprises three elements. It guides (1) "how things are viewed" ("semantics"); (2) "how things are done" ("pragmatics"); and (3) "how these activities are institutionally arranged" ("grammar"). In the original anthropological use, conceiving of culture as a frame echoes a synchronic comparative perspective, related to different societies, places, communities. "[S]ocial semantics, social pragmatics, social grammar" (Hutter et al. 2015), hence, constitute "analytical dimensions with regard to observing society" that emphasize dissimilarities and similarities between different social contexts.

More recently, Rammert (2010) as well as Hutter et al. (2015) have applied this comparative framework explicitly to the study of innovations. The authors translate the discursive, the practical, and the institutional dimensions of cultural framing—i.e., "semantics, pragmatics, and grammar"—into what they refer to as three "observation forms" (p. 37) of innovation. In other words, the authors transform the synchronic view of (inter-) cultural comparison into a diachronic perspective of cultural change. Consequently, innovation implies a change of cultural frame: things are viewed in a novel way; done in a novel way; and these activities might also be institutionally arranged in a novel way. Moreover, the authors see interrelations between these three perspectives of change: discourses, practices and institutional arrangements may diverge, but also override or mutually influence each other.

This widened perspective of seeing innovation as essentially cultural change, for one thing, helps address the alleged lack of innovativeness in the construction industry. The focus on discursive frames, routinized "patterns of practice" (Rammert 2001, p. 175), and institutional arrangements displays innovation rather as an exception than the rule. For another and more importantly, this research approach offers a suitable way to conceptualize innovation in a more comprehensive fashion, beyond the mere development of novel technology[1]. Innovation, then, not only embraces a process during which novelty arises and proves to be (commercially) useful and viable (e.g., Amabile 1996; Roberts 1988). Innovation also essentially includes overcoming the barriers that hinder the change of cultural frames. In other words, on top of developing and implementing novelty, innovation is also about

1 Of course, also classic technological innovation processes comprise more than the mere technological

legitimation and persuasion—or about what Garud and Karnøe (2001, p. 14) refer to as "mobilizing minds."

Our key argument is that large-scale construction projects establish key arenas where cultural frames in construction are likely to change. Large projects support the development and implementation, as well as the legitimation, of novel ideas, techniques and practices as they, in a way, encourage and enforce interactions between the different dimensions of cultural frames. The projects, hence, enable and encourage those in the industry to *mobilize* "cultural orientation" (Rammert 2001, p. 178), experience and expertise, and rules from their discursive, pragmatic and institutional context; to *enact* those resources by re-shuffling concrete ways of doing; and to eventually *translate* changed ways of doing back into the (discursive, pragmatic and institutional) context. We therefore refer to large projects as potential frame changers in the construction industry.

Our analysis concentrates on the actual practices of *mobilization, enactment* and *translation* that are performed in the six construction projects examined here. Hence, we look into (1) how project actors *mobilize* orientation, experience and expertise, and rules from existing discourses, practices and institutions and either apply or deliberately avoid applying them; (2) how the project participants *enact* these resources in the actual projects, in this context facing a series of problems that the confrontation of novelty with a standardized project process and rigid material and institutional boundary conditions engenders; (3) how they *translate* ways of doing back into modified discourses, practices and institutions, either being pushed by project participants or pulled by context actors. Our use of "translation" here is inspired by how Latour (1986) refers to it: as a counter concept to "diffusion" that conceives of actual practices as drivers of dissemination of change.

This chapter, first and foremost, provides a novel contribution to the literature on construction projects and innovation, but also on the role of projects and innovation more broadly. In particular, by emphasizing the inherent context-relatedness of construction projects, we specify the usually taken for granted idea that innovation in construction takes place in projects (Boland Jr. et al. 2007; Clegg and Kreiner 2014; Dubois and Gadde 2002; Gann and Salter 2000). We find that not every construction venture by itself creates its own "experimental workshop" (Dubois and Gadde 2002, p. 628), unless it succeeds in mobilizing and enacting resources from its discursive, pragmatic and institutional context. And, by stressing discursive and institutional aspects, we also provide a novel way of conceptualizing this context, as compared to the relational approach that prevails in extant project management literature (e.g., Davies and Brady 2000; Engwall 2003; Gann and Salter 2000; Grabher 2004).

In addition, and as an application of the "semantics, pragmatics and grammar"-framework for a primarily empirical research, the chapter also offers points of departure for more general discussions about how to frame and analyze innovation and change. In particular, it provides an additional lens when it comes to framing the relation between inertia and openness that has been discussed now for decades in a variety of fields in social science (e.g., Reckwitz 2003).

The empirical analysis put forward in this chapter is based on the total of the six case studies that we conducted. The material that we actually processed was assembled in two steps. First, out of a total of eighty-six interviews we selected those with the four types of core project actors (project managers, clients representatives, architects and engineers). Second, we reduced the original code set to those codes that were related to the conceptual framework of *semantics, pragmatics* and *grammar.* We reorganized the codes according to these three terms. In so doing, we discovered that the number of codes relating to *pragmatics* exceeded significantly the number of those associated with *semantics* and *grammar.*

Through both steps, we retrieved a total of 1,192 interview passages as basic material for further analysis. The starting point of interpretation was the *pragmatics* dimension. We looked carefully into all *pragmatics*-related codings and into how these relate to the two other concepts. In several rounds we categorized and interpreted the data by going back and forth between conceptual literature and empirical material, and through multiple steps of re-coding (using code words from our extensive analysis of literature on innovation, practices and projects). New codes included, among others, "formal—informal," "codified—implicit," "material—social," "push—pull." Building both on the three dimensions and on these re-codings we unpacked the empirical material in a first chapter draft. This draft provided the basis for us to condense our findings into three different sets of practices that are performed in the process of changing cultural frames in construction: *mobilization, enactment* and *translation.* In the second draft, we outlined how *mobilization, enactment* and *translation* took place in the six examined projects, again going back to the empirical material and recalibrating the starting points derived from the literature. This last round of analysis eventually informed the analytical structure of the chapter.

The chapter proceeds as follows. The following three sections comprise the results of our empirical analysis: *mobilization, enactment* and *translation.* We focus in detail on these three different sets of practices, how they are actually performed and how they relate to the analytical dimensions of semantics, pragmatics and grammar. In the final section, we summarize our findings and emphasize the contribution of our work for further research on innovation in (construction) projects. Additionally, by reflecting upon the restrictions of our (methodological) approach, we also relate our work to the book's remaining chapters.

Mobilization: Application and Avoidance

Large-scale construction projects are exceptional occurrences within the largely routinized project-to-project trajectories that individuals and organizations in the industry usually follow. Inevitably, coalitions of actors for each large venture are assembled just for that project (Grabher and Thiel 2015); timeframes of projects occupy large parts of professionals' and firms' biographies; often, size and complexity of the task exceed the requirements of what involved actors experience in their everyday business. As a consequence, large-scale projects cannot build on an existing stock of capabilities, tools or ideas in a straightforward fashion. Mobilizing necessary resources from beyond the boundaries of the actual project is therefore not only essential with regard to doing things in ways different from what is usual, but also simply in order to carry out the projects at all.

We conceptualize what is meant by "beyond the boundaries" according to the three analytical dimensions "semantics, pragmatics and grammar" (Hutter et al. 2015). Practices of mobilization, hence, comprise cultural orientation, experience and expertise, as well as rules that project participants need to activate from the discursive, practical and institutional context. Our findings revealed two contrasting main mechanisms that were inherent in mobilization practices and that encouraged novelty: the refined application and the deliberate avoidance of existing ways of seeing, doing, or institutionally arranging.

Semantics: Mobilizing Cultural Orientation

Construction is a professional activity, but also a "public business" (Gann and Salter 2000, p. 962), given that every building contributes to the shape of public space. As a consequence, construction projects reflect discourses in the professional realm as well as in the public arena.

In the context of the projects that we examined, the mobilization of discourses as orientations usually happened purposefully and selectively. On the one hand, project actors sought to apply and refine the established mainstream. The actual project was to be an exemplary solution for a particularly well-acknowledged way of addressing the built environment and architecture. On the other, project actors explicitly sought to achieve the contrary. The actual project then served as a proof of the successful deviation from standard ways of dealing with construction.

Mobilization as refined application occurred particularly in the four cases for which iconicity played an important role (Elbphilharmonie, European Central Bank, Berlin Central Station, Wehrhahn Subway Line). In those cases, the public perception of ambitious architecture and its impact on the positioning of cities and organizations established important narratives based on which the design for the buildings was developed. These narratives provided incentives, both for clients to be demanding with regard to design quality and for involved individuals and organizations to contribute to something exceptional:

This is what Elbphilharmonie achieved. The building has set a benchmark, as a large-scale project that supported the marketing of the city, similar to the Sydney Opera House (C2_Oth2).

The project is simply an icon. … And when I experienced it more closely, there was—over the whole period—incredible enthusiasm (C1_Proj1).

Mobilization as avoidance took place mainly in the engineering-driven projects, i.e., the two bridges, and related to professional discourses. These discourses concerned, for instance, the design of a new type of high-speed railway bridges, as an alternative approach that seeks a better integration of new infrastructures in existing landscapes:

… when we as planners dare something and really try to introduce a new philosophy into bridge building, saying that design quality is an important point for acceptance and design is not contradictory to price—this was in our heads (C4_Oth1).

Another illustrative example of a deliberate attempt to change discourses relates to the recently growing market for bridge maintenance and reinforcement that is in fact less appealing than the mainstream of, for instance, "building a stayed girder bridge in Japan or a bascule bridge over the Suez Canal" (C6_Eng2):

I remember a talk with Mr. [X] … . And he said: "You plan to get involved in maintenance? … . This is out of the question for us. … . We don't do shotcrete" (C6_Eng2).

Pragmatics: Mobilizing Expertise and Experience

Mobilizing expertise and experience from elsewhere, that is, mostly from previous projects, does not imply a smooth transfer of knowledge from project to project. Against the backdrop of their temporary nature, projects exhibit what Gann and Salter (2000, p. 961) refer to as "broken learning and feedback loops" that create structural barriers to project-to-project learning (e.g., Grabher 2004; Swan and Scarbrough 2010). Furthermore, even if this process of transferring experiences between projects happens, it is likely to foster stability rather than support innovations.

We found, nevertheless, that large-scale projects can facilitate the mobilization of expertise and experiences in a way that is productive for the generation of innovations. Such mobilization processes varied between different types of organizations and followed contrasting patterns. When mobilization implied the use and refinement of existing expertise and experience in the context of a new project, the mobilization process often included a process of deliberate and critical reflection on previous experiences, both positive and negative:

… there are certain areas of interest which we have been following now for quite a long time. … . And, of course, we can benefit from the experiences we made in previous projects and develop them further (C1_Arch4).

... we of course learnt from the previous collaboration with [the architects]. ... . We had to improve the planning quality and cooperation modes. ... . And so we held a workshop at the very beginning ... just for team building (C2_Eng2).

In some cases, mobilization crossed boundaries between different knowledge bases, thereby connecting previously disparate professional worlds. For instance, the European Central Bank (ECB) as owner organization brought in its reporting and control capabilities:

... take the controlling which is actually bank-controlling ... , then organization and risk management, that exist in a bank anyway and that was transferred to the construction project (C2_Own3).

Deliberate deviation from previous experience and capabilities proved particularly true for the architectural practice that is often defined by the permanent search for new and unconventional solutions, despite appreciating expertise and experience as important for the quality of their work:

... it's important to start new things ... with openness, but also with a certain naivety ... . While experiences are important ... at some point they are also a limitation (C1_Arch1).

Grammar: Mobilizing Rules

Considering the enormous importance of security issues, such as stability and fire safety, the production of the built environment is shaped by numerous rigid norms, standards and regulatory frameworks. For instance, the making and implementation of any atypical building details or elements require a thorough process of approval and permission-seeking. Construction, hence, is a highly regulated industry. The wide range of binding regulations tends to define, but also to secure, a very specific scope of actions: as explained by one of the engineers involved in the execution of the Main Station in Berlin, "provided there were no norms and directives that you could relate to, we would have to develop everything on our own ... , with tests and so on ... there would be no end to it" (C3_Supp2).

Regulatory frameworks, thus, seem to be "both constraining and enabling" (Giddens 1984, p. 25) with regard to the generation of innovations. Across the six case studies we encountered two opposing mechanisms of how this pool of possibilities (and limitations) could be mobilized in a productive way. For instance, existing rules could be utilized as a reference when rules did not exist at all. Take the case of the covered bridges that formed the station platforms of Berlin Central Station, where the existing rules for uncovered bridges were mobilized as an analogy and orientation for a regulated implementation of novelty:

... we have a covered bridge, and the prescription does not address covered bridges. What it addresses, is a bridge where the sun shines from above and where the top is warmer than the bottom ... . We then translated this specific setting in design loads with lower differences in temperatures (C3_Oth2).

However, existing rules can also set rigid limits, so providing an incentive, in particular for engineers, to deviate from existing norms and standards, and potentially exceed hitherto often unquestioned boundaries:

But this is precisely the engineer's task ... to go to the limits and then to decide: Now I depart from the prescriptions" (C5_Eng5).

... so you—or I—sometimes infringe rules, so as to make it more exciting (C2_Eng1).

Enactment: Tackling Self-Induced Problems

While existing cultural orientations, experience and expertise, and rules afford important resources for the generation of novelty in construction projects, the actual proof of innovativeness occurs through "innovative acts" (Rammert 2010, p. 35), that is, through what is actually done in a project. Novel ways of doing things, hence, have to be enacted against the backdrop of the boundary conditions that usually shape the practice of performing construction ventures. In this context, changing how things are done encounters routinized "patterns of practice" (Rammert 2001, p. 175), i.e., ways of working through a construction process. What is more, an intention to deviate from routines faces restrictive conditions of material feasibility and an institutional setting that is not a priori supportive of change. Above all the architects among the interviewees complained that this restrictiveness is particularly notorious in Germany:

Well, I mean, the architecture in Germany looks as it looks, since the common or garden architect simply works with this set of rules and regulations. And around that, there is not much to design. It's almost like a catalogue for pre-fabricated elements. And that is in fact, that is alarming (C1_Arch4).

As a consequence, across all case studies the desire and ambition to do things in a novel way usually conflicted significantly with the existing restrictive nature of the construction industry. This clash exerted new demands and requirements on the actors involved, spurring them to deal with and confront the rigid material and institutional boundary conditions. Enacting mobilized resources in order to change patterns of practice, in a way, engendered self-induced problems that the involved actors and organizations inevitably needed to tackle.

The practices of problem-solving that were triggered when confronting new ideas with restrictive boundary conditions related to different areas in the process of planning and implementation: first of all, guaranteeing material feasibility required a continuous conversation with *artifacts* of different scales (from one-to-one mock-ups to paper made samples and architectural models) and natures (haptic and digital). When ideas about novel ways of doing came up, the involved actors needed to thoroughly probe into detail at an early stage in order to grasp whether and how the actual making of non-standard solutions was possible. Across the different projects, therefore, the work with haptic and digital objects forced and enabled architects and engineers to develop new quantitative models and to calculate ambitious design loads, and to conduct numerous experiments—including the development of completely new test methods, for instance, with regard to testing the load-bearing capacity of curved glass:

> ... *usually you put the glass pane in a frame and place sandbags on it. And you check, quite primitively, with how many sandbags the glass cracks. But this way did not work with such a curved geometry ... so we came up with the idea of a vacuum load. ... . We then placed the pane on top of a box, sealed that box, and then sucked the air off (C1_Eng6).*

In the course of testing and inquiring, mostly the firms in the supply chain, but also ambitious architects, as in the Elbphilharmonie case, produced partly abstract and visualized, partly tangible intermediate results that served as testbeds for the remaining development process. During the design and decision-making processes, such intermediate objects and simulations proved pivotal milestones in the process of introducing novelty: on the one hand, the artifacts enabled the actors to actually see and potentially re-think and scrutinize initial ideas; on the other, intermediate results could illustrate the feasibility of products, solutions and approaches and thereby convince critical or less ambitious actors:

> And you perhaps need to take a small extra-step in order to prove to the industry that what you have designed is possible. As a consequence, we often invest in advance, by building one-to-one models ourselves and experimenting with these models. Sometimes we also find firms that support us in that (C1_Arch4).

> ... and you also need images and models to achieve certainty for yourself. Particularly when you choose non-standard (C1_Arch2).

Second, professionals needed to develop and employ novel *skills and tools* when tackling self-induced problems. In this way, they were often propelled to move beyond their disciplinary field and the methods and tools to which they were accustomed. For instance, architects needed to gain a profound understanding of technical issues and challenges, such as glass bending, or the cut-cover-method for underground tunnels. Additionally, involved actors often needed to acquire—sometimes even produce—and work intensively with tools that exceeded their existing repertoire. New tools comprised both machinery (e.g., furnaces for glass bending, CNC machines) and self-made and one-off tools (e.g., algorithms, parametric tools, silicone syringe). Adapting working approaches and employing new tools disrupted significantly the established routines of firms and professionals. Introducing novel practices therefore presupposed a willingness to take risks and shoulder responsibilities, and to invest immense amounts of time and money. Yet, the size of the project often rendered these investments profitable, in the short or in the long run:

> Well, [firm X] introduced digitalized production processes. But, with an order of such a size, firms are of course willing to extend their facilities (C5_Oth1).

> And the next step ... was that single firms took the effort to optimize processes and then acquire general approval for their products (C1_Eng6).

Third, in order to realize their ambitious plans, actors needed to actively craft their *networks of cooperation*. The search for partners who would help implement novel ideas was, on the one hand, determined by the limitation of available firms that were capable of delivering sophisticated solutions at all and were also willing to participate in an experimental process:

> ... it is helpful to have ... a partner who is also interested to jointly answer a small puzzle game. ... [firm X], who had the interest to not always do run-of-the-mill projects on a square meter base (C1_Arch1).

On the other hand, particularly for architects often long-standing relations with partners that share similar priorities and values were important. Therefore, they sometimes even sought to bend rigid procurement and tendering regulations. Take the case of the ECB, where the principal designer's perseverance and reputation eventually secured collaboration with the desired planning engineers:

> He said: ... . "We did that project with them and we need to continue with them, no matter what the rules and regulations are." And he really banged his fist on the table. And so, we in fact got in (C2_Eng4).

Finally, bending the rules happened not only with regard to assembling project coalitions, but also with the implementation of novel construction solutions in the face of a rigid *institutional environment*. Manipulating this environment by "mobilizing minds" (Garud and Karnøe 2001), in order to overcome or bypass rigid rules, was of central importance. Such practices of manipulation related in particular to regularly communicating with external experts, surveyors and verification engineers or even influencing their selection and appointment:

> When we do something that is innovative, we intensely propose to the project owner: "Let us agree on the verification engineer with the Federal Railway Authority and let us include him already in the design process. And, let us look for somebody who has enough backbone to push this through with us." If you don't do that, and if you just concentrate on technical aspects, every innovation fails from the very first moment. You have no chance to get it through (C4_Oth1).

Translation: Push and Pull

While mobilization practices mostly related to what was needed in the respective projects, the translation of novel practices out of a project into concrete lessons from novel practices, or even changing discursive framings and regulatory frameworks, proved much more contingent and open-ended. As construction projects usually establish custom solutions, a straightforward transfer beyond the project boundaries is difficult. In addition, the temporary coalitions that accomplish planning and implementation of large-scale projects dissolve once a building is finalized. There is, hence, no proper entity responsible for drawing and multiplying lessons. Disseminating and perpetuating innovations that materialize in large-scale construction projects therefore require actors to actively engage in translating novel practices into modified orientations (semantics); enhanced experience of involved actors (pragmatics); and new sets of rules and regulations (grammar).

Our findings show that practices of translation occur in two directions. On the one hand, involved actors strategically *push* innovations in order to leverage reputation benefits, re-use novel practices, or standardize tailored solutions to facilitate future benefits. On the other, discourse-related structures (e.g., professional journals, conferences), future project coalitions, or regulatory bodies take up novel solutions and practices and, in a sense, *pull* them out of the project to make them visible and available elsewhere.

Semantics: Modified Orientations

In public and professional discourse, all six case studies were framed as new references (of "best practice"). These projects were considered to attest to the feasibility of unorthodox technical and ambitious aesthetic solutions, and to the value of large-scale construction projects for and beyond the construction industry. The motives for this discursive re-orientation, however, referred not only to particular novel practices, techniques or solutions, but also essentially to the projects as a whole. In professional and public discourses, hence, projects are perceived as bundles of rich expertise and experience across disciplines and sectors.

Push dynamics occurred through involved actors, in particular through architectural offices that sought to reinforce and thereby leverage the positive perception of their work by means of deliberate actions and long-term engagement. Actors pursued push strategies regardless of their status. Celebrity architects such as Herzog & de Meuron have long-established strategies for enhancing the visibility of their projects, including the publication of a richly illustrated book on the Elbphilharmonie. Also, emerging players such as the "underdog" architects of the Wehrhahn Line hired an advertising agency to promote the project after its completion (besides also publishing a similar book):

> Here we hired a really professional public relations agency to do this work. And the result was really good communication. Take this catalog that communicates this entire project, the entire interdisciplinary project ... if we had left this to the city administration's PR department, the result would have been different (C5_Oth3).

More important were pull dynamics with regard to how the projects achieved reference status. A significant number of articles was published in specialist journals (architectural and engineering). Acknowledgement and recognition (especially for the contributions of architects and engineers) were bestowed by diverse professional associations in the form of honorable mentions and institutional awards. Interestingly, both bridge projects, while explicitly going against mainstream discourses, obtained one of the highest honors in the field of bridge engineering and construction in Germany:

> This did not happen accidentally or because there was no other structure available. The engineering community acknowledged the project as a milestone and as a really extraordinary structure (C4_Oth1).

In particular, and significantly, the projects with exceptional symbolic qualities developed by celebrity architects attracted the attention of the daily press (Elbphilharmonie, ECB, Berlin Central Station[2]) and thereby achieved public recognition.

In addition to the classic drivers of recognition, there were a multitude of smaller formats through which knowledge and information about the projects influenced how things are seen in the construction industry. Such formats included lectures, talks, presentations in professional and academic contexts, high quality

2 Also the projects surrounded by the highest levels of controversy.

publications, but also consultancy for the development of future projects, and guided tours making the project accessible to professionals and the wider public:

> I have meanwhile given so many talks and conducted so many guided tours for professionals, next week there will be another tour for engineers. It will be about acoustics and oscillations (C1_Cont1).

Pragmatics: Enhanced Expertise and Experience

With regard to the benefits in terms of experience and expertise, interview partners across all cases as well as professional fields described how the work in the respective projects changed their ways of doing things, for instance, developing "a completely different way of thinking" and "a sharper look" (C2_Supp2), or learning to "explore new avenues" (C2_Eng3). Especially for firms in the supply chain that were often required to adapt their working approaches and to acquire new technologies and tools, the successful translation of experiences and expertise for future endeavors was considered a way to enhance their competitive position in the marketplace.

One way of securing that expertise and experience would be available also outside the project at hand was through pushing lessons learnt. In all cases, independently from firm, organization or sector, the involved project partners actively and deliberately sought to strategically use experience and new expertise by means of long-established and formalized channels, such as intranet, libraries and databases, workshops and training sessions, or within comprehensive knowledge management systems. In some cases, organizations codified processes employed in the project and adopted these processes as new standards:

> Well, we set standards for calls for tenders ... Before we started to plan, we standardized all processes related to procurement, and we still use these processes and guidelines in the (owner organization) today (C2_Own3).

However, the actual re-use of expertise and experience obtained in the projects examined here was different: mainly through pulling them into follow-up ventures in a purposeful fashion. Here, translation occurred selectively, driven by the specific needs of new projects. Interviewees argued that such a selective use is necessary, as drawing on the full stock of accumulated expertise and experience would produce "a certain blockage" (C5_Arch1). In addition, pull dynamics followed primarily informal ways, that is through interpersonal relations and face-to-face encounters:

> However, the best way of transferring knowledge is of course through real people. You have the people here, you can talk to them, and you get explanations about the solutions that were developed (C2_Eng2).

Informal channels, hence, support the selectivity and purposefulness that are necessary for the translation of lessons for new ventures.

Grammar: New Sets of Rules and Regulations

The translation of project-related innovations into new rules and regulations for the wider construction sector usually takes time. The sedimentation of novel pragmatics in the industry's grammar (through codification, standardization and patenting of specific details and single building elements) is an incremental process that follows predefined steps and fulfills certain formal requirements. Especially engineers working in the supply chain and thus often involved in codification processes emphasized how lengthy, effortful and resource consuming the processes of approval can be:

> And there is the option of applying for individual approval. It takes at least three months ... . It can be a first step to a general authorization. But the way to such an authorization is long, expensive and not fully certain (C1_Eng4).

Therefore, translations into grammar were actively and deliberately pushed by project actors, often guided by (professional and economic) interests. In particular, companies in the supply chain were keen to translate tailored solutions into "regulated products" (C1_Eng6) in order to reap long-term benefits from one-off investments. This translation proves highly productive for future projects, as it expands the scope of actors' action and potentially advances the execution of novel solutions:

> We had done the precursor project—we had all approvals, we had delivered all proofs—and of course those proofs were used again. The proofs exist in several versions. And such a re-use of proofs also occurred in projects that drew on our bridge project (C4_Proj1).

However, there are also instances of pulling novelty into new rules and regulation. Such pull was driven by regulatory bodies, in particular by the public administration. Governments and the industry reflected upon and reacted primarily to negative experiences. For instance, the City of Düsseldorf translated experiences garnered during the development of the new subway line into new and more comprehensive criteria for decision-making concerning future contract allocations:

> We changed that for the next subway project ... we say: "Okay, the price accounts only for seventy-five percent ... ." We have developed additional criteria ... . And then we sometimes find: "Okay, we do not necessarily select the cheapest tender" (C5_Own1).

Similarly, new measures to improve project planning and cost control in the form of a government document followed the cost escalations related to Hamburg's Elbphilharmonie project. Yet, such broad changes in regulatory frameworks cannot solely be traced back to one individual project. Regulatory change is always influenced by diverse experiences, and the efforts of numerous actors and organizations feed into the decision processes from which new rules arise.

Discussion and Conclusion

In a way, this chapter has had a double objective: the first was primarily conceptual. Based on a broad framework that conceives of innovation in the construction industry as a change of "cultural frames" (Rammert 2001), our intention was to show how large-scale projects perform as frame changers. We argued that large construction ventures not only encourage the generation and exemplary implementation of novelty, but also afford the necessary legitimating impulse that helps novelty to be accepted in an otherwise rigid environment. Large projects enable and enforce an enhanced interaction between the three analytical dimensions in which cultural frames materialize—"how things are viewed" ("semantics"); "how things are done" ("pragmatics"); and "how these activities are institutionally arranged" ("grammar") (Hutter et al. 2015; Rammert 2001, 2010). More specifically, construction ventures enable project participants to *mobilize* discursive, practical and institutional resources, *enact* these resources and *translate* them back into the discursive, practical and institutional context. The second objective was to undertake a methodological exercise, trying out an empirical application of the "semantics, pragmatics, and grammar"-framework for innovation based on a comprehensive analysis of large-scale projects in the construction industry.

When it comes to the first objective, our evidence corroborates and clarifies the argument. Figure 1 summarizes our argument and the main findings, illustrating the practices of frame changing.

In our view, two overarching themes stand out that provide novel insights for the study of innovation in construction and the role of large projects with regard to innovation and change more generally. The first relates to the difference between practices of mobilization and translation, on the one hand, and practices of enactment, on the other. Mobilization and translation practices follow an exogenous logic. Project participants leverage the project context as they build on and engender references (both in a positive and negative manner), be it in a discursive, practical or institutional logic. Enactment practices, in contrast, unleash an endogenous dynamic of indispensable problem-solving. This dynamic resembles what Hirschman (1967) refers to as the "principle of the hiding hand." Managers start off large projects with an idea and a plan, but without knowing exactly what will happen once work is underway. During the journeys through these projects they encounter problems, but are forced and enabled to develop the creativity to solve them. It would be fruitful to examine this problem-solving dynamic and its implication for innovations in a more thorough fashion.

The second theme concerns the relation between novelty generation and legitimation as two different key aspects in innovation processes. Our findings show that,

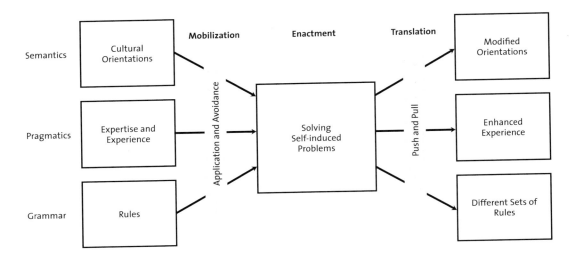

Semantics — Cultural Orientations

Mobilization · Enactment · Translation

Pragmatics — Expertise and Experience

Grammar — Rules

Application and Avoidance

Solving Self-induced Problems

Push and Pull

Modified Orientations

Enhanced Experience

Different Sets of Rules

Figure 1: Frame Changing Practices Through Large-Scale Construction Projects

in practice, both are intricately interwoven. Each testing procedure, for instance, embodies the search for an optimized solution as well as an act of legitimation. Also here, more research would be needed in order to see more clearly different modes and patterns of how novelty creation and novelty legitimation interact.

When it comes to the methodological exercise, we found that employing the "semantics, pragmatics, and grammar" framework has been highly productive. However, we also encountered some challenges. One challenge is methodological in a narrow sense. It relates to the classification of instances as semantics, pragmatics, or grammar. When, for example, a rule of allocating contracts within an organization changes, it depends on the scale of analysis whether this change applies to how things are done (pragmatics) or how they are institutionally arranged (grammar). The decisions we have made about assigning instances to the observation forms of innovation are therefore necessarily contingent. A second challenge relates to the limitations of the approach more generally. Despite proving extremely fruitful when it comes to looking into mostly understudied facets of innovation and, particularly, exploring the relation between innovation and routinized behavior, there are some aspects that remain unexplored and undertheorized within our analysis. This refers particularly to time, actor networks and materiality. It seems obvious that the three analytical dimensions "semantics, pragmatics, and grammar" as well as the different practices exhibit varying temporalities—take the incremental process of translating novelty into changed regulations.

Also, the impact of practices clearly depends on the position of actors vis-à-vis others. Finally, the construction projects essentially constitute processes of gradual materialization. Looking into how dealing with this materiality on different scales and in varying natures influences the generation of novelty requires a much more thorough analysis than we could provide here.

Some of these aspects will be discussed in the following chapters. One chapter deals explicitly with temporalities, another one with materiality. The time aspect is also addressed in the chapter on problem formulation that looks into what happens in the early stages of a project cycle. The materiality aspect—connected to the immobility of the material output—is also an important element in the chapter on geographies. Actor networks are tackled in a specific perspective—with regard to the transformation of distinct professional cultures in the process of innovation generation. Together, these chapters engender a more complete picture of how large-scale projects drive innovation in the construction industry.

References

Amabile, T. M. (1996). *Creativity in Context: Update to the Social Psychology of Creativity.* Boulder, CO.

Boland Jr., R. J., K. Lyytinen, and Y. Yoo (2007). "Wakes of Innovation in Project Networks: The Case of Digital 3-D Representations in Architecture, Engineering, and Construction." *Organization Science* 18.4: pp. 631–647.

Butzin, A. and D. Rehfeld (2013). "The Balance of Change in Continuity in the German Construction Sector's Development Path." *Zeitschrift für Wirtschaftsgeographie* 57.1-2: pp. 15–26.

Clegg, S. and K. Kreiner (2014). "Fixing Concrete: Inquiries, Responsibility, Power and Innovation." *Construction Management and Economics* 32.3: pp. 262–278.

Davies, A. and T. Brady (2000). "Organisational Capabilities and Learning in Complex Product Systems: Towards Repeatable Solutions." *Research Policy* 29.7-8: pp. 931–953.

Dubois, A. and L.-E. Gadde (2002). "The Construction Industry as a Loosely Coupled System: Implications for Productivity and Innovation." *Construction Management and Economics* 20.7: pp. 621–631.

Ekstedt, E., R. A. Lundin, A. Söderholm, and H. Wirdenius (1999). *Neo-Industrial Organising. Renewal by Action and Knowledge Formation in a Project-Intensive Economy.* London.

Engwall, M. (2003). "No Project is an Island: Linking Projects to History and Context." *Research Policy* 32.5: pp. 789–808.

Gann, D. M. and A. J. Salter (2000). "Innovation in Project-Based, Service-Enhanced Firms: The Construction of Complex Products and Systems." *Research Policy* 29.7-8: pp. 955–972.

Garud, R. and P. Karnøe (2001). "Path Creation as a Process of Mindful Deviation." R. Garud and P. Karnøe, eds. *Path Dependence and Creation.* Mahwah, NJ.

Giddens, A. (1984). *The Constitution of Society. Outline of the Theory of Structuration.* Berkeley; Los Angeles

Grabher, G. (2004). "Temporary Architectures of Learning: Knowledge Governance in Project Ecologies." *Organization Studies* 25.9: pp. 1491–1514.

Grabher, G. and J. Thiel (2015). "Projects, People, Professions: Trajectories of Learning through a Mega-Event (the London 2012 case)." *Geoforum* 65: pp. 328–337.

Hirschman, A. O. (1967). "The Principle of the Hiding Hand." *The Public Interest* 6: pp. 10–23.

Hutter, M., H. Knoblauch, W. Rammert, and A. Windeler (2015). "Innovation Society Today. The Reflexive Creation of Novelty." *Historische Sozialforschung* 40.3: pp. 30–47.

Latour, B. (1986). "The Powers of Association." J. Law, ed. *Power, Action and Belief: A New Sociology of Knowledge?* London.

Rammert, W. (2001). "The Cultural Shaping of Technologies and the Politics of Technodiversity." K. Sörensen and R. Williams, eds. *Shaping Technology, Guiding Policy.* Cheltenham.

Rammert, W. (2010). "Die Innovationen der Gesellschaft." J. Howaldt and H. Jacobsen, eds. *Soziale Innovation. Auf dem Weg zu einem postindustriellen Innovationsparadigma.* Wiesbaden.

Reckwitz, A. (2003). "Grundelemente einer Theorie sozialer Praktiken. Eine sozialtheoretische Perspektive." *Zeitschrift für Soziologie* 32.4: pp. 282–301.

Rehfeld, D. (2012). "Innovationsbiographien in der Bauwirtschaft." A. Butzin, D. Rehfeld, and B. Widmaier, eds. *Innovationsbiographien: Räumliche und sektorale Dynamik* (1 ed., Vol. 1). Baden-Baden.

Reichstein, T., A. J. Salter, and D. M. Gann (2005). "Last among Equals: A Comparison of Innovation in Construction, Services and Manufacturing in the UK." *Construction Management and Economics* 23.6: pp. 631–644.

Roberts, E. B. (1988). "What We've Learned: Managing Invention and Innovation." *Research-Technology Management* 31.1: pp. 11–29.

Swan, J. and H. Scarbrough (2010). "Why Don't (or Do) Organizations Learn from Projects?" *Management Learning* 41.3: pp. 325–344.

How Small Deviations Can Trigger Greater Transformations. Comparing Innovation Biographies in the Construction Industry

Werner Rammert

Framing an Innovation Study in a Slowly Renewing Field: A Diachronic Perspective of Cultural Change

The construction industry is an underestimated field of innovation studies in comparison to others such as the automotive, computer, or communication industries. Disruptive core technologies, creative start-ups, and big players are not as visible as elsewhere. Instead, this field knows piecemeal improvement, long-term collaboration with heterogeneous partners and project-based network forms of organization. Innovation is often visible only after a decade or more, when new practices and cultural orientations have materialized in paradigmatic buildings. Significant examples are the Gothic cathedrals, Eiffel's iron constructions, and the serial Bauhaus-settlements. Present-day examples

are the computer-designed iconic buildings that blend steel, concrete and glass to unique skyscrapers, terrific airports, or fantas-
tic concert halls.

Taking into account these features of the construction industry, it was a reasonable design decision of the *Constructing Inno-*
vation research enterprise (a) to compare six large-scale projects
to discover the manifold roots of small-scale novelties, and (b) to
compare their biographies over a longer timeframe to uncover
the rise of a greater innovation. The design follows a diachronic
perspective of cultural change that emphasizes practices and processes of doing innovation in a highly heterogeneous field. In this
respect, it deviates from the mainstream synchronic perspective
that favors institutional, socio-economic and technological structures to explain the rates of innovation between different fields,
sectors, or nations. Surely, both perspectives have their illuminating insights as well as their blind spots. My comments, however,
focus on the questions of whether and how this particular theoretical framing and the empirical results may advance the state of
the art in innovation studies (Rammert 2021). I shall concentrate
my questions on (1) how to determine the subject of innovation
studies, (2) on how to elicit where innovations come from, and (3)
on how to meet some challenges of the framework.

Determining the Subject of Innovation Studies: Novelties,
Innovations, and Cultural Change

Innovation studies often start with a seemingly certain knowledge about the phenomenon of innovation and a clear definition
of the subject that justifies the selection of the specific research
sample. As a consequence, they prefer fields of high innovativeness. They even treat scientific breakthroughs as completed innovations. They focus on obvious technological gadgets. In short,
they follow the standard spectrum of novelties, which ahead of
time are labeled as innovation.

Constructing Innovation starts in a field of seemingly low
innovativeness and, indeed, with little knowledge of it. In contrast
to the above studies, the researchers are interested in all kinds of
novelties and even in the smallest variations of ideas, techniques,
and practices that make differences. Their chosen "cultural shaping"-approach expands the usual technological or economic perspective on innovation. Its theoretical frame distinguishes
between how things are viewed (concepts and discourses), how
things are done (constellations and material practices), and how

things are instituted (state of the art and institutional regimes). It also distinguishes between times of the project and between respective practices of mobilization, enactment, and translation. Hence, it enables a diachronic and comparative view on different innovation biographies in a particular field. The subject of this kind of study is the process of doing innovation in a longer time perspective and under conditions of greater material and social diversity (Grabher 2004).

In my view, this research design also advances the state of the art in innovation studies in general; it is not solely an appropriate approach to the particular field of the construction industry and its large-scale projects (Butzin and Rehfeld 2009). The expanded view for all kinds of novelties enriches the search for roots and relevant drivers of later innovation. The applied theoretical frame differentiates between times and kinds of practice, which is why it allows a fine-grained reconstruction of the transformations from novelty to innovation.

Searching for Where Innovations Come from: Entrepreneurs, Organizations, or Fields of Heterogeneous Inter-Agency

How innovation comes into being can be observed at different levels of agency: the individual, the collective, and the societal. A simplified history of innovation theory shows us a stepwise shift from single ingenious individuals and role models to techno-scientific communities and big corporations to heterogeneous networks and fragmented fields of innovation (Rammert 2006).

The early work of Schumpeter condensed all the necessary attributes of an innovative person in the figure of the "entrepreneur." This figure connects the features of the visionary creator, the passionate rule-breaker, the high risk-taker, and the restless project-maker. Today it is entirely justified to translate these features into practices and to search for such novelty-creating practices everywhere, namely among all participants in heterogeneous large-scale projects. The figure of the innovative entrepreneur cannot be confined to economic players, to star architects, or to smart project-managers.

Schumpeter later came to realize that it is large corporations that have become the prime drivers of innovation. They were able to accumulate the necessary risk capital for the next generation of innovation; to acquire the necessary skills; they wielded the power and were in a position to control the long-term course of innovation, from early exploration to late exploitation.

Since the 1980s, a growing body of research into innovation has noted significant changes to a "post-Schumpeterian mode of innovation": a shift from the individual entrepreneur to social networks of innovators, from disciplines and domains to mixed communities of practice, and from large corporations to heterogeneous networks of organizations. Finally, it shows a move from a technology-centered approach to a reflexive "innovations of society"-frame relating to all kinds of novelty-creating practices and referring to valuation criteria beyond the economic (Passoth and Rammert 2018).

What, then, are the consequences of this shift for the design of innovation studies? In my view, one has to expand the zone of innovation beyond innovative figures, communities and organizations and over a longer time span, since heterogeneous networks and multiple arenas of negotiation are now the main driving forces of innovation. One should also focus on the practices of deviation, creation and translation between diverse cultural orientations. That means paying close attention to micro changes in the doing and undoing of innovation, such that one is interested in the reconstruction of the situational, material and gradual transformations that finally lead to an "individual biography" of innovation with "multiple identities" and that no longer follow a "standard path" of innovation (Lenzen 2020; Lettkemann 2016).

Constructing Innovation constitutes an excellent example of this process-oriented and micro-funded design. It compares the deviations and developments of a sample of six large-scale projects within one highly heterogeneous field. Every working practice is included and analyzed during the phases of mobilization, enactment, and translation. It follows the many small variations in the different professional practices and at different times, intended and unintended, explicit and implicit. In this way the researchers have uncovered the multiple loci, the different tempi of novelty-creation and the constellations for successful developments. They convincingly demonstrate that even following the patterns of routines and professional rules can lead to small acts of innovation, e.g., when one unconsciously performs the practice in a slightly different way or when one occasionally deviates from the norm in order to adapt to a difficult situation. The most impressive insight seems to me to be that neither the contracted network nor one of its dominant participants can be seen as the critical authority from where innovation comes. They build the necessary context. The critical driving forces, however, are the actions of the heterogeneous inter-agencies in the field.

Meeting the Challenges of the Framework: How to Conceive the Agential, Material, and Temporal Aspects

The contributors to this chapter analyzed 1,192 interview passages from ninety-five people. In the main, they received a very detailed and highly differentiated picture of the micro changes when they employed the "semantic, pragmatics, and grammar"-framework. They do, however, report experiencing problems of classification when they had to ascribe instances such as "changing a rule" to one of the three aspects. In my view, this theory of praxis has a blind spot: it fails to recognize deliberative and individual action as a source of agency. The category of practice already implicates a pre-structured form of action, one which is, too, already halfway to transforming into more consolidated habits and fixed units of institutions and cultures. On the other hand, theories of action, creativity, and experimental interactivity (Rammert 1999; Schulz-Schaeffer and Rammert 2019) also assume a first transformation from spontaneous agency to a routinely repeated practical action. This assumption completes the second transformation from mostly implicit forms towards explicit ones, such as codes of law, professional rules, or standards of regulation. It might well be helpful to employ a gradual concept of agency that can distinguish between (a) one-off acts, (b) slightly repeated routines or practical actions, (c) often and consciously followed actions, and (d) officially coded or materially incorporated rules of agency.

A second methodological challenge would be to supplement the expert interviews with multi-sited and focused ethnographical studies. Such collected observational data would strengthen the statements about the performances ("how things are done") in comparison to the interview narratives ("how things are viewed"). The fact "that the number of codes relating to pragmatics exceeded significantly the number of those associated with *semantics and grammar*" (Thiel et al. in this volume) confirms my theoretical position that discourses are over-valued and misleading if not controlled by actions and materialized rules (Rammert 2010).

The term "materialized rules" transfers to a third challenge: how could the under-explored "materiality aspect" be integrated into the frame? The construction industry seems to have especially narrow engagement with the material aspect. Its large and long-time projects can almost be seen as processes of gradual materialization: from the first plans, designs and models to the construction stages to the building in use and in converted use, and finally, before demolition, as a ruin or cultural monument. The more the materialization advances, the less chance there is to remove the material output or to reverse the built structure.

A classical concept of materiality, however, risks overemphasizing the resistance of physical things and the irreversibility of materialized structures. A relational "form/media"-concept of technicization and materialization (Rammert 2001) could open the research space for the analysis of various forms of effective connections as well as for multiple material media that make differences. A research unit is the complex constellation of physical things, bodies, and signs; the question is how it is set in action, how it is put together, and how it is changed (Rammert 2012). A research unit is neither a practice nor a product. Innovation can be discovered everywhere, especially when the practices change the relations between the various parts and move the interagency between the media that make differences. Examples are a new technique of connecting curved glass and steel frames, the conversion of old buildings and industrial quarters into luxury lofts and public spaces for art and culture, or the new combination of organic material with smart skyscrapers that turns them into "greenhouses." These long-term transformations emerge out of earlier small changes in practice, such as experimenting with various kinds of material and techniques, testing different uses and impacts, avoiding the resistance of materials and regulations, or recombining all the parts into new constellations.

The materialization processes also refer to a fourth challenge: how can one conceive and grasp the varying temporalities? This challenge concerns the horizontal differentiation of temporalities, not the longitudinal differentiation. The horizontal one refers to the tempi and time cycles of the heterogeneous participants, cultures and institutions; the longitudinal one cuts the time into periods. The research team found a more sophisticated way that avoids the usual model of a linear innovation development by instead loosely ascribing the practices of mobilization, enactment, and translation to different stages of the project flow. Another step forward would have been possible, had the team compared the different tempi of innovation across professional cultures and institutional contexts. Such a comparison would have also allowed them to analyze how the different tempi of innovation synthesize to a joint rhythm and how this confluence is orchestrated by the respective projects (Rammert 2000). As a consequence, the research space would then extend to the whole ecology of innovations.

References

Butzin, A. and D. Rehfeld (2009). *Innovationsbiographien in der Bauwirtschaft: Endbericht*. Stuttgart.

Grabher, G. (2004). "Temporary Architectures of Learning: Knowledge Governance in Project Ecologies." *Organization Studies* 25.9: pp. 1491–1514.

Lenzen, K. (2020). *Die multiple Identität der Technik. Eine Innovationsbiographie der "Augmented Reality"-Technologie*. Bielefeld.

Lettkemann, E. (2016). *Stabile Interdisziplinarität. Eine Innovationsbiographie der Elektronenmikroskopie*. Baden-Baden.

Passoth, J.-H. and W. Rammert (2018). "Fragmental Differentiation and the Praxis of Innovation: Why is There an Ever-Increasing Number of Fields of Innovation?" W. Rammert, A. Windeler, H. Knoblauch, and M. Hutter, eds. *Innovation Society Today*. Wiesbaden.

Rammert, W. (1999). "Weder festes Faktum noch kontingentes Konstrukt: Natur als Produkt experimenteller Interaktivität." *Soziale Welt* 50.3: pp. 281–296.

Rammert, W. (2000). *Ritardando and Accelerando in Reflexive Innovation, or How Networks Synchronize the Tempi of Technological Innovation*. TUTS-WP-7-2000. TU Berlin.

Rammert, W. (2001). "Relations that Constitute Technology and Media that Make a Difference: Towards a Social Pragmatic Theory of Technicization." H. Lenk and M. Maring, eds. *Advances and Problems in the Philosophy of Technology*. Münster.

Rammert, W. (2006). "Two Styles of Knowing and Knowledge Regimes: Between 'Explicitation' and 'Exploration' under Condition of Functional Specialization or Fragmental Distribution." J. Hage and M. Meeus, eds. *Innovation, Science, and Institutional Change: A Research Handbook*. Oxford.

Rammert, W. (2010). "Die Pragmatik des technischen Wissens oder: 'How to Do Words with Things'." K. Kornwachs, ed. *Technologisches Wissen*. Berlin.

Rammert, W. (2012). "Distributed Agency and Advanced Technology, or: How to Analyze Constellations of Collective Inter-Agency." J.-H. Passoth, B. Peuker, and M. Schillmeier, eds. *Agency Without Actors? New Approaches to Collective Action*. London.

Rammert, W. (2021). "Technology and Innovation." B. Hollstein, R. Greshoff, U. Schimank, and A. Weiss, eds. *Soziologie – Sociology in the German-speaking World*. Berlin.

Schulz-Schaeffer, I. and W. Rammert (2019). "Technik, Handeln und Praxis. Das Konzept gradualisierten Handelns revisited." C. Schubert and I. Schulz-Schaeffer, eds. *Berliner Schlüssel zur Techniksoziologie*. Wiesbaden.

Mobile Knowledge, Sticky Products: Geographies of Innovation in Large-Scale Construction Projects

Johannes Dreher/Joachim Thiel/Gernot Grabher/ Monika Grubbauer

Introduction

Without any doubt, the role of time in projects has enjoyed a clear epistemological privilege in project management research. From the basic definition of projects as "temporary organizations" with "institutionalized termination" (Lundin and Söderholm 1995) to recent attempts to overcome this original closed temporal orientation (for a synthesis, see Thiel and Grabher in this volume), projects have largely been framed as modes of "temporal structuring in organizations" (Orlikowski and Yates 2002). In contrast to this prevailing focus on time, however, there are few contributions that seek to conceptualize the spatialities of temporary organizing in a systematic fashion. The few existing examples focus on micro-geographies of team work (Bosch-Sijtsema and Tjell 2017), distance as a reason for boundary spanning activities (Maaninen-Olsson and Müllern 2009), or locational decisions as elements of inter-organizational politics in mega-project consortia (van Marrewijk and Smits

2014). In addition, some studies address dispersed work in project teams and thereby implicitly touch on spatial categories such as face-to-face interaction (e.g., Aaltonen and Turkulainen 2018; Sapsed and Salter 2004).

The persistent neglect of space and geography in research on project organizations is surprising given recent shifts in project management research toward examining cross-boundary constellations. For instance, academics have increasingly emphasized the interplay between projects and their contexts (e.g., Engwall 2003; Grabher 2004; Stjerne and Svejenova 2016). Other studies systematically address inter-organizational or even transnational patterns of project organization (e.g., Jones and Lichtenstein 2008; Orr et al. 2011; Sydow and Braun 2018). Investigation of such constellations seems to suggest that geographical categories—e.g., scale, place and location, mobility and immobility, proximity and distance—should provide useful analytical categories to better understand how projects work in practice.

Our focus in this chapter is on the geography of large (and inevitably inter-organizational) construction projects. Following the thread running through this book, we seek to establish a link between these geographies and innovation processes. More specifically, our intention is to show how innovation processes within large-scale projects unfold across geographical space and how the geography contributes to these innovation processes.

Conceptually, we are inspired by the rich body of literature on geographies of innovation. In particular we draw on a recent line of inquiry that proposes a nuanced understanding of the patterns of mobility and immobility as well as of proximity and distance that may support or obstruct knowledge creation and innovation (e.g., Crevoisier and Jeannerat 2009; Nygaard Tanner 2018; Rallet and Torre 2017; Rutten 2014, 2017). While this literature is helpful with regard to identifying sources of immobility (against a backdrop of omnipresent mobilization and logics of proximity in the light of increasingly distanciated interaction), it does not cover two crucial features of the construction industry: its essentially project-based nature, and the genuine immobility of its final product (e.g., Butzin and Rehfeld 2013).

Empirically we draw on the total of the eighty-six semi-structured interviews that we conducted for our six case studies. In addition, we made use of firm address lists that we partly received from project owners and partly self-assembled as a by-product of contact-making for the interviews. From the interview material we analyzed codes that provided answers to three guiding questions: (1) how the geography of collaboration in the inter-organizational project networks emerged through the firm selection process; (2) how the actual (and multi-locational) process of collaboration was organized over distance; and (3) what role the immobile construction site played in this multi-locational process of collaboration. Our main emphasis was on particularly ambitious and technically complex solutions that required specialized and highly qualified suppliers and a high degree of inter-organizational coordination. We used the address lists for two purposes: first, to simply map the multi-locational patterns of all six cases; and, second, to trace the shifting geographies of collaboration for one characteristic building element: the glass façade of Hamburg's new Elbphilharmonie.

Following on from this introduction, we provide an overview of recent shifts in the literature on innovation geographies and relate this literature to our subject of research: large-scale construction projects. The empirical part unfolds the findings of our analysis governed by the three guiding questions that helped us to unpack our empirical material. In a concluding section, we summarize the main insights of our research and propose further lines of inquiry.

Large-Scale Projects and Multi-Locational Innovation Processes

The interactive nature of innovation processes has become a commonplace in innovation studies. Novelty, so the argument goes, has neither a single source—e.g., Schumpeter's heroic entrepreneur—nor is it unidirectional—as a technology push or a demand pull—but arises out of interactive processes that can comprise entire value chains or even go beyond them (Cohendet and Simon 2017). Starting from this observation, the literature on geographies of innovation seeks to look into "the spatiality of the means of interaction" (Faulconbridge 2017, p. 675) that is favorable for such novelty to arise and diffuse (for an overview, see Bathelt et al. 2017; Faulconbridge 2017). For quite a long time, the pertinent academic debate was dominated by an inherently territorial approach. The so-called "territorial innovation models" (TIMs) (Moulaert and Sekia 2003) emphasized "localized learning systems" (Bathelt et al. 2017, p. 10) as major sources of novelty generation. More recently, however, a more differentiated literature has developed that has sought to come to grips with "varied spatial configurations of social practice" (Amin and Roberts 2008, p. 29) and their connection to learning and innovation. Against the backdrop of continued globalization processes and proliferating communication technologies, the emphasis has shifted to multi-locational and multi-scalar dynamics (e.g., Crevoisier and Jeannerat 2009; Nygaard Tanner 2018) through which interactive processes unfold. Also, conceptual lenses have changed—from focusing on the structural conditions that favor or disfavor interactive learning to stressing the actual practices of knowing and learning (e.g., Amin and Cohendet 2004; Ibert 2007).

While the TIMs emphasized the relative immobility of production factors relevant for innovations—in particular, of (tacit) knowledge and (localized) trust built in face-to-face interactions—and the importance of physical proximity for interactive learning, multi-locational innovation processes involve contingent combinations of mobile and immobile elements as well as of nearby and distanciated interactions (Crevoisier and Jeannerat 2009). The relevant literature has sought to identify patterns of mobility and immobility as well as modes of interrelation between proximity and distance that might contribute to knowledge creation and innovation.

When it comes to the relation between *mobility* and *immobility*, there is a strong focus on mobile innovation-related activities (e.g., Nygaard Tanner 2018) and the possibility of temporarily sharing tacit knowledge (e.g., Rallet and Torre 2017). Scholars identify two sources of immobility: for one thing, literally immobile elements such as scientific laboratories (Ibert 2007) or other specific material infrastructures. For another, there is a recent line of thought that has advanced a more comprehensive reading of the immobility of tacit knowledge. In particular, discussions revolve around the geographical "anchoring" (Crevoisier and Jeannerat 2009; Rutten 2017) of knowledge and knowledge creation. Rutten (2017, p. 162), for instance, attributes anchoring to the fact that "individuals are spatially sticky to the place where they live and work."

While, according to the author, the individual's knowledge is local, actual "knowledge creation is not local because social interaction happens across geographical space" (p. 162), occurring, hence, both in *proximity* and over *distance*. There is a large body of work that focuses precisely on how interaction across space actually materializes between these two poles. Three strands of inquiry can be distinguished. First, there are studies that discuss the relation between physical proximity and other forms of proximity (e.g., relational, organized, cognitive) (Boschma 2005; Moodysson and Jonsson 2007) or emphasize similar features, such as "relational capital" (Aaltonen and Turkulainen 2018) or "social affinity" (Gertler 2008) that may function as a substitute for geographical closeness or may even outweigh physical proximity. Two salient points can be extracted from this literature: the ambivalent impact of all kinds of closeness on learning and innovation (e.g., Boschma 2005; Ibert 2010), and the role of geography as a mediator of other forms of closeness rather than as an enabler of knowledge creation on its own. In project collaborations at a distance, for example, face-to-face is considered as "the 'richest' form of interaction" (Sapsed and Salter 2004, p. 1516) that helps generate "trust, respect, credibility, commitment" (p. 1517)—these social-capital related aspects being the actual sources of interactive learning.

A second group of studies seeks to identify sources of variation with regard to when physical proximity matters for interactive learning and knowledge creation. Gertler (2008), for instance, maintains that the need for nearby interaction varies between different "knowledge bases" (e.g., Asheim et al. 2007). Brinks et al. (2018) put the need for proximity down to actors' capacity to specify their own ignorance. Finally, Nygaard Tanner (2018) as well as Ibert and Müller (2015), among others, observe varying needs for geographical proximity in different phases of innovation processes. While, according to Nygaard Tanner (2018, p. 2307), particularly the early periods of idea generation require close local interaction, later stages tend to allow the substitution of physical proximity by organized proximity.

A third strand of inquiry looks into the impact of online technologies on the need for physical proximity and face-to-face interaction (e.g., Grabher and Ibert 2017). Grabher et al. (2018), for instance, drawing on Knorr Cetina's (2009) concept of the "synthetic situation," observe "an increasing simultaneity and amalgamation of presence/absence and physical/virtual" (Grabher et al. 2018, p. 250) in collaborative settings of knowledge creation. The authors argue that interactive processes build less on mere presence ("being there") and more on mutual awareness ("being aware"). Hence, physical proximity might generate less closeness than the collaboration between professionals across distance via virtual technologies.

Taken together, recent research on the multi-locational nature of innovation processes provides useful insights for the analysis of the innovation geography of large-scale construction projects. These insights in particular relate to (a) sources of immobility and stickiness in an otherwise mobile environment of interaction; and (b) the role of physical proximity in interactive processes of knowledge creation in or across value chains. And yet, the current literature on geographies of innovation does not cover two specific features of the construction project geographies: first, construction is an inherently project-based industry—interaction across geographical space is therefore essentially temporary; second, immobility and stickiness refer not only to production-related aspects (such as knowledge or material facilities and infrastructures), but fundamentally to the output—the locally bounded building (e.g., Butzin and Rehfeld 2013).

Multi-Locational Innovation Processes: Insights from Six Large-Scale Construction Projects

It goes without saying that large-scale construction projects cannot be accomplished "unilaterally" (C1_Supp2). Large projects are, in essence, temporary collaborations. Examining the (innovation) geography of six large-scale projects, hence, implies exploring the "inter-organizational landscape" and the "interaction processes within and between both permanent (i.e., firms) and temporary organizations (i.e., projects)" (Havenvid Ingemansson et al. 2019, p. 5) that occur within this landscape. In what follows, we outline the dynamic geography of six temporary inter-organizational landscapes by delving into three formative elements of this geography: (1) the genesis of the multi-locational project geographies of involved organizations; (2) the interactions across space in the multi-locational innovation processes that unfold during project implementation; (3) the "stickiness" of the construction site as center of gravity—and key output—around which all activities revolve. Our aim is to show how innovation processes unfold in the interplay of these three formative elements.

Multi-Locational Project Geographies: Ambitions as Restrictions

The assemblage of the temporary coalition that eventually produces a large building is a critical moment in the project cycle. Recent research on innovation in large-scale projects describes this moment as one of four "windows of opportunity" (Davies et al. 2014) which provide an enhanced chance for innovations. The argument is that the so-called "engaging window" (p. 26) has the potential to widen the repertoire of practices and solutions by opening the process to unusual proposals and hitherto unknown firms and by incentivizing potential suppliers to propose innovative solutions.

However, our findings do not corroborate the idea of a chance for openings in the engaging window. On the contrary, the scale and complexity of the projects as well as the ambition linked to the technical, organizational, or design related features, rather posed restrictions with regard to the selection of potential partners at various stages in the supply chain of each case study. We identified three types of such restrictions. The first, and most important one, referred to the (in particular technical) *capabilities* of recruited actors:

> ... the bidding field tends to become smaller for the technically more demanding large-scale projects. So that it is no longer the masses that participate, but rather a lot of specialization is required (C6_Cont1).

Across all case studies interview partners mentioned a "highly limited market" (C5_Eng2) with "bottlenecks" (C2_Arch4); "there are not many [options]" (e.g., C2_Eng1). Expressed in figures, the possibility for selecting potential project partners or suppliers for specific tasks was limited, for example, to ten (C1_Cont2; C4_Proj1), four (C6_Eng1), two (e.g., C3_Eng3) or even only one option (e.g., C1_Supp1):

> There's just this one company that does that. You don't have to search for a long time... these one-suppliers are usually the ones with the somewhat innovative topics (C2_Proj1).

Thus, the more complex the task and the more uncommon (i.e., innovative) the required solution, the smaller the number of available project partners.

The second type of restrictions concerned the *relational entanglement* of firms. Potential project partners were involved in other bidding consortia and therefore not available (C1_Cont2). In other cases, there was a "shadow of the past" (Swärd 2016, p. 1841) that narrowed the choice of potential partners. Hence, companies did not collaborate either because they had never worked together before or because they had had negative experiences in previous collaborations (C1_Supp1; C1_Supp2).

The third type of restrictions related to the *willingness* of potential suppliers. In the words of an interviewee, "it is not easy to inspire firms for large-scale projects" (C5_Oth3). Lack of willingness sometimes hinged on disagreements about the terms of the contract, such as allocation of commercial risk, but also on a lack of financial muscle to take risks (C1_Supp1; C1_Supp2). And, in fact, even though large-scale ventures seem to be attractive for potential partners—as "once in a lifetime opportunities" (Grabher and Thiel 2015)—such complex and ambitious projects also entail substantial risks that not all small and medium construction enterprises are willing to take (C3_Supp3; C3_Supp4; C3_Supp5; C4_Proj1). The implementation of often novel solutions means entering an uncertain process during which it cannot be predicted if, how, when, and under which conditions solutions might be found. Uncertainties translate into contractual risks of not being able to deliver the promised results at all or not in time (e.g., C1_Arch5; C1_Supp1; C1_Supp2), or into financial risks (C5_Oth3)—closely connected to the first ones—as it is simply not possible to calculate the resources needed. "Extra" efforts such as conducting experiments, producing mock-ups and models, developing new tools, applying new software, etc. are largely based on good will and require the intrinsic motivation of partners to depart from routines (e.g., C1_Arch1; C1_Arch2; C1_Supp1). Mutual trust built up in long-lasting collaborations enhances such motivation (C1_Supp2) but in turn engenders its own restrictions.

The processes of setting up the project networks in our six case studies show that there was—especially for complex and highly specific tasks—hardly any choice of possible partners. Project geographies were therefore strongly pre-structured by the fact that suitable partners had to be found at all. Figure 1 provides an overview of how the project supply networks extend over Germany or even beyond. Although only displaying parts of the networks, the maps show multi-locational and widespread project geographies. Involved firms are anchored to the places where they are located—for whatever reason—and closeness to the construction site is not a criterion for being part of project networks. The Kochertal Bridge is an exception to this spatial pattern. Although comprising a demanding task—the maintenance and reinforcement of a bridge listed for preservation—the work was largely accomplished through a local coalition. This exception may be due to the fact that the same (local) actors, who designed and built the bridge in the 1970s, were commissioned for its maintenance. These actors were particularly eager to be involved, as the bridge is an outstanding structure of its kind and time, and the original builders wanted to see their corporation's name on the construction site (C6_Cont1).

Multi-Locational Innovation Processes: Proximity, Distance, and the Role of Models
The widespread multi-locational project networks necessarily involved interactions across geographical space that took place both by way of face-to-face encounters of project partners and at a distance.

Physical co-presence of professionals from different firms was important both in the processes of selecting the rare suitable partners and later on, when existing coalitions had jointly to develop the solutions that could fulfill what had been initially conceived. Before actual collaborations started, therefore, project leaders involved in planning processes (primarily architects and engineers) visited the production sites of potential suppliers in the construction industry to identify suitable partners. Some visits involved travel over longer distances (e.g., from Germany to Spain and Italy), mainly organized as day-trips. Such production-site visits were crucial to inspect production conditions, as well as to increase mutual

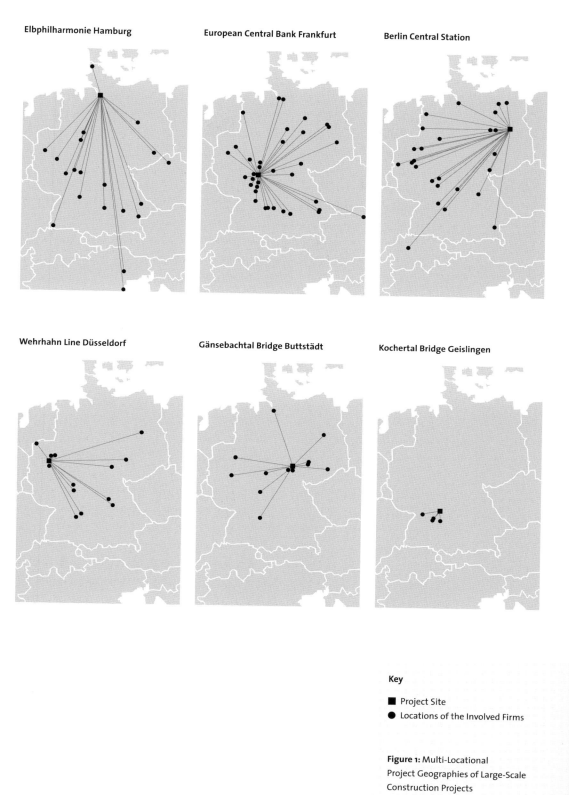

Elbphilharmonie Hamburg

European Central Bank Frankfurt

Berlin Central Station

Wehrhahn Line Düsseldorf

Gänsebachtal Bridge Buttstädt

Kochertal Bridge Geislingen

Key

■ Project Site
● Locations of the Involved Firms

Figure 1: Multi-Locational Project Geographies of Large-Scale Construction Projects

understanding of processes and thereby to assess what was feasible (C5_Supp3; C5_Own2):

> We have been to all the factories. We were in all the glassworks, looked at the glass production, we looked at all the bending possibilities. ... we know the plants of all the factories. So, also through our personal knowledge: Who is eligible? Then you have conversations with each firm (C1_Supp1).

> It´s important to really see such production. How is glass bent and coated? It's just important that you understand the processes and also the physical limits of how things are being done right now. Especially when you go to the interface, or to the limits of feasibility, it is very important that you understand that, otherwise we are speaking at cross purposes (C1_Arch1).

Visiting production plants was often connected with the production of samples and served to check whether potential partners could be relied upon to meet their commitments:

> Yeah, there's a phone call at two: "Sorry, glass is broken. What's broken? It's broken? What do you think first? They are lying to me. I don't believe that. So, leave it there. Please, leave the glass. Book a flight Friday at noon, fly there, I have to go there. Saturday morning in Spain, I want to see that. So, we checked it on the spot: Where's the glass? Why did this happen? ... Did it break at all ... did they cool it [the pane] the wrong way ... or you realize, they didn't bend it at all (C1_Supp1).

Once a partner had been chosen, temporary face-to-face interaction facilitated mutual learning and joint solution finding as it helped the parties understand working methods and assess possibilities of project partners (C1_Arch2; C5_Own2; C5_Supp3). Physical co-presence not only materialized among professionals or between professionals and production facilities, but very often included models. Models offered important tools in the joint working process as they helped assess various aspects of perception (like aesthetics of design, materiality), and also served as testbeds for technical performance (through, for instance, acoustics, fire-safety, climate and weather tests, and load testing, as well as tests of physical and chemical reactions, and mutual compatibility of materials). Models served as "boundary objects" (Carlile 2002) that enabled communication between professionals from various disciplines. Working with models therefore repeatedly brought together different experts in order to jointly find solutions for crucial components, especially at interfaces between different kinds of expertise (e.g., C1_Arch4; C2_Eng4; C5_Eng2). While models in the early phase were still small and were used at different places, over time they became larger and immobile (e.g., C1_Arch5; C3_Eng3; C5_Eng2). The presence of immobile models increasingly determined the places where professionals met:

... as I said at the beginning of this workshop, it was small models ... I would say table models ... but these were more like these workshop formats. And then we had this big search where we just had to rebuild the stations individually, rebuilt in a one-to-one model. That was huge. That was such a cutout here like half a room, three meters ceiling, three meters wall and three meters of ground. You could virtually walk through it and you could touch it and everything (C5_Eng2).

Apart from being beneficial for the joint development process, models were also essential to convince skeptical project partners of the feasibility of novel solutions (e.g., C1_Arch1; C3_Eng3; C5_Supp3):

There was a big round and the client also came. And then you could see with the help of the model that the daylight was falling all the way down. And then they believed us (C3_Arch2).

In the most extreme form, mock-ups (i.e., one-to-one models) were used for tests in order to demonstrate that the construction would meet the required security standards and functionality (C1_Eng4; C1_Supp1; C1_Supp3; C4_Eng1; C4_Oth2; C4_Proj1). Large-scale models also provided the proof of whether developed solutions met the desired high-quality standards (e.g., acoustics tests for the Elbphilharmonie concert hall with a 1:10 model; C1_Arch2; C1_Arch4; C1_Arch5; C1_Supp6). Tests with models took place at production sites, special testing facilities, and partly on or near the construction site, and always brought together various experts involved in finding a solution (C4_Proj1). Mock-ups or large samples (e.g., "three by four meters," C5_Oth1), showrooms and even finished building components also offered important meeting points for the different actors. There, design solutions were assessed and selected, and involved professionals could get haptic and spatial impressions and control the quality of execution (e.g., C1_Arch3; C1_Supp2; C1_Supp5; C2_Eng3; C5_Oth1; C5_Own2).

However, the development of non-routine solutions also included periods of working separately at the headquarters and in workshops of involved companies at different locations. Such isolation helped professionals to concentrate on further developing details. When interaction was needed during such periods, digital models and diverse channels of communication offered substitutes for face-to-face:

It is always easier to say something in a conversation [referring to physical co-presence] than if you write it down in an e-mail. On the other hand, you also need the concentrated work and an e-mail and a 3D model. In the case of the hall, we also sent back and forth a lot of complicated things with the company ... and then we looked at them together and made a phone call ... (C1_Arch2).

Using one of the most outstanding and technically ambitious elements in the context of our cases studies—the glass façade of the Elbphilharmonie—as an example,

Maps A to E in Figure 2 portray the multi-locational process of developing an innovative building element over the project cycle. The process comprises a shifting geography, including varying patterns of mobility and immobility as well as of distanciated and face-to-face interaction: from short-time inspection visits to production plants in the pre-selection phase (Map A); through concentrated elaboration at separate places (Map B); planners' one-day visits to the production-site to increase their understanding of the production process and assess intermediate products (Map C); visits of core project partners at the test facility (Map D); to long-term stays of specialized planners at the production site over the entire fabrication process (Map E).

The Sticky Product: The Construction Site as Center of Gravity
While the production of the six large-scale structures under investigation came about in spatially extended project networks, each of the networks had a particular geographical focus: the site where the structure should materialize. Even before construction work began, every construction site was already a center of gravity for the respective project network. Contracted actors had to inspect the site in order to prepare tasks. Architects had to visit the construction site in its specific context in order to check the local boundary conditions of their design drafts. Structural engi-

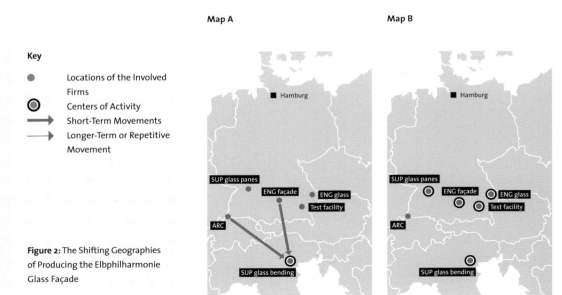

Figure 2: The Shifting Geographies of Producing the Elbphilharmonie Glass Façade

neers had to carry out soil investigations in order to design and calculate the load-bearing structure (C4_Oth2; C5_Eng1;). In later planning stages architects set up showrooms, models, and mock-ups at the construction site to decide on the final design and material in an authentic setting (e.g., for the Wehrhahn Line in a disused underground tunnel close to the construction site, C5_Eng2). Engineers had to undertake large-scale tests on one-to-one models to ensure that their calculations fulfilled security requirements and worked under real conditions on site (e.g., C4_Proj1; C5_Eng2). Contracted partners also had to visit the site to verify whether and how the planned solutions would work there:

> If the construction site is in Berlin, then I can think of great things in Munich, when you see it in real life, it's a completely different feeling. People always say that a reinforcement with a diameter of twenty-eight is a line on the paper. When you see that on site, weighted in all directions, there's hardly any concrete that fits in there, then you get a different feeling. So, visits to construction sites were one of the main reasons for checking whether what we were thinking about at the green table made sense at all (C3_Oth2).

The recruitment of local project partners responsible for execution planning, for instance, enabled the lead architects—particularly in the iconic projects Elbphilharmonie and ECB—to continue working from distance in the early planning stages and to tap into the knowledge concerning local building authorities (C1_Arch5; C2_Arch4).

Map C   Map D   Map E

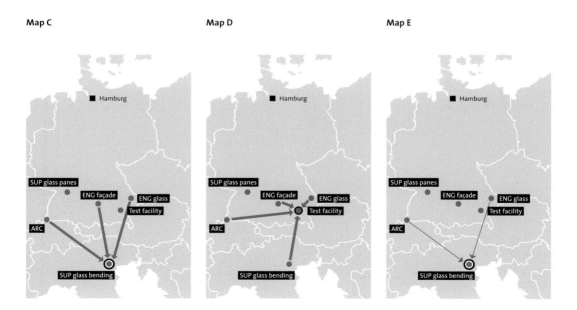

During the actual construction phase, many of the involved firms moved their project teams close to each other and close to the construction sites. The sites now definitely became the focal points of activity, for countless contractors and subcontractors, project management experts as well as architects and engineers who sought to ensure the required quality of execution. For many involved firms the construction phase implied moving project planning functions into temporary offices close to the site. In this way each firm was able to make sure that related professionals could quickly co-locate with others to tackle suddenly surfacing problems (e.g., C2_Arch4; C3_Oth2; C3_Proj4; C6_Cont1). Such temporary face-to-face interaction on the construction site was, however, also indispensable even when there was no need to solve sudden problems. Functional and sequential interdependencies between the various trades involved required continuous coordination, particularly when it came to crossing organizational and professional boundaries. This was especially crucial for novel solutions that were realized for the first time and therefore entailed a higher risk of unforeseen problems (C4_Eng2). Being physically co-located both to the project and to other project partners allowed the identification of problems in a more precise fashion and more quickly. Thus, the (co-)presence of involved staff onsite allowed for better problem assessment and so helped minimize risks (C4_Cont1):

... if you are anywhere else, you'll get papers on your desk. You can decide that too. But whether what's in there, whether that's really the problem, or whether the problem is perhaps a completely different one, of course you'll only find out about that when you're outside on the spot ... at the pulse of time ... [and] if we are supposed to keep it [the project] going, then we have to make the right decisions quickly (C2_Proj1).

It is always important to look at it [the problem] on the spot, at the construction site. And then you get the first overview. Then everyone involved is there. The construction company is there, the construction management is there. And if necessary, our planning office again, so that we can also be there. And then you take a look at it. What is the problem, what did it depend on and then you think of solutions (C6_Own1).

The high degree of uncertainty linked to non-routine activities also entailed a higher density of meetings and temporary physical co-presence (e.g., C1_Eng1; C1_Eng2):

We have put ourselves in a relatively rigid corset of routines, which was also enforced by the project steering: sometimes weekly in the hot phases and monthly in the regular periods ... there were weeks in which such routines happened on a daily basis, when there was too much buzz around ... and we thought: "now we have to keep our fingers on the pulse" so that the whole thing would stay within the time frame (C2_Oth1).

Critical moments required a high concentration of professionals, not only at operational but also at managerial level (C1_Supp1; C4_Eng2):

Well, of course I [interviewee from senior management] was repeatedly at the construction site, but then I had to overcome some problems at the construction site, where we got together, also internally and discussed how to get the problems under control (C1_Arch3).

The construction site was not only the center of gravity for practical reasons such as quick problem solving, task coordination and control of critical construction phases (C1_Eng3; C1_Supp3; C4_Eng1; C4_Eng2), but also for the various routine tasks of different project partners. So jours fixes were often held on site and many of the involved professionals regularly appeared there. Such routine engagement with the site helped "identify" with the gradually materializing product (C2_Arch4). In addition, the regular presence of individual professionals helped them get a comprehensive idea of project implementation, by ensuring they did "not ... lose the feeling and understanding for the construction" (C3_Proj1); they were "able to assess the varying production conditions, such as qualification and ability of the workers, weather, storage conditions, material quality" (C1_Arch4); and they could check construction quality and progress (e.g., C1_Eng3; C2_Supp2; C3_Proj3; C5_Proj2). Physical co-presence on the construction site was also necessary to show one's own availability as a contact person (C2_Own2) and to build mutual trust between the project partners (C1_Supp6).

Identification with the project and relations of trust among the on-site team were also supportive elements when projects went through hard times. While, for instance, the Hamburg City Administration and the general contractor for the Elbphilharmonie works went to court to settle their argument about the escalation of the project's costs, there was always a positive atmosphere among those responsible for construction (C1_Arch4; C1_Own2). However, one interviewee (C2_Arch4) also stressed downsides of a too close and too trustful interaction. Particularly when there were conflicts, too much trust hindered a clear allocation of responsibilities and thereby could hamper effective problem-solving.

The centripetal forces that were coming from the construction sites during the project implementation stage did not stop when the structures examined in these pages were eventually completed. Once planners as well as construction managers had left, the eventual hype—produced (or at least disseminated) by public media and specialist journals—rendered each large-scale construction project "a place of pilgrimage for experts" (C2_Own1). Professionals visited the structures on site, taking part in guided tours and learning from project participants about the innovative practices and solutions that had been adopted (e.g., C2_Own2). In this way, the structures have served as reference objects for subsequent projects (e.g., C1_Supp1). In a sense, then, the sticky product of large-scale construction projects not only shapes the generation and implementation of innovations, but also their diffusion—at least on a discursive level.

Discussion and Conclusion

This chapter started from two research gaps: a lack of geographical thinking in project management research, and a privileged attention that knowledge-intensive services and high-tech industries—and not construction, with its project-based nature and local boundedness—have received in recent work in innvovation geography. To address these gaps, our strategy involved an empirical analysis of large-scale construction projects that drew on the conceptual apparatus of recent literature on the geography of innovation.

The chapter has shown that our findings—presented in the preceding section—provide novel insights that may enhance both project management research and work related to a geography of innovation. More specifically, we would like to highlight four key points that exemplify the results of our research and enrich and/or challenge the common understanding of how projects work in geographical terms and how innovation processes unfold across space.

First, it seems that innovative ambition in (or through) large-scale projects engenders interaction over distance. Unlike the discussion in the geography of innovation literature, the point here is not whether innovation and knowledge creation need proximity or how innovation processes deal with distance. In our cases—with one (specific) exception—distance is an inevitable by-product of innovation. The difficult search for and selection of partners that are capable of implementing innovations simply reduces the likelihood of co-location when it comes to involved actors. It would be interesting to look into whether this "compulsion of distance" is specific to construction or whether it also holds for other types of innovation processes (not only) in large inter-organizational projects.

Second, we identified the huge importance of temporary face-to-face interaction in distanciated project networks—for a variety of reasons—that largely corroborates extant knowledge from geographies of innovation and the literature on management of dispersed project teams. Face-to-face is, in fact, "the 'richest' form of interaction" (Sapsed and Salter 2004, p. 1516). More interesting, however, is that moments of keeping distance also matter in order to ensure concentrated further development of specific elements. This evidence seems to be more in line with Ibert's (2010), Nygaard Tanner's (2018), and Ibert and Müller's (2015) argument that the need for face-to-face interaction varies, depending on the phases in innovation processes. And we noted that, during periods of collaboration over distance, online communication and joint work on digital models underpin interaction, which also supports Grabher et al.'s (2018) point that mutual awareness might sometimes be more important than actual co-presence.

The role of models as joint objects of collaboration—both over distance and in co-presence—implies the *third* key result that we would like to highlight here. Models, mock-ups, and other intermediate results of the design and development process afford occasions for encounters—virtually, but often face-to-face. Such intermediate artifacts are partly immobile, partly evade a joint exploration at a distance and thereby impose co-present interaction. In addition, immobility tends to increase over the course of the project. The role of these artifacts in the large-scale construction projects that we studied here resonates with the role of prototypes as boundary objects in product development processes (e.g., Carlile 2002). However, the boundary objects here not only facilitate collaboration beyond knowledge boundaries but also draw people together geographically. It would, therefore, be worthwhile to examine the geography of and around boundary objects—also in other industries—in a more systematic fashion.

Fourth, our findings provide a first impression of how the local stickiness of the final product shapes interactions and their geographies in multiple ways. The role of the construction site resembles what Knorr Cetina (2001) calls an "epistemic object"—an artifact that a scientist works with in the lab and that requires his or her permanent care. Temporarily locating close to the site—as many of the involved firms in our cases did during construction work—enables them to be there quickly to provide this care: by solving embryonic problems, grasping the complexity of the entire work, feeling the materiality, touching, smelling. Presence at the construction site not only shapes the relation between individual professionals and the emerging building. Being there is also a source of joint identity and mutual trust within the project network. In a sense, the site serves as a stage on which participants in the project can mutually prove their commitment to the joint task. And once the building is completed, the site translates its centripetal force into a "place of pilgrimage" for professionals who were not involved in the actual project.

Taken together, the interactive processes out of which innovations in large-scale construction projects arise seem to oscillate between two opposing geographical dynamics: on the one hand, a centrifugal force inherent in putting together an inter-organizational network of rare firms that are able to fulfill the ambition linked to each project; on the other, the centripetal force coming from the construction site as the center of gravity of this network. Particularly the latter point, that is, the attracting force of the end-product, is a novel aspect for economic (or innovation) geography that deserves further scrutiny, not only in research on construction.

References

Aaltonen, K. and V. Turkulainen (2018). "Creating Relational Capital Through Social-ization in Project Alliances." *International Journal of Operations & Production Management* 38.6: pp. 1387–1421.

Amin, A. and P. Cohendet (2004). *Architectures of Knowledge—Firms, Capabilities, and Communities*. Oxford.

Amin, A. and J. Roberts (2008). "The Resurgence of Community in Economic Thought and Practice." A. Amin and J. Roberts, eds. *Community, Economic Creativity, and Organization*. Oxford.

Asheim, B. T., L. Coenen, and J. Vang (2007). "Face-to-Face, Buzz, and Knowledge Bases: Sociospatial Implications for Learning, Innovation, and Innovation Policy." *Environment and Planning C: Government and Policy* 25.5: pp. 655–670.

Bathelt, H., P. Cohendet, S. Henn, and L. Simon (2017). "Innovation and Knowledge Creation: Challenges to the Field." H. Bathelt, P. Cohendet, S. Henn, and L. Simon, eds. *The Elgar Companion to Innovation and Knowledge Creation*. Cheltenham.

Bosch-Sijtsema, P.M. and J. Tjell (2017). "The Concept of Project Space: Studying Construction in Project Teams from a Spatial Perspective." *International Journal of Project Management* 35.7: pp. 1312–1321.

Boschma, R. (2005). "Proximity and Innovation: A Critical Assessment." *Regional Studies* 39.1: pp. 61–74.

Brinks, V., O. Ibert, F. C. Müller, and S. Schmidt (2018). "From Ignorance to Innovation: Serendipitous and Purposeful Mobility in Creative Processes—The Cases of Biotechnology, Legal Services and Board Games." *Environment and Planning A: Economy and Space* 50.8: pp. 1742–1763.

Butzin, A. and D. Rehfeld (2013). "The Balance of Change in Continuity in the German Construction Sector's Development Path." *Zeitschrift für Wirtschaftsgeographie* 57.1-2: pp. 15–26.

Carlile, P. R. (2002). "A Pragmatic View of Knowledge and Boundaries: Boundary Objects in New Product Development." *Organization Science* 13.4: pp. 442–455.

Cohendet, P. and L. Simon (2017). "Concepts and Models of Innovation." H. Bathelt, P. Cohendet, S. Henn, and L. Simon, eds. *The Elgar Companion to Innovation and Knowledge Creation*. Cheltenham.

Crevoisier, O. and H. Jeannerat (2009). "Territorial Knowledge Dynamics: From the Proximity Paradigm to Multi-Location Milieus." *European Planning Studies* 17.8: pp. 1223–1241.

Davies, A., S. MacAulay, T. DeBarro, and M. Thurston, M. (2014). "Making Innovation Happen in a Megaproject: London's Crossrail Suburban Railway System." *Project Management Journal* 13.4: pp. 25–37.

Engwall, M. (2003). "No Project Is an Island: Linking Projects to History and Context." *Research Policy* 32.5: pp. 789–808.

Faulconbridge, J. R. (2017). "Relational Geographies of Knowledge and Innovation." H. Bathelt, P. Cohendet, S. Henn, and L. Simon, eds. *The Elgar Companion to Innovation and Knowledge Creation*. Cheltenham.

Gertler, M. S. (2008). "Buzz without Being There? Communities of Practice in Context." A. Amin and J. Roberts, eds. *Community, Economic Creativity, and Organization*. Oxford.

Grabher, G. (2004). "Temporary Architectures of Learning: Knowledge Governance in Project Ecologies." *Organization Studies* 25.9: pp. 1491–1514.

Grabher, G. and J. Thiel (2015). "Projects, People, Professions: Trajectories of Learning Through a Mega-Event (the London 2012 case)." *Geoforum* 65: pp. 328–337.

Grabher, G. and O. Ibert (2017). "Knowledge Collaboration in Hybrid Virtual Communities." H. Bathelt, P. Cohendet, S. Henn, and L. Simon, eds. *The Elgar Companion to Innovation and Knowledge Creation*. Cheltenham.

Grabher, G., A. Melchior, B. Schiemer, E. Schüßler, and J. Sydow (2018). "From Being There to Being Aware: Confronting Geographical and Sociological Imaginations of Copresence." *Environment and Planning A: Economy and Space* 50.1: pp. 245–255.

Havenvid Ingemansson, M., Å. Linné, L. E. Bygballe, and C. Harty (2019). "In Pursuit of a New Understanding of Innovation in the Construction Industry: The Significance of Connectivity." M. Havenvid Ingemansson, Å. Linné, L. E. Bygballe, and C. Harty, eds. *The Connectivity of Innovation in the Construction Industry*. London.

Ibert, O. (2007). "Towards a Geography of Knowledge Creation: The Ambivalences between 'Knowledge as an Object' and 'Knowing in Practice'." *Regional Studies* 41.1: pp. 103–114.

Ibert, O. (2010). "Relational Distance: Sociocultural and Time–Spatial Tensions in Innovation Practices." *Environment and Planning* A 42.1: pp. 187–204.

Ibert, O. and F. C. Müller (2015). "Network Dynamics in Constellations of Cultural Differences: Relational Distance in Innovation Processes in Legal Services and Biotechnology." *Research Policy* 44.1: pp. 181–194.

Jones, C. and B. Lichtenstein (2008). "Temporary Inter-Organizational Projects: How Temporal and Social Embeddedness Enhance Coordination and Manage Uncertainty." S. Cropper, M. Ebers, C. Huxham, and P. S. Ring, eds. *The Oxford Handbook of Inter-Organizational Relations*. Oxford

Knorr Cetina, K. (2001). "Objectual Practice." T. R. Schatzki, K. Knorr Cetina, and E. V. Savigny, eds. *The Practice Turn in Contemporary Theory*. London.

Knorr Cetina, K. (2009). "The Synthetic Situation: Interactionism for a Global World." *Symbolic Interaction* 32.1: pp. 61–87.

Lundin, R. A. and A. Söderholm (1995). "A Theory of the Temporary Organization." *Scandinavian Journal of Management* 11.4: pp. 437–455.

Maaninen-Olsson, E. and T. Müllern (2009). "A Contextual Understanding of Projects—The Importance of Space and Time." *Scandinavian Journal of Management* 25.3: pp. 327–339.

Moodysson, J. and O. Jonsson (2007). "Knowledge Collaboration and Proximity: The Spatial Organization of Biotech Innovation Projects." *European Urban and Regional Studies* 14.2: pp. 115–131.

Moulaert, F. and F. Sekia (2003). "Territorial Innovation Models: A Critical Survey." *Regional Studies* 37.3: pp. 289–302.

Nygaard Tanner, A. (2018). "Changing Locus of Innovation: A Micro-Process Approach on the Dynamics of Proximity." *European Planning Studies* 26.12: pp. 1–16.

Orlikowski, W. J. and J. Yates (2002). "It's about Time: Temporal Structuring in Organizations." *Organization Science* 13.6: pp. 684–700.

Orr, R. J., W. R. Scott, R. E. Levitt, K. Artto, and J. Kujala (2011). "Global Projects: Distinguishing Features, Drivers, and Challenges." W. R. Scott, R. E. Levitt, and R. J. Orr, eds. *Global Projects. Institutional and Political Challenges*. Cambridge.

Rallet, A. and A. Torre (2017). "Geography of Innovation, Proximity and Beyond." H. Bathelt, P. Cohendet, S. Henn, and L. Simon, eds. *The Elgar Companion to Innovation and Knowledge Creation*. Cheltenham.

Rutten, R. (2017). "Beyond Proximities: The Socio-Spatial Dynamics of Knowledge Creation." *Progress in Human Geography* 41.2: pp. 159–177.

Sapsed, J. and A. Salter (2004). "Postcards from the Edge: Local Communities, Global Programs and Boundary Objects." *Organization Studies* 25.9: pp. 1515–1534.

Stjerne, I. S. and S. Svejenova (2016). "Connecting Temporary and Permanent Organizing: Tensions and Boundary Work in Sequential Film Projects." *Organization Studies* 37.12: pp. 1771–1792.

Swärd, A. (2016). "Trust, Reciprocity, and Actions: The Development of Trust in Temporary Inter-Organizational Relations." *Organization Studies* 37.12: pp. 1841–1860.

Sydow, J. and T. Braun (2018). "Projects as Temporary Organizations: An Agenda for Further Theorizing the Interorganizational Dimension." *International Journal of Project Management* 36.1: pp. 4–11.

van Marrewijk, A. and K. Smits (2014). "Projectscapes: The Role of Spatial Settings in Managing Complex Megaprojects." *International Journal of Complexity in Leadership and Management* 2.4: pp. 278–292.

Advancing Geographies of Innovation in Large-Scale Construction Projects

Maude Brunet/Patrick Cohendet

The analysis of the geography of innovation in large-scale projects, the topic of the chapter by Dreher et al., is rather original, since the literature on large-scale construction projects, while focusing on their temporalities, mostly tends to neglect their geographies. Drawing on six empirical case studies of large-scale construction projects in Germany, this contribution aims to expand the literature specifically about geography of innovations, by analyzing in detail the multi-locational process of knowledge and innovation generation of these projects and highlighting the role of the final construction site.

The contributions from the careful examination of this literature are important as they seek to understand the geographies of project networks (the collaborators and suppliers of the projects), and the process of innovation as spatially bounded and evolving over time as the projects unfold. The chapter leads to some key findings that are highly significant for the sector.

First, large-scale construction projects can be seen as multi-locational processes of knowledge creation over distance, in which the physical co-presence of diverse actors is temporarily organized at different locations. Physical co-presence is important to identify potential/capable partners, to inspect the conditions of production, and to increase mutual understanding of the working methods/construction processes.

Second, intermediate products (digital platforms, virtual communication, models, mock-ups, prototypes, etc.) play a key role in helping project teams elaborate these large-scale projects (Van den Ende et al. 2015). As the processes of materializing planning progress, these intermediate products grow in scale, models become increasingly static, and these intermediate products/outputs/material objects temporarily determine places of meetings and joint knowledge generation.

Third, as the project progresses, the construction site/place of final consumption is not only the place to which all activities are directed, but it becomes increasingly central, as core organizations move their project teams close to each other and close to the project in order to plan and implement it. Physical co-location on the construction site is indispensable as the various trades involved in the realization of the common material product are functionally and sequentially interdependent. Additionally, the construction sites serve as reference objects for subsequent projects.

Fourth, as emphasized here, there is a need for the development of large-scale project studies to delve into broader social science research to enrich current thinking. Knowledge culled from tailored research into geography, land use planning, urbanism, innovation and network theories could usefully serve to approach large-scale construction projects from a multidisciplinary perspective (e.g., Hubert et al. 2014). For example, a recent book by European researchers (Chatzis et al. 2017) investigated the metamorphosis of infrastructures through a multidisciplinary lens, as the intersection between the concrete and the digital spheres. While construction projects are important landmarks anchored in a context, a geographical and a political space, they are also weighted with important cultural, social, and virtual dimensions to be explored and understood contextually. As an example, in their analysis of life stories of megaproject leaders, Drouin et al.

(2021) mobilize the dimension of "place" as an important component of their conceptual framework. Within this dimension they include the cultural context, the political context, and the environmental complexity, as well as stakeholder management, risk management, and innovative processes.

Lastly, the use of maps as visual artifacts in the chapter has been carefully considered: visual representation helps readers to understand the location of the project sites and of the other organizations involved (see Figure 1, p. 93). Figure 2, p. 96–97, takes the example of one of the projects to illustrate the multi-locational process of knowledge creation as the project unfolds. As suggested by Siemiatycki (2017), projects develop through cycles, impacting local networks, innovations, and local communities. One of the main limitations of these geographies of innovation has been identified by the present authors (and their interviewees) as related to the contractual arrangements and delivery modes chosen for the projects; some are more open than others to allowing for innovation (Davies et al. 2019).

While this chapter opens up some important new avenues for research, some of its recommendations for further improvements could be usefully addressed, in particular in the perspective of temporary organizations mentioned by the authors.

First, the role of the project managers as chief executives of the temporary organization (Turner et al. 2003; Sydow and Braun 2018) could be clarified. Their role consists not only in setting objectives and motivating team members or in planning and executing work, but also in considering the influence of politics, the economy, society, the public, and the media on organizational behavior. The dynamics of their career, after the project's successful completion, could also be further investigated. For example, Mark Thurston, CEO of the High Speed 2 megaproject was appointed after his initial involvement with other important megaprojects including Railtrack, Metronet, The Nichols Group, London Olympics, Crossrail, and, CH2M Hill (Sergeeva and Davies 2021).

Second, the structure and dynamics of the teams involved in such large-scale projects could bear further elaboration. As suggested by Grabher and Ibert (2011), it would be interesting for future studies to explore wider communities of practice (e.g., NETLIPSE—Network for the dissemination of knowledge on the management and organization of large infrastructure projects in Europe) and their impact on the dissemination of knowledge and innovation in the construction industry. Large-scale projects could also be the occasion for the formation of impromptu teams that could initiate significant spin-offs from such projects (Jacobsson and Hällgren 2016).

Third, as mentioned earlier, there are few studies in the literature on the geographies of large-scale construction projects, however, some of those that exist could fruitfully have been dealt with in greater detail. As an example, we refer to Van Marrewijk and Smits (2014), who carried out an ethnographic study of two megaprojects (the Dutch High Speed Train megaproject and the Panama Canal Expansion Program). In their study, which deals with two different intersections of spatial design and organizational development around location of project headquarters and spatial distribution of project locations, they suggest the concept of "projectscape," which has been developed to analyze the entanglements of spatial settings and the organizing of megaprojects. This concept, which allowed the inclusion of environmental dimensions of ambient conditions, spatial layout, and symbols and artifacts, would have benefited from a more detailed discussion.

Fourth, in the six projects under review, a few have collaborators from other countries (Spain, Italy, Switzerland, etc.). While regulations and legislation might not be impacted as these are likely uniform across the European Union, it would be useful to investigate geographies of innovation when several countries are involved, for example with Sweden's Öresund bridge (Löfgren 2008) or the Hong Kong–Zhuhai–Macao Bridge (Shi et al. 2020). The diffusion of innovation from the developed world to the developing world is also of interest when addressing geographies of innovation in megaprojects. For example, the megaproject of the Nagpur Metro Rail in India used BIM (Building Information Modeling) technologies after the CEO made a visit to the megaproject site of Crossrail in the UK (Mahalingam 2021).

Lastly, besides the comparison with other large-scale construction projects, we would benefit from lessons learned from other industrial domains such as mechanics, the automotive sector, aeronautics, etc. In the domain of aeronautics, for instance, the place of the construction site is key, and the management of large-scale projects that combine multi-locational processes of knowledge creation with a final assembly site offers some similarities with large-scale construction projects. As an example, in the case of the production of the Stealth bomber plane in the U.S., Argyres (1999) highlighted the role of the choice of a common information system to facilitate multi-site coordination, by establishing a "technical grammar" for communication, and creating social conventions. In the domain of space, some studies focus on the key role of spaceports such at the Kourou center for the European Space Agency launchers in French Guyana (Martin 2020) and on how it contributes both to the economic development and the educational plan of the country. At this level, project organizations are no longer isolated and closed systems, but are associated with larger industry systems, political systems as well as cultural systems, in forming super-organization networks, supply chain networks, and organizational environments.

Aside from the instances of success of large-scale projects (which is the case for the six projects analyzed here), it would be important to better understand some of the limitations of megaprojects: how, for instance, to balance the governance power of government and private companies; how to design institutional systems to avoid poor performance; how to avoid the occurrence of systematic corruption in megaprojects, etc.

In conclusion, the topic of geographies of innovation in large-scale projects merits further exploration and thus we have made the case for this neglected area of research to be seen as a source of insightful discoveries. Large-scale construction projects are not disembodied, they are entangled within their physical location and have importance for local communities. We have also provided examples to illustrate how this might be done through the use of rich empirical material from the six project case studies.

References

Argyres, N. S. (1999). "The Impact of Information Technology on Coordination: Evidence from the B-2 'Stealth' Bomber." *Organization Science* 10.2: pp. 162–180.

Chatzis, K., G. Jeannot, V. November, and P. Ughetto, eds. (2017). *Les métamorphoses des infrastructures, entre béton et numérique.* Brussels.

Davies, A., S.C. MacAulay, and T. Brady (2019). "Delivery Model Innovation: Insights from Infrastructure Projects." *Project Management Journal* 50.2: pp. 119–127.

Drouin, N., S. Sankaran, A. Van Marrewijk, and R. Müller, eds. (2021). *Megaproject Leaders Reflections on Personal Life Stories.* Chelthenham.

Grabher, G. and O. Ibert (2011). "Project Ecologies: A Contextual View on Temporary Organizations." P. W. G. Morris, J. K. Pinto, and J. Söderlund, eds. *The Oxford Handbook of Project Management*. Oxford.

Hubert, M., P. Lewis, and M. M. Raynaud, eds. (2014). *Les grands projets urbains: Territoires, acteurs et stratégies*. Montréal.

Jacobsson, M. and M. Hällgren (2016). "Impromptu Teams in a Temporary Organization: On Their Nature and Role." *International Journal of Project Management* 34.4: pp. 584–596.

Löfgren, O. (2008). "Regionauts: The Transformation of Cross-Border Regions in Scandinavia." *European Urban and Regional Studies* 15.3: pp. 195–209.

Mahalingam, A. (2021). "Megaproject Leadership in the Developing World: An Indian Perspective" N. Drouin, S. Sankaran, A. Van Marrewijk, and R. Müller, eds. *Megaproject Leaders Reflections on Personal Life Stories*. Cheltenham, UK.

Martin, A.-S. (2020). "Kourou: The European Spaceport and Its Impact on the French Guyana Economy." A. Froehlich, ed. *Space Fostering Latin American Societies*. Cham.

Sergeeva, N. and A. Davies (2021). "Storytelling from the Authentic Leader of High Speed 2 (HS2) Ltd. Infrastructure Megaproject in the United Kingdom" N. Drouin, S. Sankaran, A. Van Marrewijk, and R. Müller, eds. *Megaproject Leaders Reflections on Personal Life Stories*. Chelthenham.

Shi Q., M. Hertogh, M. Bosch-Rekveldt, J. Zhu, and Z. Sheng (2020). "Exploring Decision-Making Complexity in Major Infrastructure Projects: A Case Study from China." *Project Management Journal* 51.6: pp. 617–632.

Siemiatycki, M. (2017). "Cycles in Megaproject Development." B. Flyvbjerg, ed. *The Oxford Handbook of Megaproject Management*. Oxford.

Sydow, J. and T. Braun (2018). "Projects as Temporary Organizations: An Agenda for Further Theorizing the Interorganizational Dimension." *International Journal of Project Management* 36.1: pp. 4–11.

Turner, J. R. and R. Müller (2003). "On the Nature of the Project as a Temporary Organization." *International Journal of Project Management* 21.1: pp. 1–8.

Van den Ende, L., A. Van Marrewijk, and K. Boersma (2015). "Machine Baptisms and Heroes of the Underground: Performing Sociomateriality in an Amsterdam Metro Project." *Journal of Organizational Ethnography* 4.3: pp. 260–280.

van Marrewijk, A. and K. Smits (2014). "Projectscapes: The Role of Spatial Settings in Managing Complex Megaprojects." *International Journal of Complexity in Leadership and Managment* 2.4: pp. 278–292.

Embracing Temporal Ambiguities? Innovation and the Temporalities of Large-Scale Projects

Joachim Thiel/Gernot Grabher

Introduction

Large-scale projects, it seems, challenge extant ideas about time in temporary organizations. In particular, durations of a decade and more render debatable whether temporariness is the decisive aspect that structures the temporalities of large ventures (Brookes et al. 2017). Hence, the classic view of project time as "always running out" (Lundin and Söderholm 1995, p. 439), that has prevailed in project management research and professional practice for quite a long time, only partially holds for large-scale projects. Large projects do not engender the experience of continuous time pressure, and project participants will not perceive a project timespan of ten years and more as a "linear"—and therefore "predictable and plannable"—episode in an otherwise "continuous time-flow" (p. 450). Moreover, large-scale projects are relatively permanent vis-à-vis a volatile organizational, relational, and institutional environment (Brookes et al. 2017). Therefore, also the idea of a duality between temporary organizations, on the one hand, and more permanent contexts, on the other, that has dominated recent approaches to project temporalities (e.g., Bakker 2010; Davies and Brady 2000; Engwall 2003; Grabher 2004; Sydow et al. 2004) applies only to a limited extent to large (and therefore long-term) ventures.

This chapter starts from this incongruity of large-scale projects with traditional understandings of project time. More specifically, we seek to examine how the temporalities of large construction projects contribute to the generation of innovations during the process of designing, planning, and implementing such projects. We maintain that addressing the conjunction between temporalities of large projects and innovation is particularly promising as the specific features of these temporalities reveal interesting parallels to how time is framed in the research on innovation processes (e.g., Garud et al. 2016; Garud and Karnøe 2001; Garud et al. 2013). In contrast to project management's obsession with temporariness, the pertinent research on innovation processes describes these as inherently contingent and open-ended (Garud et al. 2016). Innovation times are regarded as essentially complex. Innovation processes involve "backing and forthing" (p. 458), varying rhythms and paces, and time is perceived "as a resource" that can be "mobilized" (Garud and Karnøe 2001).

Against this backdrop we argue that large-scale projects essentially exhibit *temporal ambiguities*. In large-scale project organizations several temporalities coexist. Innovation processes unfold within this coexistence and through the complementary—and not conflicting—interplay between these temporalities. Large-scale projects, hence, encourage the generation and implementation of innovations as they allow for embracing—and not eliminating—temporal ambiguities.

The ambiguities play out along two different dimensions of addressing time in large-scale projects: as *long-term processes* and as *long-term episodes*. Long-term processes refer to what happens over the project lifecycle. Large-scale project cycles embrace different and varying process dynamics, that is, they both afford temporal leeway for the exploration and consolidation of novelty, and generate urgency and momentum that operate "to get a project through" (Garud and Karnøe 2001, p. 22). Long-term episodes relate to the interplay between temporary structures and a more permanent environment. Large projects—as temporary episodes—can affect this environment. However, given that they establish relatively stable structures as compared to this environment (Brookes et al. 2017), large ventures necessarily face context changes and may be able to leverage them.

In our view, the findings that we present on the following pages will contribute in particular to the recent work on temporalities of large-scale projects (Brookes et al. 2017) that challenges the idea of temporariness as decisive structuring factor in the light of projects' long durations. Our focus on temporal ambiguities provides a more nuanced understanding of the interplay of properties of permanence and temporariness that are inherent in large projects. In addition, our research provides new insights with regard to the conjunction of project temporalities and innovation. We hold that the findings go beyond the often taken for granted assumption that projects per se—as temporary organizations—are "a key way of organizing innovation" (e.g., Brady and Hobday 2011; Davies 2014). We demonstrate that it is particularly the complementary interplay of ambiguous temporalities through which novelty can arise and materialize. Moreover, large-scale projects not only afford temporal ambiguities, but also allow for embracing them.

The empirical analysis of this chapter is based on the records of all eighty-six interviews that we conducted across the total of six case studies. We assembled the material that we actually processed in our analysis in two steps. First, we retrieved 350 interview segments that were explicitly coded as "temporal aspects." Second, we performed a keyword search with various time-related keys such as "urgent," "durable," "suddenly" in order to capture text segments that were somehow related to time and temporality (and not explicitly coded as "temporal aspects"). Through both steps, we selected around 450 codings as basic material for our analysis. We recoded this material, using codes that we had taken from our extensive analysis of literature on projects, time, and innovation. Codes comprised, for instance, "urgency," "momentum," "availability of time," "episode," or "context change." Based on this recoding we categorized the segments in several rounds, starting with the new keywords and then reducing the number of categories by moving back and forth between conceptual literature and the empirical material, partly even going back to interview records in order to contextualize coded quotes. This iterative process extended into the actual draft writing. As a result, we developed the analytical structure of this chapter, based on the two conceptualizations of time in large projects—*long-term processes* and *long-term episodes*. We emphasized the diverse and ambiguous effects that both temporalities have on the projects and the innovative impulses that originate from these effects.

The chapter proceeds as follows. In the following second section, we discuss the literature on project temporality and innovation, focusing in particular on the temporalities of large-scale projects. Here we develop and unpack the two basic conceptualizations: *long-term processes* and *long-term episodes*. The third section comprises the results of our empirical analysis. In the final section, we summarize the findings and suggest some avenues for further research.

Innovation and the Temporal Ambiguities of Large-Scale Construction Projects

Projects, regardless of their size, are "temporary organizations" (Bakker 2010; Lundin and Söderholm 1995). Based on this assumption project management research has developed two different ways of discussing how the temporary nature of projects translates into an understanding of project time. The first conceives of this time as a *process* that is largely decoupled from history and future. The related research traditionally addresses management-related topics such as the optimization of time management; risks of cost and time overrun; or the assessment of success or failure, but also, more recently, varying process dynamics, such as different pacings and rhythms within the project (e.g., Gersick 1989; Gersick 1994; Jones and Lichtenstein 2008; Söderlund 2011).

The second research approach reaches beyond the idea of a temporal decoupling of projects by placing emphasis on the interdependencies between temporary projects and the more permanent organizational and institutional contexts in which they operate (e.g., Bakker 2010; Davies and Brady 2000; Engwall 2003; Grabher 2004; Stjerne and Svejenova 2016; Sydow et al. 2004). Projects here primarily constitute *episodes* in longer-term developments. From the contexts, on the one hand, project participants draw key resources of expertise, legitimation, and reputation; on the other, projects are supposed to have an impact on their contexts, by encouraging non-routine agency and thereby driving renewal and change (e.g., Lundin and Midler 2012).

There has been comprehensive, separate research on both ways of dealing with project times. There is also recent work that tackles both approaches jointly with regard to time by unpacking different "temporal tensions" related to the project process as well as to the project's connection with past and future (Stjerne et al. 2019). However, surprisingly little work has been done that (a) connects project temporalities to innovation and (b) addresses the temporalities of large-scale projects. As an exception to the former, there is an extensive and controversial debate on whether and how the impact projects are supposed to have beyond their temporal boundaries in fact materializes, i.e., on whether and how renewal and change diffuse into the project context (Boland Jr. et al. 2007; Davies and Brady 2000; Prado and Sapsed 2016; Scarbrough et al. 2004; Swan and Scarbrough 2010). As an exception to the general neglect of the temporalities of large projects, Brookes et al. (2017), by emphasizing the long-term nature of large projects, call into question whether temporariness is decisive at all when it comes to understanding (large) project times. We take up these authors' emphasis on long duration and frame large-scale projects, therefore, as *long-term processes* and *long-term episodes*.

Large-Scale Projects as Long-Term Processes

There are two main features that shape the process dynamics of large-scale projects: the first is simply duration. Time in large-scale projects is neither "scarce" nor "predictable and plannable" (Lundin and Söderholm 1995). Envisioning a time horizon of more than a decade, at least in the early stage, resembles more starting a venture into the unknown than planning an accelerated, but well-defined period ahead. That large projects are notoriously over time (Flyvbjerg 2011) also proves the difficulties of predefining the time horizons connected to them. The second feature relates to the inevitably inter-organizational nature of large ventures. Large-scale projects require the involvement of a large number of individuals and organizations, each of them entailing their own temporal regularities, time constraints, and "timing norms" (Dille and Söderlund 2011) that might be independent from and even compete with the project time. Taking both features together, hence, the process dynamics of large projects embrace the concurrence of various temporalities over a hardly predictable period.

Extant project management research therefore emphasizes the need to "synchronize" (e.g., Stjerne et al. 2019) the different temporalities. In addition, synchronization in large-scale projects mainly functions as what Sayles and Chandler (1971, p. 207; Söderlund 2012) refer to as the "organizational metronome" that creates the "beat" all involved actors have to follow. Long-lasting projects, hence, entail the development of routinized and recurring work processes similar to those of permanent organizational structures (Grabher and Thiel 2015, p. 333). However, long-term projects also involve shifting rhythms and tempos that build on particular milestones and varying work periods over the project cycle (e.g., Pemsel and Söderlund 2019). With regard to shifting rhythms, Jones and Lichtenstein (2008, p. 236) distinguish between different "pacing techniques": "event-based pacing"—"based on attaining key milestones towards a goal"—and "chronological pacing"—based on a detailed management of work packages and deadlines. According to the authors, in large-scale engineering and construction projects pacing techniques change from event-based to chronological when a project moves from a phase of problem-framing and planning to design and implementation (p. 248). Whereas, hence, in the early stages of a project the perception of time is rather based on qualitative criteria, the execution stage follows a straightforward clock- or calendar-based time conception.

A juxtaposition of different time conceptions holds also for innovation processes, even though not clearly connected to specific stages of the project cycle. On the one hand, innovation builds on a qualitative understanding of what you do with the time. Time is seen as a "resource" (Garud and Karnøe 2001) that has to be mobilized—and that is needed for "the exploration of ideas" (p. 22). On the other, however, also innovation processes involve periods of speeding up and carefully managing time in order to consolidate or conclude the development of novelty (p. 22).

Large-Scale Projects as Long-Term Episodes

That projects establish particular episodes within otherwise stable structures and thereby encourage non-routine agency is a basic assumption behind the often taken for granted idea that projects are "a key way of organizing innovation" (Brady and Hobday 2011, p. 273; Davies 2014). This assumption applies to large-scale construction projects in a specific way: construction projects per se are the actual routine of most involved actors. For these individuals and organizations, each project is, hence, one step in a trajectory of episodes. Large-scale projects establish exceptional episodes in such trajectories. Like "rare events" (Christianson et al. 2009), large ventures in particular challenge the capacities of involved actors, and they may also generate impulses for doing things in ways different from the routine. These impulses scatter through a diffuse context of individual career paths and personal networks (e.g., Grabher and Thiel 2015), or through institutional contexts and organizational fields (Thiel and Grabher 2015; Tukiainen and Granqvist 2016).

At the same time, given their long-term nature, large-scale projects can only in part be framed as an episodic impulse. According to Brookes et al. (2017), the extended timeframe of large-scale ventures turns the classic analytical differentiation between temporary episodes and a relatively stable permanent context upside down. Large-scale projects, the authors maintain, are, in a way, permanent—for some (considerable!) time; rather, a lack of permanence exists in their "drifting environments" (Kreiner 1995). Large projects, hence, tend to "outlive their organizational milieu" (Brookes et al. 2017), as well as possibly face the changes of other important boundary conditions, such as technological or regulatory standards. As the projects remain entangled with their environment, such context changes engender imperatives for project activities. In a sense, then, projects cannot only drive context change, but context change can also drive projects.

Temporal Ambiguities?

Large-scale projects blend long duration and temporariness. They therefore exhibit features of both permanent and temporary organizations when it comes to how time is addressed and perceived. Large-project organizations enact routinized and recurring processes and take time to find common goals or develop new solutions. At the same time, all these processes remain directed towards finalizing a joint task. Large-scale projects can afford an episodic impulse whose effects survive the temporary venture and resonate in the relational, organizational, and institutional project context. However, as a project may survive parts of this context, context changes may afford episodic impulses for the project.

Temporalities of large-scale projects are therefore "relative" (Brookes et al. 2017), i.e., they call into question the difference between temporary and permanent. In addition, the temporalities of large-scale projects are also ambiguous. Different, but equally important conceptions and perceptions of time necessarily coexist (Reinecke and Ansari 2015) and mutually influence each other. In what follows we seek to reveal how innovations can unfold within these temporal ambiguities.

Findings: Innovations and the Ambiguous Temporalities in Six Large-Scale Construction Projects

Five out of our six study cases spanned a period from first idea to handover to operation of between fourteen and seventeen years, and the planning and realization happened in huge inter-organizational networks. The Kochertal Bridge—the only case that comprised exclusively the maintenance and reinforcement of an existing construction—is an exception. The period was considerably shorter—two-and-a-half years—and the number of involved actors comparably small—the entire project coalition comprised four organizations. Timespans of the five long-term projects partly included idle times—e.g., a two-and-half-year suspension of construction work on the Elbphilharmonie site and even a twelve-year break after the planning framework for high speed railway projects in Eastern Germany had been established for the Gänsebachtal Bridge. Nevertheless, we can legitimately frame the projects under study here as embracing long-term processes and constituting long-term episodes.

Long-Term Processes: Ample Time and Varying Dynamics

The long project durations implied and enabled varying process dynamics over the entire project cycle. When it comes to the generation and implementation of novel strategies, practices, or technologies the projects exhibited contrasting effects.

Long duration simply increased the amount of available time that could be "mobilized" (Garud and Karnøe 2001) for a variety of purposes. Project trajectories of around fifteen years afforded leeway for all kinds of exploratory activities; produced periods of "dead time" (C5_Eng2), e.g., during approval processes, that enabled the specification, refinement, or testing of intended solutions; provided time for ideas to mature; and also time to "mobilize minds" (Garud and Karnøe 2001, p. 14)—that is, to collect supporters and win over critics and approving agencies. "In ordinary projects you are in a straitjacket of temporal and financial restrictions, and you cannot escape from that" (C4_Oth1). The option to mobilize time occurred particularly in the earlier phases of the project cycle, hence corresponding to what Jones and Lichtenstein (2008) describe for "event-based pacing." However, as large-scale projects are also finite undertakings, spending a lot of time on experimental practices at the beginning also had its downsides: in some cases, it created time pressure toward the end. For instance, when for Berlin Central Station an immovable deadline for final delivery was fixed in conjunction with the Football World Championship in 2006, the strong up-front investment in development and approval of exceptional solutions eventually squeezed time for delivery. As a result of time pressure, parts of the exceptional elements—for instance, the design of platforms as covered bridges—were not fully implemented (C3_Oth3). Similarly, in the case of the Wehrhahn Line, taking a lot of time for the development and implementation of art projects for the interior finish put substantial pressure on the transport operator, whose work packages were the last to be realized (C5_Own3).

Long duration, however, also entailed variations in process dynamics, particularly with regard to the temporal structuring of collaboration between the different actors in the project settings. Variation above all concerned what Sayles and Chandler (1971) refer to as the "organizational metronome:" the routinized "beat" all actors involved in a project have to follow. This metronomic beat is mainly enacted through systems of regularly recurring meetings—jours fixes—that take place at varying intervals according to the hierarchical position of related issues and related actors. Such meetings are an ordinary element of every project management and governance process at all levels, but their importance and seriousness may differ between projects. We found the strictest enactment of a cyclical governance process in the European Central Bank (ECB) project where the meetings of the steering committee and the bank's governing council established decisive external clocks to which all important decision processes in the project had to be aligned (C2_Own3).

Variations in this routinized and cyclical pattern occurred according to two logics. For one thing, approaching milestones, i.e., structuring elements that derive from the actual task, but also imminent high-level meetings, create count-down periods of

Table 1: Large-Scale Projects as
Long-Term Processes

urgency that engender a particular momentum. When it comes to innovations such accelerated periods ahead of critical moments accomplish two functions in the examined projects: (a) urgency can push developments forward; and (b) urgency helps to create irreversibilities, by safeguarding compromises and pushing decisions.

For another thing, collaboration intensity may increase. The project's beat can speed up when intervals between regular meetings shorten and additional meetings related to specific problems are set up. Even continuous interaction through co-locating work becomes relevant in certain periods. Growing intensity arose for three reasons: (a) to cope with enhanced requirements of coordination (this coordination is particularly relevant when the planning for sophisticated solutions has to be specified); (b) to enable control for particularly critical elements, e.g., the spherically bent glass elements for the Elbphilharmonie façade; and (c) to shorten reaction times. This is particularly relevant during construction, when myriads of small problems on-site require quick responses.

Long-Term Episodes: Project Push and Context Push
Notwithstanding the long duration of our project cases, the projects examined here are also entangled in developments that go beyond their temporal boundaries. In some cases, the episodic nature of a project afforded a concrete impulse within an "innovation journey" (Garud et al. 2013). Such episodic impulses could concern new technologies, but also changes on a field level with regard to technological development (e.g., glass bending) or institutional change. In the case of Düsseldorf's new Wehrhahn Line, the project provided the seedbed out of which a novel technique in fact arose: a concrete mixture with integrated glass beads that would afford a special light reflection. The application of the mixture eventually did not materialize in that project, but the involved actors developed the technology further (C5_Arch2; C5_Oth1). In other cases, later stages of innovation processes—such as the development and consolidation of a new technology, technique, or organizational practice—were affected. The spherical glass bending for the glass façade of the Elbphilharmonie exemplifies an episodic impulse in the development stage. Spherical glass bending did exist before, and studies about its stability were already underway (C1_Eng6). Hamburg's new architectural icon enabled the deployment of this technology on a larger scale and with additional features.

Long-Term Process Effect	Innovative Impulse	Exemplary Data
Ample time	Exploring ideas	When we had the order, I said: "I need another four months." ... . That was clear. And I eventually needed three to four months until we had set up the sawing technology in order to implement the thing properly. And I got this timespan. C5_Supp3
	Refining ideas	In the dead time, when the project does not proceed anyway as the plans are at the authorizing agency. Normally you simply lose that time ... . [here] it was used to ask the planning group for a detailed design, much more detailed than usual. C5_Eng2
	Possible downside: moving time pressure to the final phases	However, one of the aspects is... it takes a lot of time until you have planned and realized everything, and obtained approval. The consequence was, that there were many delays. C3_Eng2
Varying process dynamics: urgency	Pushing developments	A few days before my summer vacation, there was a request and there was money. I was asked to produce a 30 square meter mock-up at extremely short notice. I managed to start that before my holidays, but had to return one week earlier than planned to actually produce the slabs. C5_Supp3
	Forcing decisions and maintaining compromise	... there was stress everywhere, as we were in a phase in which things had to be nailed down. And this happened regularly. Again and again, things had to be finalized, and these things were fixed then ... . In such a large project, you cannot always switch over to, say, another material or so, once you have reached an agreement. C5_Oth3
Varying process dynamics: intensity	Facilitating coordination	We had to be at one table with the artist, and with representatives of the firms, not with those who sell products and services, but with the actual technicians and engineers. We tried, then, to find out how we can actually realize it. These were really tough times. C5_Arch1
	Enabling control	The glass production company organized the whole process, and Mr. [X] ... every Monday morning got in his car, went to [where the production was carried out] and stayed until Friday. And whenever I meet him, I say: "Those three glass panes there, they were manufactured when you were on vacation. You see the streaks?" C1_Arch5
	Responding to problems	There were weeks, in which such routines happened on a daily basis, when there was too much buzz around ... and we thought: "now we have to keep our fingers on the pulse." C2_Oth1

More important, however, were the impacts that the large projects were having as exceptional episodes in the biography of all the organizations and individuals involved. The exceptionality even functioned as a key incentive for many to get involved. The unique quality related particularly to two aspects of project involvement: the requirements actors had to accomplish the job and the organizational structures in which they worked.

With regard to exceptional requirements, all the projects we studied exhibited to different degrees challenges that went beyond what the professionals involved usually had to deal with. Such extraordinary demands were related to particular technical complexities, such as the construction of two office buildings that would span Berlin Central Station like a bascule bridge (C3_Supp4). Projects also called for extra efforts and particular commitment, e.g., with sixty-hour weeks over long periods of time, or for presence on the construction-site also at weekends (C2_Own2). In any case, involved actors assessed these exceptional requirements as particular enlightening episodes in individual career paths, but also in the trajectories of their organizations. Large construction projects, it seems, offer opportunities "to explore limits" (C1_Eng3) and thereby establish valuable occasions for learning and self-affirmation in the industry.

Interviewees' positive references to their experience in the projects often also related to the exceptional structures in which they worked. Much of the planning, but also of the project management work, took place in structures set up deliberately and exclusively for the project, both in project-based firms and in owner organizations. Such in-house project groups or temporary collaborations of several consultancies afforded a complete and exclusive focus of teams on the project at hand, in some cases over the entire project cycle, in others only during the planning period. For those project-based organizations that perform the bulk of work in construction, projects of a particular size both require and enable an exclusive focus—"the only possibility … to get such a project off the ground in such a short period of time at all" (C5_Eng6). Hence, large projects allow actors to circumvent the usual trade-offs inherent in work time allocation between competing projects in the firm portfolio (Winch 2014, p. 727) and facilitate synchronization of team members' activities.

In addition to establishing an episode, however, the projects also revealed the opposite dynamic: instead of generating a push, through which a project affected the longer-term context trajectory,

Projects as drivers of change	Incubation and consolidation in innovation trajectories	The design implied many surfaces that should be reflective. And... there was no material available... . And I thought: Why not develop our own? From that idea we brought together concrete and micro glass beads, but we decided to decouple this development process from the actual project... . But the Wehrhahn Line was of course a catalyst.
		C5_Oth1
		And it's not: "Elbphilharmonie led to new norms." But the trials that we performed for the Elbphilharmonie occurred in a period when many people had started to think about the ...problem of stability.
		C1_Eng6
	Exceptional requirements: learning incentive and opportunity for self-affirmation	Well, what we definitely have to mention: at least we had the possibility to do that [the tilting]. If, nowadays, you invited tenders for something like that, you would not have a chance, as the call is fixed. And we did something that was not part of the call.
		C3_Supp4
		Yes, this is our incentive. We find it exciting to explore limits.
		C1_Eng3
	Exceptional structures: focus, concentration, attractiveness	...I mean that's old-fashioned but still innovative as it is the only possibility... to get such a project off the ground in such a short period of time at all: you create an own project office and cram all the responsible people into one office room. That's what we did.
		C5_Eng6
		And, for such an exceptional project ...some planners did that for themselves. They said: "I definitely want to join, no matter from where I work ... . For such an exceptional project you can afford that for a certain period of time.
		C1_Cont1
Context as driver of change	Changing (technological and regulatory) boundary conditions as windows of opportunity	One could argue that some of the details were only possible as so much time passed ... . Take the 3D planning, if we had started ten years before it wouldn't have been there. That is, while you would have been able to produce this building, you do not know in what a timeframe as there wouldn't have been a chance to prefabricate.
		C1_Cont1
		Why did we use the new directive at all? .... Why didn't we stick to the old one? Simply as the new directive provided, for some proofs, at least a certain flexibility ... .
		C3_Oth2

the instability of this context afforded changes that the project organizations involved had to tackle. During fifteen-year project timeframes, many boundary conditions changed, particularly with regard to technology and regulation. And in some cases, these changes in fact provided windows of opportunity for implementing things in ways different from what had been standard before.

Concerning technology, for instance, there was huge progress in 3D-technology (not only) during the planning and construction of the Elbphilharmonie. If the architects had had to build the iconic building at the time when they developed the design, the construction of the "white skin"—the famous wall covering of the big concert hall—would have been a real challenge: around 10,000 individually cut and routed plaster slabs assembled at the walls of an amorphously designed hall. Only a parametric design tool and the connection between design program and machinery eventually rendered the production viable (C1_Cont1; C1_Eng7).

When it comes to regulation, Berlin Central Station is a good case in point. Changes of directives at the Federal Railway Authority happened while the project was already underway. Usually projects have to follow the prescriptions that are valid when a project starts. In the Berlin case this practice was changed as the new guidelines offered "greater flexibility" that was more suitable with regard to the implementation of the complex construction (C3_Oth2).

Interactions: Conflicts and Complementarities

Temporal ambiguities in projects do not imply a simple co-existence of different, but isolated temporalities. The different temporal effects that we identified interact. There are two opposing modes of these interactions: they can be either conflicting or complementary. Conflicts occur, for instance, between the mobilization of time for exploration and increasing urgency toward the end of projects, as illustrated for Berlin Central Station, where the time spent at the beginning that was necessary to develop and consolidate extraordinary design elements eventually compressed the time for implementation toward the end.

When it comes to innovations, it seems, complementary relations between different temporalities are more important. Take the case of the extra-dense concrete slabs that would cover the walls of Düsseldorf's Wehrhahn Line stations: the artist who had the design idea and the leading architects were at pains to discover a way of producing what they had envisioned and did not give up before they found both a suitable material and a capable supplier (*ample time, intensity*); the supplying firm had to develop the way to manufacture and a mock-up that proved feasibility in a very short period of time (*urgency*); the managing director then asked for additional time for exploration and testing production on a larger scale, and that time was granted (*ample time*); finally, the size of this contract enabled the firm to invest in digital technologies which in turn had a substantial effect on the longer-term trajectory of the organization (*exceptional requirements*). This investment was also encouraged through the progress in digital technology that had occurred during the long timeline along which the project proceeded (*changing boundary conditions*).

Discussion and Conclusion

This chapter started with two key assumptions: first, that large-scale projects exhibit temporal ambiguities, i.e., that different, but equally valued temporalities coexist in these projects; and, second, that innovations evolve in the interplay between these temporalities. We argued that due to their relative longevity, large projects, in a way, embrace temporal properties of both temporary and permanent organizations. While being finite and operating toward a final goal and deadline, large ventures develop routines and allow leeway for exploration. While being able to push change in their relational, organizational, and institutional context, projects of a particular size are likely to be more durable than this context, and they are themselves pushed to adapt to changing boundary conditions.

The empirical insights that we have presented in the preceding section illustrate the variety of temporalities that exist alongside each other in large projects, as well as the different roles that the structuring and perception of time play in innovation processes. Most importantly, however, our findings show that innovation processes seem to be favored when different temporalities interact in a complementary, and not in a conflicting fashion. Temporal trade-offs, it seems, hinder the generation and implementation of novel strategies, techniques, or practices. Our research suggests that large-scale projects, given their potential to embrace different temporalities, offer the opportunity to avoid such trade-offs. It is therefore the very fact that large projects are able to incorporate and harness temporal ambiguities that renders them drivers of innovation. Unlike what is suggested in extensive project management research, temporal ambiguity is also an asset and not just a problem that managers have to solve through massive efforts of synchronization or temporal alignment.

Our findings provide arguments that help further develop the ongoing debates on temporalities of large-scale projects, particularly in two respects. First, we offer a clarification of what Brookes et al. (2017) refer to as "relative temporalities." In these authors' understanding "relative temporalities" refer to the relative temporariness of a temporary organization when the temporary is more durable than the seemingly permanent. We hold that temporariness is still important, also in projects with a long duration. In our view, it is the combination of finiteness and longevity that makes up the temporalities of large-scale projects. It would be promising to dig deeper into how the different vectors of temporary vs. permanent and short-term vs. long-term interrelate. Second, we can also differentiate Jones and Lichtenstein's (2008) account on shifting "pacing techniques" over the project cycle. Secondary to the differentiation between event-based and chronological pacing in planning and implementation, respectively, there are much more fine-grained changes of rhythm and tempo according to milestones, deadlines, or periods of particular intensity.

In addition, our research helps frame the conjunction between (large-scale) project temporalities and innovation. Traditionally, temporary organizations are supposed to afford episodic pushes that drive non-routine agency (and thereby generate innovations) in otherwise routinely operating environments. The big question here has been whether and how the non-routine agency in fact operates to translate into long-term change (Boland Jr. et al. 2007; Davies and Brady 2000; Prado and Sapsed 2016; Scarbrough et al. 2004; Swan and Scarbrough 2010). Through the focus on ambiguities our research offers a more varied approach to time and innovation in large-scale projects. There are various coexisting temporalities inherent in these projects, and project size (and duration) allow for the interplay of temporalities in a complementary and not a conflicting fashion. Large projects involve both time for exploration and time to nail down and safeguard decisions; they both push their environment *and* are pushed by the same environment. Hence, large-scale projects facilitate embracing—instead of eliminating—temporal ambiguities, and thereby help novelty to arise and to materialize.

References

Bakker, R. M. (2010). "Taking Stock of Temporary Organizational Forms: A Systematic Review and Research Agenda." *International Journal of Management Reviews* 12.4: pp. 466–486.

Boland Jr., R. J., K. Lyytinen, and Y. Yoo (2007). "Wakes of Innovation in Project Networks: The Case of Digital 3-D Representations in Architecture, Engineering, and Construction." *Organization Science* 18.4: pp. 631–647.

Brady, T. and M. Hobday (2011). "Projects and Innovation: Innovation and Projects." P. W. G. Morris, J. K. Pinto, and J. Söderlund, eds. *The Oxford Handbook of Project Management*. Oxford.

Brookes, N., A. Dainty, G. Locatelli, and J. Whyte (2017). "An Island of Constancy in a Sea of Change: Rethinking Project Temporalities with Long-Term Megaprojects." *International Journal of Project Management* 35.7: pp. 1213–1224.

Christianson, M. K., M. T. Farkas, K. M. Sutcliffe, and K. E. Weick (2009). "Learning Through Rare Events: Significant Interruptions at the Baltimore & Ohio Railroad Museum." *Organization Science* 20.5: pp. 846–860.

Davies, A. (2014). "Innovation and Project Management." M. Dodgson, D. Gann, and N. Phillips, eds. *The Oxford Handbook of Innovation Management*. Oxford.

Davies, A. and T. Brady (2000). "Organisational Capabilities and Learning in Complex Product Systems: Towards Repeatable Solutions." *Research Policy* 29.7-8: pp. 931–953.

Dille, T. and J. Söderlund (2011). "Managing Inter-Institutional Projects: The Significance of Isochronism, Timing Terms and Temporal Misfits." *International Journal of Project Management* 29.4: pp. 480–490.

Engwall, M. (2003). "No Project Is an Island: Linking Projects to History and Context." *Research Policy* 32.5: pp. 789–808.

Flyvbjerg, B. (2011). "Over Budget, over Time, over and over Again: Managing Major Projects." P. W. G. Morris, J. K. Pinto, and J. Söderlund, eds. *The Oxford Handbook of Project Management*. Oxford.

Garud, R., J. Gehman, A. Kumaraswamy, and P. Tuertscher (2016). "From the Process of Innovation to Innovation as Process." A. Langley and H. Tsoukas, eds. *The SAGE Handbook of Process Organization Studies*. Los Angeles; London; New Delhi; Singapore; Washington DC; Melbourne.

Garud, R. and P. Karnøe (2001). "Path Creation as a Process of Mindful Deviation." R. Garud and P. Karnøe, eds. *Path Dependence and Creation*. Mawah, NJ.

Garud, R., P. Tuertscher, and A. H. Van de Ven (2013). "Perspectives on Innovation Processes." *The Academy of Management Annals* 7.1: pp. 773–817.

Gersick, C. J. (1989). "Marking Time: Predictable Transitions in Task Groups." *Academy of Management Journal* 32.2: pp. 274–309.

Gersick, C. J. (1994). "Pacing Strategic Change: The Case of a New Venture." *Academy of Management Journal* 37.1: pp. 9–45.

Grabher, G. (2004). "Temporary Architectures of Learning: Knowledge Governance in Project Ecologies." *Organization Studies* 25.9: pp. 1491–1514.

Grabher, G. and J. Thiel (2015). "Projects, People, Professions: Trajectories of Learning through a Mega-Event (the London 2012 case)." *Geoforum* 65: pp. 328–337.

Jones, C. and B. Lichtenstein (2008). "Temporary Inter-Organizational Projects: How Temporal and Social Embeddedness Enhance Coordination and Manage Uncertainty." S. Cropper, M. Ebers, C. Huxham, and P. S. Ring, eds. *The Oxford Handbook of Inter-Organizational Relations*. Oxford.

Kreiner, K. (1995). "In Search of Relevance: Project Management in Drifting Environments." *Scandinavian Journal of Management* 11.4: pp. 335–346.

Lundin, R. A. and C. Midler, eds. (2012). *Projects as Arenas for Renewal and Learning Processes*. New York.

Lundin, R. A. and A. Söderholm (1995). "A Theory of the Temporary Organization." *Scandinavian Journal of Management* 11.4: pp. 437–455.

Pemsel, S. and J. Söderlund (2019). "On the Verge of Times: Temporal Shifts in Temporary Organizations." Paper presented at the 35th EGOS Colloquium, Edinburgh.

Prado, P. and J. Sapsed (2016). "The Anthropophagic Organization: How Innovations Transcend the Temporary in a Project-Based Organization." *Organization Studies* 37.12: pp. 1793–1818.

Reinecke, J. and S. Ansari (2015). "When Times Collide: Temporal Brokerage at the Intersection of Markets and Developments." *Academy of Management Journal* 58.2: pp. 618–648.

Sayles, L. R. and M. K. Chandler (1971). *Managing Large Systems: Organizations for the Future*. New York; Evanston; San Francisco; London.

Scarbrough, H., J. Swan, S. Laurent, M. Bresnen, L. Edelman, and S. Newell (2004). "Project-Based Learning and the Role of Learning Boundaries." *Organization Studies* 25.9: pp. 1579–1600.

Söderlund, J. (2011). "Theoretical Foundations of Project Management. Suggestions for a Pluralistic Understanding." P. W. G. Morris, J. K. Pinto, and J. Söderlund, eds. *The Oxford Handbook of Project Management*. Oxford.

Söderlund, J. (2012). "Project Management, Interdependencies, and Time: Insights from Managing Large Systems by Sayles and Chandler." *International Journal of Managing Projects in Business* 5.4: pp. 617–633.

Stjerne, I. S., J. Söderlund, and D. Minbaeva (2019). "Crossing Times: Temporal Boundary-Spanning Practices in Interorganizational Projects." *International Journal of Project Management* 37.2: pp. 347–365.

Stjerne, I. S. and S. Svejenova (2016). "Connecting Temporary and Permanent Organizing: Tensions and Boundary Work in Sequential Film Projects." *Organization Studies* 37.12: pp. 1771-1792.

Swan, J. and H. Scarbrough (2010). "Why Don't (or Do) Organizations Learn from Projects?" *Managment Learning* 41.3: pp. 325–344.

Sydow, J., L. Lindkvist, and R. Defillippi (2004). "Project-Based Organizations, Embeddedness and Repositories of Knowledge: Editorial." *Organization Studies* 25.9: pp. 1475–1489.

Thiel, J. and G. Grabher (2015). "Crossing Boundaries: Exploring the London Olympics 2012 as a Field-Configuring Event." *Industry and Innovation* 22.3: pp. 229–249.

Tukiainen, S. and N. Granqvist (2016). "Temporary Organizing and Institutional Change." *Organization Studies* 37.12: pp. 1819–1840.

Winch, G. M. (2014). "Three Domains of Project Organising." *International Journal of Project Management* 32.5: pp. 721–731.

Temporal Ambiguities in Large-Scale Projects

Jonas Söderlund

In many respects, large-scale projects challenge some of the very foundational ideas about project-based organizing, as pointed out in Thiel and Grabher's chapter; in particular, those large-scale projects that are of long duration. Such projects constitute rather peculiar kinds of economic organizations that call for considerable managerial intervention and support, without which they might well run the risk of breaking apart or going on for much longer than is financially warranted. They are fragile as several strong organizations participate with contrasting views on what and how to do things, and they are plagued with cooperation and coordination difficulties as has been reported in research spanning several decades.

It should be pointed out that while we know a great deal about large-scale projects, there are still many things that we do not know. I personally think that the issue around time and temporality is one of the most important yet historically most overlooked issues in the study of large-scale projects, despite the fact that their entire raison d'être to a great extent revolves around this very issue. Frankly, to better understand why they exist, how they behave, and how they differ—then we need to further explore issues around temporality. In that respect, this chapter is very much a welcome contribution.

As much of the literature on temporary organization has pointed out, the deadline—the awareness of an end date—is essential to breathe life into the project. Without a deadline, there is no real pressure to get things going, to act in the moment (Lindkvist et al. 1998). What is needed to make deadlines work, to make the deadline breathe life into a project? First, the time needs to be relatively short—there needs to be some kind of time pressure involved, otherwise there would be only a modest degree of challenge. Second, there needs to be some negative consequence for actors not keeping to the deadline, otherwise what difference would a deadline make? In that respect, I would claim that long-duration projects can definitely have deadline pressure if there is a severe consequence of not sticking to the deadline, for instance a fine, the loss of reputation or a missed opportunity of significant economic value. Especially if this is paired with a relatively short time span to complete the project, then even a multi-year project would sense the deadline pressure already from the start and begin focusing on that point to get the action going.

As for the relationship with innovation, it is quite interesting to note another pair of issues. First, deadline pressure, if handled appropriately, would make people rethink their current way of doing things—and thus make them depart from established routines, as suggested by Obstfeld (2012). Projects are in that regard clearly vehicles for innovation in relation to how things are done within the organization. In their contribution, Thiel and Grabher underline the capacity of projects to function as "enlightening episodes"—that make people think and rethink. Second, projects play a central role as mechanisms for the organization of innovation. Too little time available may undoubtedly run the risk of making people locally oriented and staying close to what they know will work. As a consequence, they may engage in time-urgent behavior and seek solutions at low degrees of innovation (Waller et al. 2001). This is also seen in the chapter, as lost time toward the end may lead to actions of a less innovative degree than might otherwise have been chosen. The question is, however, when does it lead to reflexive behavior and when does it lead to local-centric behavior?

Projects and Innovation

Prior research has clearly emphasized the close bond between projects and innovation (Brady and Hobday 2011). Projects in themselves are novel and should spur rethinking in terms of what is being done and how things are done. Innovation is a central part of most large-scale projects, and historically we have seen a number of technological innovations coming out of such projects also in the construction industry. Moreover, projects should not only spur innovation with regard to products and technologies, they should also contribute to new ways of organizing. In that respect, the intention with many large-scale projects is to make people collaborate differently and to enact different kinds of institutions, for instance with regard to the collaboration within a particular industry. For example, in one of the hospital projects we studied, the goal was not only to build a new, top-of-the-range hospital with up-to-date technologies and systems, but also to get people to collaborate in research projects in novel ways, and to change the entire conception of what a hospital actually is (Pemsel and Söderlund 2020). This is indeed a rather different way of perceiving innovation in large-scale projects in the construction industry. Moreover, new district and urban development to achieve sustainability is another example of a similar kind (Hallin et al. 2021). This "project innovation ambition" is especially critical for large-scale projects as these projects are often set in motion, because they call for new forms of collaboration and new ways of doing things, to establish collaboration among participants who have not collaborated in the past so that bringing them together would constitute an innovation in itself (Pemsel and Söderlund 2020). Interestingly, my experience is that project innovation is strongly associated with how central project actors relate to time—that their temporal conception and temporality will change as part of the project. Thus, it is interesting to consider the spectrum of innovation in the context of projects—that projects stimulate and should sometimes bring about product, process, and technological innovation, but equally important is their role to stimulate project innovation in terms of how projects are done.

Processes and Episodes

According to the authors, the temporal ambiguities could be addressed as two different dimensions: as long-term processes and as long-term episodes. In their framework, these are the most central conceptualizations of time in the context of large-scale projects. They suggest that long-term processes are those that happen over the project lifecycle—from initiation to completion of the actual project; these seem to be more internal to the temporary organization (Engwall 2003).

The long-term episodes, on the other hand, are those that relate to the interplay between temporary and permanent structures. These seem to be more external to the temporary organization and capture to a greater extent how the temporary organization relates to its environment (Lundin and Söderholm 1995).

First, concerning the issue of projects as long-term processes, it is clearly so that the idea with project-based organizing is to set a specific pace to the implementation of these activities. The deadline establishes a sense of interdependence and thereby a need for coordination. In that respect, people might become, if done mindfully, more aware of one another's activities, more aware of how their own work relates to other people's work. Becoming more aware and more mindful about other people's interests, contribution and knowledge would thus constitute a central issue of projects as long-term processes. In that respect, the issue of projects as long-term processes addresses their process dynamics—how the project moves from initiation to completion, the various rhythms and temporalities involved in bringing the project to fruition. As for the temporality problems, then respecting the fact that people might adhere to different rhythms and paces would clearly be critical for effective project implementation. An important task for those in charge of managing the project is thus to economize on these differences and synchronize and influence whenever possible and necessary.

As for the idea of projects as long-term episodes, projects may clearly change their institutional settings, establish new norms and function as "institutional projects" (Holm 1995), but most projects are, rather, victims dictated to by institutional norms that they need to obey (Dille and Söderlund 2011). As for temporalities, one could thus argue that some projects may clearly act as mechanisms to change people's perceptions of time, whereas other projects are instead adaptive systems that need to respond to people's rigid perceptions of time. Zerubavel (1981) suggested a temporal framework that is highly relevant also for the project context. He analyzed temporality as duration, location (timing), frequency (speed), sequence, and rhythm. In that respect, one might argue that there is a dynamic involved in terms of projects needing to respect certain rules of the game, yet given their size and sometimes ambition they are also set to act as institutional entrepreneurs and influence the rules of the game, as suggested by Holm (1995).

The distinction between processes and episodes sheds new light on a classic dilemma frequently observed by project scholars as well as managers of projects—namely to secure timely and efficient implementation whilst simultaneously upholding the project's legitimacy to external stakeholders. This presents a dilemma with regard to the trade-offs between internal and external efficiency and legitimacy—a dilemma often alluded to in research on projects and temporary organizations. The question is, however, to what extent there might be a conflict between these two forces. Are prioritization of temporalities and balanced temporalities among the participating organizations in the project in conflict with the temporal legitimacy that might be essential to ensure acceptance for the delivery and results of the project? In what sense is it possible to work efficiently and prioritize what is best for internal affairs, irrespective of how this might negatively impact the project's external legitimacy?

Temporality and Innovation

Continuing with the issue of temporality and innovation, I would claim that much of the idea underlying project-based organizing is exactly this—to arrange, to cope with conflicting temporalities, and to create synergies out of these contrasting temporalities— rather than create a difficult situation in which collaboration would be hard to bring about. In that regard, one could argue that the underlying raison d'être of project-based organizing is to handle the fact that people may have very different ideas about when things should be done, how fast things should be done, and in what order things should be done (Zerubavel 1981). One could thus say that projects as organizational forms take on the role of arranging for these contrasting temporalities and bring about innovation.

As evidenced in the chapter by Thiel and Grabher, large-scale projects with long duration involve both time for exploration as well as time to "nail down and safeguard decisions." In that respect, the authors demonstrate how they interactively shape and are shaped by their context. Accordingly, the authors maintain that temporal ambiguities may in fact spur innovation. This is clearly an interesting point that deserves further attention in order to uncover in what respect temporal ambiguities may promote or hinder innovation.

References

Brady, T. and M. Hobday (2011). "Projects and Innovation: Innovation and Projects."
P. W. G. Morris, J. K. Pinto, and J. Söderlund, eds. *The Oxford Handbook of Project Management*. Oxford.

Dille, T. and J. Söderlund (2011). "Managing Inter-Institutional Projects: The Significance of Isochronism, Timing Norms and Temporal Misfits." *International Journal of Project Management* 29.4: pp. 480–490.

Engwall, M. (2003). "No Project Is an Island: Linking Projects to History and Context." *Research Policy* 32.5: pp. 789–808.

Hallin A, T. Karrbom-Gustavsson, and P. Dobers (2021). "Transition Towards and Of Sustainability— Understanding Sustainability as Performative." *Business Strategy and the Environment*: pp. 1–10.

Holm, P. (1995). "The Dynamics of Institutionalization: Transformation Processes in Norwegian Fisheries." *Administrative Science Quarterly* 40.3: pp. 398–422.

Lindkvist, L., J. Söderlund, and F. Tell (1998). "Managing Product Development Projects: On the Significance of Fountains and Feadlines." *Organization Studies* 19.6: pp. 931–951.

Lundin, R. A. and A. Söderholm (1995). "A Theory of the Temporary Organization." *Scandinavian Journal of Management* 11.4: pp. 437–455.

Obstfeld, D. (2012). "Creative Projects. A Less Routine Approach Towards Getting New Things Done." *Organization Science* 23.6: pp. 1571–1592.

Pemsel, S. and J. Söderlund (2020). "Who's Got the Time? Temporary Organising under Temporal Institutional Complexity." T. Braun and J. Lampel, eds. *Tensions and Paradoxes in Temporary Organizing (Research in the Sociology of Organizations, Vol. 67)*. Bingley

Waller, M., J. Conte, C. Gibson, and M. Carpenter (2001). "The Effect of Individual Perception of Deadlines on Team Performance." *Academy of Management Review* 26.4: pp. 586–600.

Zerubavel, E. (1981). *Hidden Rhythms: Schedules and Calendars in Social Life.* Chicago.

What Was the Problem Again? How Problem Formulation Affects Innovativeness in Large-Scale Projects

Lennart Fahnenmüller/Johanna Ruge/
Annette Bögle

Introduction

In this chapter, we focus on the early stage of large-scale projects and trace how it influences their success. More specifically, we analyze how *problem formulation* at the very beginning of large-scale projects spurs or hinders innovations in the course of the project. We understand problem formulation as the consistent *formulation* of a *problem*, for which the proposed structure constitutes a solution. As such, the problem formulation summarizes expectations and boundary conditions, restricts or opens the space for possible solutions, typically functions as the first common ground for all stakeholders and serves as an input for the subsequent process of solving that problem. Problem formulation has a profound impact on projects, as it shapes the initial stage of decision-making, where a slight change of direction can lead to an entirely different outcome (Volkema 1983). We argue that a high-quality problem formulation executed consciously ultimately allows for greater innovation in large-scale projects, as it draws attention to the characteristics of the problem, the actors involved in and affected by the problem formulation, the resulting solution space as well as to the solution as a function of the problem formulation. One objective of this chapter is therefore to apply the lens of problem formulation to large-scale projects as a new perspective to analyze them.

Problem formulation has been studied either in relation to design problems in the context of the development of new products (e.g., von Hippel and von Krogh 2016; Volkema 1983), or in relation to strategic problems in the context of long-term organizational strategies (e.g., Baer et al. 2013; Lyles 2014). We argue that large-scale projects unite characteristics of both design and strategic problems: on the one hand, a practical design problem—to design and build a product in the form of a building or structure—has to be solved. On the other, the context of these large-scale projects often makes them strategic: for instance, they can be part of a city development strategy or of an overarching infrastructural program. Additionally, the timescales involved in large-scale projects—to completion but also to the end of life of the "product"—are so long that factors such as knowledge management or organizational learning become intertwined with the project. Their timescale allows the emergence of a *storyline* around the problem formulation, as different actors and stakeholders interpret, adapt, and collaborate on the problem formulation. A second objective of this chapter is thus to examine whether large-scale projects can be suitably described as *hybrid* problems and how they could be used to advance problem formulation theory.

To this end, we focus specifically on how the problem formulation affects the structural engineer's work in large-scale projects. This is of particular interest as the engineer is typically perceived as a "problem solver" (e.g., Koen 2009); somebody else formulates the problem. Engineering literature mostly deals with the activity of problem solving, whereas the activity of problem formulation or the problem itself is seldom questioned. Instead, the structural engineer tends to understand boundary conditions that define the solution space such as costs, safety, material resources, or architecture as given and unchanging parameters. It is our aim to challenge the view of the engineer as problem solver and to examine instead the different ways in which engineers are involved in problem formulation processes and when they can contribute their problem-solving skills in an optimal way.

When applying the logic of problem formulation to large-scale projects, the structure constitutes the outcome or solution of the latter-stage problem solving process: "A mega-project is a solution" (Priemus and Wee 2013). As von Hippel and von Krogh (2016) suggest "basing studies upon samples of solutions ... implemented rather than problems formulated," we analyze the problem formulation and its implications in four case studies of large-scale projects by developing an ex-post linkage between the problem formulation and the solution that was realized. The case studies are the Elbphilharmonie, the European Central Bank (ECB), the Gänse-bachtal Bridge, and the Kochertal Bridge (for descriptions and pictures of these case studies, see pages 34–37 and 42–45). While the first two represent projects that were strongly influenced by architectural designs, the latter two are structures designed solely by engineers. Thus, the engineers played different roles in the first two and the latter two projects, which provides an opportunity to investigate how the engineer deals with a given problem formulation or even participates in its development. The analysis of two cases for each project type provides the opportunity to develop robust findings for each type, while also enabling cross-checking the validity for the respective other type. For the analysis, we scanned the interviews of the four cases for codings related to the field of problem formulation. This included direct codings ("problem formulation," "reformulation") but also related codings such as "collaboration" or "tender procedure." We then aimed to synthesize a consistent storyline describing the pathway from problem formulation to solution implementation from various players. Depending on the interviewee, their involvement in the early project phase varied. However, each player described their entry into the project, which included pointers to the problem formulation at this respective stage. Features of the problem formulation named by several players are abstracted in the results below, while anecdotal evidence given by one player only is cited and processed at the periphery of the overall research result.

The chapter proceeds as follows. In the next section, we present a theoretical background to problem formulation and the pathway from problem to solution. We then describe the problem formulation storylines of the four cases based on the empirical data. This is followed by a cross-case analysis, which focuses on the hybridity of the problem, the actors involved in the problem formulation, the resulting engineering problem, the solution space, and the solution as a function of the problem formulation. In the conclusion, we explain how the lens of problem formulation could guide future large-scale projects. Advancing problem formulation theory, we present an understanding of how solution spaces open and confine as the project progresses, complementing previous findings of early volatile stages and complexity reduction measures.

From Problems to Problem Formulations to Solutions: Theoretical Background to Problem Formulation

Problem formulation can be understood as a vision or challenge within the early stages of any project or strategic development. It encompasses properties of the actual underlying problem and ways in which this problem has been formulated to fulfill needs and constraints or spark innovation. The problem formulation storyline—the activity of problem formulation itself and the pathway from problem formulation to solution, including developments as the project evolves—is largely shaped by different actors and stakeholders, the evolution of the solution space, and decision-making.

The literature on problem formulation currently focuses on two distinct problem typologies. Firstly, the field of problem formulation in product development, planning and design scrutinizes problem formulation for New Product Development (NPD) in consumer products (e.g., von Hippel and von Krogh 2016; Volkema 1983). In this context, "design" does not refer solely to artistic or architectural design, but is understood in a broad and abstract sense and thus also incorporates areas such as product or service design and business model design. Within this context, a product owner or innovation manager formulates a problem for and with design and product development teams in order to design or develop a product or offering. In this way the problem formulation acts as a proxy for customer needs and requirements, value propositions, or market opportunities. Volkema (1983) situates problem formulation between the "problem detection" stage and the latter stages of the planning and design process, which typically already focus on the solutions rather than the problem. The problem formulation is a measure to "both specify the design problem a priori and fix the solution set," thereby providing the designer with a specification to "search for the best designs" (von Hippel and von Krogh 2016).

Secondly, other scholars have focused on abstract, strategic issues in the field of strategic problem formulation (e.g., Baer et al. 2013; Lyles 2014). This field scrutinizes how organizations tackle long-term, strategic challenges, thereby building a bridge toward corporate strategy and organizational learning. It is important to understand that strategic problem formulation addresses the "formulation of strategic problems" and should not be misunderstood as "strategically formulating (design or NPD) problems." Unlike NPD problems that relate to a single product, these strategic problems are "of critical importance to a firm's success" (Baer et al. 2013) and are characterized by Teece (1994) as "quasi-irreversible commitments." As in this case problem formulation is embedded into the process of strategic decision-making, the involved actors and stakeholders are different to the NPD scenario: a strategic problem is formulated by top management and involves various disciplines throughout its formulation (and later, solution). Strategic problems invariably carry a large amount of complexity—they have "characteristics that the mere sum of [their] parts cannot reproduce" (Volkema 1983). In sum, strategic problems "are complex and ill-structured; ... teams involved in strategic decisions consist of individuals with heterogeneous information, knowledge, and motivation" (Baer et al. 2013).

These different problem typologies illustrate that the "socio-political process" (Lyles 2014) of problem formulation is largely shaped by the different actors involved: in general, problem formulation is more successful when done in heterogeneous teams, because they assemble broadly dispersed information and knowledge sets. However, scholars argue that the members of these teams display different objectives regarding the problem formulation, which can impede consensus within the problem formulation activity (Baer et al. 2013). Spradlin (2012) criticizes that teams tend to devote too little time and resources to this process, possibly leading to rudimentary problem formulations.

Another important aspect of problem formulation is its degree of openness. A "very broad" (von Hippel and von Krogh 2016) problem formulation leads to a large degree of freedom for problem solvers such as architects or engineers with a wide range of possible solutions, while a confined problem formulation, shaped by stricter constraints, limits the breadth of solutions that fulfill these criteria. The degree of openness of the problem formulation, possibly varying over time, shapes the "domain of solutions and ideas that the representation can produce" (Volkema 1983). The problem formulation opens "an underlying space of feasible solutions [through its] several objectives that can be evaluated with regard to the feasible solutions" (Buchert et al. 2015). This "solution space" can also be understood as the multitude of conceivable solutions within the "degrees of freedom" (von Hippel 1998) that the problem formulation offers.

Thus, the problem formulation also has huge implications for the subsequent problem-solving process. A well-formulated problem is ultimately "a benchmark against which various solution attempts can be evaluated" (Nickerson et al. 2007); conversely, "proper decision making is difficult in the absence of a clear problem formulation" (Priemus and Wee 2013). As the project advances, the problem formulation can be dealt with in an adaptive, "iterative" way, "reconsider[ing] objectives and sens[ing] new opportunities for problem formulation" (Shane 2008, p. 154), actively using the problem as a lever to shape the solution space. However, the problem formulation can also remain untouched, comparable to a waterfall approach with a "linear flow" where iterations are understood as "rework" rather than advances in the project (Shane 2008, p. 159). In this case, the effect of the problem formulation on the solution is so large that Shane (2008, p.159) claims "it is absolutely essential that the initial problem formulation is done correctly." As "assumptions and constraints are added ... , [which] limit the scope of the problem and the range of possible solutions" (Volkema 1983), confining the solution space becomes more relevant. Methods to achieve this include formulation of requirements, providing information for stakeholders, formulation of metrics of success, and the decision which problem solvers are engaged and with which incentives (Spradlin 2012).

While problem formulation is the first essential step in solving any problem, the ultimate aim of it is nonetheless to inspire the best solution within the solution space. This can be triggered by opening the solution space for "a broad range of alternative solution concepts and then picking the most promising one" (Shane 2008, p. 160). Another possible approach would be for players to scan their "mind and/or the environment for need-solution pairs that might fit" (von Hippel and von Krogh 2016), thereby matching a solution to the problem formulation rather than developing one throughout the project.

Problem Formulation Storylines

In what follows, we present empirical data on the four cases in the form of problem formulation storylines as described by the interviewees. For each case we address the overall vision or problem, the initial solution space as well as the resulting task for the engineer and how the engineer perceived it, the solution space and the engineer's handling of it, the built solution, and the factors contributing to success in the engineer's problem-solving activity.

Elbphilharmonie

The city of Hamburg as client initially broadly and ambitiously declared as the goal of the Elbphilharmonie: "we want to have one of the ten best concert halls in the world" (C1_Own1). However, the client had no in-depth knowledge of "what was needed to run, to build a concert house" (C1_Proj1). Furthermore, the client consisted of two parties, one that was supposed to operate the concert hall after completion and one responsible for the construction which was initially equipped with "little human resources" (C1_Own2). This led to conflicts of interest even within the client (C1_Eng3). Moreover, the design of the Elbphilharmonie project was not awarded in an architectural competition. All in all, little time and resources were devoted to a problem formulation. Project members claimed that the design aspect was "placed very much at the forefront" of the project (C1_Eng2), which allowed the architect to develop something "special" (C1_Arch1) in terms of design, while engineers argued that at this stage the "goal was not clearly defined" (C1_Eng1).

As a consequence, the task for the structural engineer was to make the architecture feasible while "taking up little room from it" (C1_Arch6). The scant attention given to structural engineering issues is illustrated by the demand to "build a high rise, make a hole [for the concert hall itself] in the middle and then tell the structural engineers 'please continue building above'" (C1_Own2). Thus, for the structural engineers, the problem was on the one hand clear—make the building feasible—on the other hand it was not consciously formulated; instead, constraints and requirements developed in the course of the project along with the "paramount" (C1_Eng2) architectural design. These constraints included the various envisaged uses of the building, which led to multiple conflicting problems "in principle not solvable within a couple of months" (C1_Arch3), but also the difficult location, on top of an old warehouse initially not fit to carry the loads of the concert hall, and surrounded on three sides by water, making the construction of foundations a complex issue.

Instead of opening the solution space, the unclear problem formulation led the engineers to adopt a "nearly linear approach, going step by step in one direction" (C1_Eng3), in order to develop solutions for the complex problems. There was little room to influence the geometry of structurally important and complex elements such as the hall itself. The problem-solving capacity of the engineer was therefore restricted to making the building elements structurally stable.

Within the built solution, the clear priority is the architecture, including façade and interior, while structural engineering fulfills the function of materializing it. In the eyes of two of the engineers involved, the structure remains "rather conventional" (C1_Arch6; C1_Eng4). However, the successful realization of the Elbphilharmonie has provided Hamburg with a new "landmark," as anticipated in the first renderings of the building.

Due to the waterfall top-down flow of problem formulation from client to architect to engineer, little room for innovation in the field of engineering remained. One interviewee concluded that the opportunity to change this was "missed at the beginning of the project" (C1_Arch6). However, with respect to the successful implementation of the architecture, one architect claimed that the ones enabling the building were the structural engineers (C1_Arch3) with a client representative describing their achievement as "superb" (C1_Own2).

European Central Bank

In the case of the European Central Bank premises in Frankfurt, the client declared the overarching goal of a "signature building—a modern building for a modern central bank" (C2_Own1). In the architectural competition, a lot of requirements and conditions were already known and communicated: "we knew what the bank needed," stated one of the client's project managers (C2_Own1). Hard conditions like the number of working places, energy efficiency, and the utilization of the Großmarkthalle were defined, and the bank pursued a "No-Change-Policy" (C2_Own1). However, the client did not intend an early fixation on a specific solution. Instead, the client included additional soft conditions, e.g., that architects, structural and climate engineers should work together from the start and a "constructive collaboration as an ethical principle" (C2_Eng2) was prescribed.

Hence, the task for the structural engineers was "to develop concepts together with the architect" (C2_Eng1). This was perceived as "the ideal scenario" by one engineer (C2_Eng1), because during design the structural and aesthetic aspects cannot be treated chronologically: "Everything is intertwined. Because when you design, you have to think in networks and consider many aspects at the same time" (C2_Eng1).

In the design process, the solution space was on the one hand limited due to precisely defined boundary conditions. On the other hand, because these "hard conditions" were known from the start, they provided the opportunity to be creative and find "unusual solutions" (C2_Eng2). In this process, the engineers were in "very close, very close" (C2_Eng2) collaboration with the architects: geometrical corridors to place structural elements were exchanged between architects and engineers (C2_Eng2) and key aspects were "designed jointly" (C2_Eng3). The holistic approach to the project uniting architectural and engineering aspects also led to a "personal respect towards the achievement of the other [discipline]" (C2_Eng3).

In the finished building, "many details were developed, that are innovative [in the field of structural engineering], [and] that … are blueprint solutions for future buildings" (C2_Eng2). One main feature was a parametrical design process for the placement of the braces (C2_Eng3). This illustrates how the engineering challenges were solved with a strong focus on delivering the desired parameters for architect and client while at the same time striving for innovative, replicable solutions.

The successful realization of the project was made possible by a highly visible and active client, who "had two people in the highest position taking care of the project in an intense manner" (C2_Own1). Another factor contributing to success was an early co-location of engineers and architects, underlined by one of the engineers claiming that "technical innovation only works within a planning process, ... never on a drawing board" (C2_Eng3), and another who stated that "this happens only in teams" (C2_Eng4). Regarding the solution space, in the project an ideal degree of openness was found to allow for a holistic, innovative solution, while boundaries were defined in a sufficiently strict manner to comply with the client's risk aversion and financial aims.

Gänsebachtal Bridge
For the new high-speed line between Nuremberg and Berlin the Gänsebachtal valley had to be spanned. The initial problem formulation by the client German Railways (DB) was to construct a bridge according to its "Framework Planning"—a well-established standardized approach which predefines the design of the bridge's structural components and as such "naturally" limits the solution space for innovations (C4_Proj1). Additionally, in such shallow valleys as the Gänsebachtal, this bridge type appears over-dimensioned and view-obstructing (Schlaich et al. 2008, p. 9). The solution pre-formulated in the problem formulation thus was not the optimal solution for the underlying problem, which led to the integration of the Bridge Advisory Board into the project. The council was established to increase the building culture in the bridges of the German Railways by guiding structural and aesthetic improvements during early project stages. Following the advice of the Bridge Advisory Board, the tender process for the Gänsebachtal Bridge was altered: construction companies were now allowed to hand in a special proposal, as long as it did not compromise the planning permission (C4_Eng1; C4_Proj1).

Previously, for years and independently of project work (C4_Eng1), the engineer Jörg Schlaich, aware of the shortcomings of the "Framework Planning" approach, had developed an "Alternative Framework" for railway bridges (C4_Eng4) with self-set goals. He developed new slender, durable and sustainable bridge prototypes, which reflect the variety in landscape and thus meet the challenges of the specific location while optimizing both construction and maintenance costs (Schlaich et al. 2008).

After the intervention of the Bridge Advisory Board, the solution space for the Gänsebachtal Bridge—previously limited to the degree of standardization due to the "Framework Planning"—was opened to innovative design proposals. This created an opportunity to realize a semi-integral bridge according to the "Alternative Framework." The unconventional pairing of a formulated problem and an already designed solution from Schlaich's "Alternative Framework" led to only minor problem-solving activities during the design phase. However, as the "Alternative Framework" differed considerably from the well-established "Framework Planning," significant additional proofs, namely calculations and tests to assure equivalent safety, needed to be delivered.

The successful construction of the bridge can be seen as a "pilot" (C4_Cont1) for semi-integral bridges, as numerous proofs were necessary for the first time in a rather conservative sector. Another interviewee called the bridge a "milestone of bridge design," both nationally and internationally (C4_Oth1).

Several factors enabled the successful realization of the semi-integral bridge. The client played a key role on several levels (C4_Eng1; C4_Eng4; C4_Oth1; C4_Oth2; C4_Own1): the project was supported by the strong will and determination of the German Railways' chairman, the goodwill of the audit authority, and the openness to innovation and alternative solutions of the operative party DB ProjektBau. Other crucial factors of success were the feasible, available solution within the "Alternative Framework," the fact that possible difficulties at later stages of the project were anticipated due to the early involvement of technical experts (C4_Eng3; C4_Eng4), and not least the strong motivation of the lead engineers and subsequently of all project partners to realize this solution.

Kochertal Bridge

After twenty-eight years in use, deficiencies in the condition of the Kochertal Bridge were noticed during a regular bridge inspection, compromising the safety of the bridge. Additionally, the A6 highway carried by the bridge was supposed to be expanded from four to six lanes. The aim of the owner of the bridge, the Stuttgart Regional Council, was maintaining and reinforcing the bridge. This approach was favored over its demolition and replacement with a new structure, as that would have resulted in enormous costs, but also due to the bridge's high profile as an iconic and listed structure (C6_Own1).

To the client it was apparent from the beginning that maintaining and reinforcing the bridge was an ambitious aim (C6_Eng2; C6_Own1), as the deficit in the bridge's load-bearing capacity was estimated at approximately fifteen percent in a first calculation. The task for the structural engineers was therefore to determine whether the aim was achievable and, if so, how (C6_Eng2; C6_Own1).

With this fixed goal, at first glance the solution space for the engineer appears narrow. However, that was not the case: the client encouraged the engineers to propose new methods to achieve the goal, and commissioned these further investigations. The leading engineer described his team in the demanding and exciting role of "investigative engineers" (C6_Eng2), challenged to deploy the complete range of engineering knowledge. With an iterative and integral approach, the engineers translated the goal of maintaining the bridge into concrete tasks, combining analytical methods, e.g., the examination of original documents of the design and construction process, with empirical methods, consisting of material tests on the bridge (C6_Eng2).

Thus, they did not merely recalculate the bridge as a finished structure but also considered the original construction process. In doing so, the engineers took a step further from the existing guidelines for the recalculation of bridges (C6_Oth1).

All in all, the integral approach led to a re-assessment of the bridge's condition and, as a consequence, to its successful maintenance and reinforcement, with only a small amount of necessary measures, namely the replacement of the bridge bearings and the reinforcement of the box girder beam. Hence, the works carried out on the bridge were not particularly innovative (C6_Oth6). However, the approach and the effort put into the project by the engineer, which led to the successful maintenance and reinforcement, were indeed innovative and also honored with an engineering prize.

The innovative approach and the later success of the project were enabled by the client's approval and support, consisting of keeping an open mind for different approaches and commissioning expensive investigations without a guarantee as to their success (C6_Eng2).

Comparing and Contrasting Problem Formulation Aspects

In this section, we specifically compare and contrast five aspects of the cases: the *hybridity* of the problems, the *actors involved in the problem formulation*, the resulting *engineering problem*, the *solution space*, and the *solution in relation to the initial problem formulation*.

Hybridity of the Problem

All of the cases analyzed can be classified as *hybrid* problems: while they are design problems which entail concept, design, planning, and realization of the respective building or structure, they are also embedded in a larger context and exert characteristics of strategic problems (Table 1). All projects are long-term and require huge commitment from all actors. In the case of the Elbphilharmonie, it was strategically aimed at building "one of the ten best concert halls in the world"—a "landmark" for the HafenCity area. In the ECB project, the strategic goal was to invest in an own office building to reduce the fixed costs of rent, as well as to materialize the self-image of "a modern central bank" in a "signature building." The Gänsebachtal Bridge is part of the strategic program VDE8—German Unity Transport Projects 8—which was planned immediately after the German re-unification with the strategic problem to better connect the former East and West Germany. In the case of the Kochertal Bridge, the goal was to maintain the bridge instead of building a new one, with the strategic aspects to preserve the Kochertal Bridge with its high symbolic value, but also to minimize costs while keeping traffic flowing during maintenance.

Actors Involved in the Problem Formulation

The *actor* most frequently involved in the problem formulation is the client or the later user (Table 2). The bridge clients—a national railway and a regional road authority—were regular procurers of similar projects. For the Gänsebachtal Bridge,

Design Problem	Concept, design, planning, and realization of the building or structure			
Strategic Problem	Build one of the ten best concert halls, develop- ment of HafenCity area	Reduce fixed costs; materialize self-image: "modern central bank"	Part of VDE8; better connect former East and West Germany	Maintain instead of building anew; pre- serve high symbolic value; reduce costs

Table 1: Design and Strategic Problem

a predefined solution was already available in the form of the "Framework Planning." The approach of the Kochertal Bridge client was to commission investigations to learn more about the actual problem of maintaining and reinforcing the bridge before decid- ing on a concrete problem formulation. The European Central Bank as client was aware they did not possess enough technical expertise for the project. However, they were eager to generate in-house knowledge during the project and involve building experts to subsequently actively engage in the problem formula- tion. Thus, the clients of the Gänsebachtal Bridge, Kochertal Bridge, and ECB were informed, knowledgeable players, who were able to formulate their needs. This was especially acknowledged by the engineers in the ECB project, one of them highlighting the impor- tance of knowledgeable clients.

The actors who participated in the problem formulation of the Elbphilharmonie are more diverse. The project was initially pro- posed by a private investor and later directly allocated to the architects. For the city of Hamburg as client this one-off project was extremely burdensome in terms both of complexity and scale. This becomes apparent in a naïve approach to the facets of the problem, e.g., the conflicting uses within the building or its diffi- cult location. The two-fold client structure—commissioning and operating entity—posed a further challenge, weakening the cli- ent's while implicitly strengthening the architect's position.

Table 2: Actors Involved in the Problem Formulation

	Elbphilharmonie	European Central Bank	Gänsebachtal Bridge	Kochertal Bridge
Client	Public authority	Bank	Railway	Public authority
Client Knowledge	Weak	Medium (acquired)	Very strong (very experienced)	Strong (experienced)
Approach to Prob- lem Formulation	Naïve	Active, knowledge- acquiring	Solution available (Framework Planning)	Feasibility research by engineers

Engineering Problem

While both of the high-rise projects started out with ambitious early visions, they differed in how these were translated into an *engineering problem* (Table 3). The vision of a "landmark" and the overburdened client in the case of the Elbphilharmonie led to a very strong architect dominating the project with his ideas. The engineering problem was thus formulated implicitly and top-down from the architects' solution ideas, time-wise after the formulation of the architectural problem, leading to the engineers' challenging task of making the architectural design feasible. Conversely, the ECB client actively formulated a problem based on its vision of a "signature building" by setting parameters to measure what could be grasped rationally and tackling the remaining problem with a dedicated holistic approach between architects and engineers. For the engineers, the problem was therefore to design the building in collaboration with the architects, with the complex challenge to meet all hard conditions while still fulfilling the initial vision.

In the case of the Gänsebachtal Bridge the "Framework Planning" initially predefined the solution. However, some engineers saw the opportunity to realize a semi-integral bridge according to the "Alternative Framework." For them, hence, the self-set problem was to lobby problem formulators to enable a realization of this "Alternative Framework," which then succeeded. The initial problem for the Kochertal Bridge case was to define the feasibility of maintaining the bridge. Thus, in both bridge projects, we can identify a clear functional problem, opening up the search for solutions for the engineer.

Solution Space

The way an engineering problem is formulated and by whom logically shapes the *solution space* (Table 4). In the Elbphilharmonie project, the solution space for engineers was defined after the

Table 3: Engineering Problem

	Elbphilharmonie	European Central Bank	Gänsebachtal Bridge	Kochertal Bridge
Engineering Problem	Not consciously formulated; implicit problem: make architectural design feasible	Design building in collaboration with architects; challenge: fulfill all defined parameters	Officially: Implement "Framework Planning"; Self-set: realize "Alternative Framework"	Analyze feasibility of maintenance

Solution space	Confined	Open	Predefined (Framework Planning)	Predefined
Evolution	Confined	Confined (target-oriented)	Open (Alternative Framework)	Iterative emergence of solution path

Table 4: Solution Space

architectural solution was already (partly) found. Hence, the engineer's solution space was confined and remained confined, which led to an almost linear approach with little room for innovative structural solutions. In contrast, co-located activities and early joint problem development led to a greater degree of freedom for the engineers in the ECB case: architectural and engineering solution spaces were defined in parallel and influenced each other's room for innovative solutions. Clear parameters and a "No-Change-Policy" set by a strong client confined the solution space as soon as the project physically started.

The Gänsebachtal Bridge had a solution space predefined by the client's "Framework Planning." This solution space was opened up after the intervention of the Bridge Advisory Board inviting alternative solutions, leading to two distinct solution trajectories: the "Framework Planning" and the "Alternative Framework," which was later implemented. For the Kochertal Bridge, there was a predefined solution trajectory—avoiding reconstruction if possible—which converged toward the lean solution of recalculating and reinforcement. The Kochertal Bridge was tackled with a strictly functional view, where the engineer operated in the solution space predefined by the problem formulation. While the problem formulation did not change, the solution path was iteratively adapted and reframed as more and more information was added to the core issues of the problem in the course of solving it.

Solution in Relation to the Initial Problem Formulation

One main argument at the outset of this chapter was that the *solution*, materialized in the project's outcome, is influenced by the problem formulation. Therefore, we explicitly connect the typology of the engineering problem to the final outcome described in Table 5 (page 147). In the case of the Elbphilharmonie, the problem of making the architectural design feasible was solved. This was acknowledged by many interviewees and also received formal recognition through the Swiss Building Award 2017 (category: structural engineering). However, the solution for the Elbphilharmonie can be regarded as innovative only in its function to make the architectural design feasible, with little innovation from a purely structural point of view.

The holistic approach of the European Central Bank yielded an intertwined working mode and a structural solution that is in perfect symbiosis with the architectural design: one cannot be separated from the other. This can be regarded as a characteristic of a "good" structure (e.g., Schnetzer et al. 2012). Moreover, many details within the solution are deemed innovative with the possibility to deploy them in other projects. With a distinction in the German Engineering Award 2016, the structural solution of the ECB was recognized for its own sake as well as for its effective integration with the architectural concept. Thus, the overall return points to an ideal degree of openness—opened up by allowing for a holistic concept, then limited by hard parameters.

For the Gänsebachtal Bridge, it is important to highlight that as the "Alternative Framework" provided a predefined solution, most aspects of the bridge's design already existed before the problem emerged. Despite this, the requirements of the client were fully met and emerging sub-problems (e.g., proofs) were solved iteratively. The successful realization was honored by the German Bridge Construction Award 2014. This shows how an openness toward an alternative solution can be of advantage while maintaining hard parameters and metrics, as was also found in the ECB project.

In the Kochertal Bridge case, the client stuck to the problem phase for a remarkably long time while commissioning extra investigations on the condition of the bridge. This was rewarded by the successful maintenance with a minimal technical expense and honored with the German Bridge Construction Award 2016, thus highlighting how a long and detailed problem formulation phase leads to a good solution.

Conclusion

At the outset of this chapter, one objective was to illustrate that problem formulation can be a useful concept to guide large-sale projects. This hypothesis is supported by three aspects. First, the *problem formulation* itself and its *quality* proved to be crucial to the development of the large-scale projects analyzed here. In all four cases, the problem solvers—in our case the structural engineers—relate their work back to the problem formulation—e.g., "build a modern central bank" (ECB) or "make this bridge durable for the future" (Kochertal Bridge). This shows that it is important explicitly to define what the project is expected to achieve in order to stimulate the expertise of the engineer. The quality of the problem formulation proved to be relevant as well. When the functional aspect of the problem formulation is undervalued, e.g., by pre-formulating design solutions, engineers find themselves with a confined solution space that does not allow an optimal transformation of the problem with the engineer's knowledge and problem-solving

Engineering Solution	Subordinate to architectural solution	Intertwined with architectural solution	Ready-designed innovative solution	Innovative outcome after long problem phase
Structural Engineering award	Swiss Building Award 2017 (category: structural engineering)	German Engineering Award 2016 (distinction)	German Bridge Construction Award 2014	German Bridge Construction Award 2016

Table 5: Engineering Solution

capability. In contrast, a functional problem formulation spurs engineering innovativeness, if the engineer participates in transforming this functional problem formulation, as illustrated by the ECB and the two bridge projects.

Second, the preoccupation with and the activity of formulating the problem generate an awareness of the impacts of problem formulation and help to decide on measures to tame complex problems. Hence, as illustrated in particular by the ECB case, a collaborative approach with all actors can lead to a productive problem formulation in accordance with disciplinary knowledge. Moreover, we observed that a knowledgeable client tends to involve the engineer early on, which empowers them to formulate the problem according to the engineers' solving abilities. In contrast, deciding on the "what" to build without consulting the person knowledgeable about the "how" can trivially lead to cost and time overruns. The cases illustrate two ways in which the engineer was involved: while in the ECB case the engineer was invited by the client to participate in the early concept stages with the architect, the Gänsebachtal Bridge case provides inspiration for how engineers can also actively position their ideas and thus co-determine which problem they subsequently solve. In this way, the absence of an architect, as occurred in the fairly "technical" bridge projects, can strengthen the relationship between client and engineer in the early project stage.

Third, in line with this and rethinking existing structures, the engineer's problem-solving abilities could also be used to develop visions for innovative structures, which can then be matched to existing problems in the sense of need-solution pairing. A best-practice example for this was the successful realization of the innovative semi-integral Gänsebachtal Bridge. This also underlines the suitability of our theoretical approach: we find that the engineer profited from the "enriched solution landscape" (von Hippel and von Krogh 2016) that was available before pairing the solution with the specific task of spanning the valley of the Gänsebachtal. How-ever, in contrast to the idea of serendipity—fortunate coincidences—present in the innovation management literature on problem formulation, the engineer designed his solution and then *specifically searched for* an application for it.

Another objective of this chapter was to explore whether large-scale projects are appropriately classified as *hybrid*—strategic and design—problems and can thus advance problem formulation theory. In our analysis, we first showed how strategic and design issues are intertwined in large-scale projects, thus enhancing and illustrating the understanding of hybridity in such projects. The four storylines illustrate different ways in which the strategic overall problem is dealt with through solving the design problem in which it materializes.

Second, advancing problem formulation theory, our findings provide insights into the pathway from problem formulation to solution and how this process is steered. Throughout the duration of a large-scale project, we find that a "game" of first opening and then confining the solution space takes place between engineers and their client or architectural counterpart. The opening of solution spaces can be fostered by an invitation for alternative solutions or an interdisciplinary collabora-tion, e.g., with an architect, in an early project stage. Later, the solution space is confined by hard metrics, joint responsibility or a "No-Change-Policy", factors com-parable to the complexity reduction measures for problem formulations as described by Volkema (1983). When the solution space is initially opened, the engi-neer has the possibility of working in an explorative manner, developing a vision-ary solution ("what" to achieve), ideally with other project stakeholders. This early involvement ensures that the engineer finds themself with a degree of freedom appropriate to the task but also enabling them to generate innovation within. This is highlighted by the Gänsebachtal Bridge, where the task of building a high-speed railway bridge naturally implied strict regulations to ensure safety. Nevertheless, it was possible to design and build an aesthetically pleasing as well as structurally innovative bridge. In contrast, when the solution space is confined, engineering capabilities are concentrated more on "how" to reach the design goal, thereby reducing complexity and advancing on the trajectory toward the solution.

To conclude, our analysis of large-scale projects as *hybrid* problems has shown that these projects can benefit from the lens of problem formulation as it provides a visionary approach to guide the early stages of such one-off projects. Conversely, problem formulation theory can be advanced using case studies of hybrid prob-lems. In our research, we analyzed in retrospect how this hybridity has been dealt with by problem formulators who were largely unaware of the task of problem for-mulation and its implications. To gain further understanding of large-scale pro-jects as hybrid problems, an interesting approach for future research would be to scientifically accompany their problem formulation activities as they happen, for instance with an action research approach.

References

Baer, M., K. T. Dirks, and J. A. Nickerson (2013). "Microfoundations of Strategic Problem Formulation: Strategic Problem Formulation." *Strategic Management Journal* 34.2: pp. 197–214.

Buchert, T., S. Neugebauer, S. Schenker, K. Lindow, and R. Stark (2015). "Multi-Criteria Decision Making as a Tool for Sustainable Product Development—Benefits and Obstacles" *Procedia CIRP* 26: pp. 70–75.

von Hippel, E. (1998). "Economics of Product Development by Users: The Impact of 'Sticky' Local Information." *Management Science*. 44.5: pp. 629–644.

von Hippel, E. and G. von Krogh (2016). "CROSSROADS—Identifying Viable 'Need–Solution Pairs': Problem Solving Without Problem Formulation." *Organization Science* 27.1: pp. 207-221.

Koen, B. V. (2009). "The Engineering Method and Its Implications for Scientific, Philosophical and Universal Methods." *The Monist* 92.3: pp. 357-386.

Lyles, M. A. (2014). "Organizational Learning, Knowledge Creation, Problem Formulation and Innovation in Messy Problems." *European Management Journal* 32.1: pp. 132–136.

Nickerson, J. A., B. S. Silverman, and T. R. Zenger (2007). "The 'Problem' of Creating and Capturing Value." *Strategic Organization* 5.3: pp. 211–25.

Priemus, H. and B. van Wee, eds. (2013). *International Handbook on Mega-Projects.* Cheltenham; Northampton.

Schlaich, J., T. Fackler, M. Weißbach, V. Schmitt, C. Ommert, S. Marx, and L. Krontal (2008). *Leitfaden Gestalten von Eisenbahnbrücken.* n.p.

Schnetzer, H., A. Muttoni, J. Schwartz, and A. Flury (2012). "Starke Strukturen" A. Flury, ed. *Kooperation. Zur Zusammenarbeit von Ingenieur und Architekt.* Basel.

Shane, S. (2008). *The Handbook of Technology and Innovation Management.* Chichester; Hoboken.

Spradlin, D. (2012). "Are You Solving the Right Problem?" *Harvard Business Review.* September 2012.

Teece, D. J. (1994). "Profiting from Technological Innovation: Implications for Integration, Collaboration, Licensing and Public Policy." *Transnational Corporations and Innovatory Activities* 15.73: pp. 679-730.

Volkema, R. J. (1983). "Problem Formulation in Planning and Design." *Management Science* 29.6: pp 639–652.

Innovations in Bridge Design?

Steffen Marx

Germany is undoubtedly one of the countries with the highest safety standards in the world. This is true in general, but especially so of the construction industry, and that is, of course, a good thing. The collapse of buildings or bridges under normal use conditions almost never occurs in Germany. Indeed, public acceptance of such an event, particularly one involving fatalities, is virtually zero.

However, the high safety requirements have also led to a steady increase in the number of pages of regulations, guidelines and other rules, especially in bridge design. Wherever possible, in order to avoid any risks, only tried and tested, industry-approved designs are used. All designs are regulated to a very high level of detail; any deviations involve considerable effort and are high risk in terms of both expenditure and time. In the present chapter, Fahnenmüller et al. use the theoretical framework of "Problem Formulation" to analyze how the early stages of construction projects can influence the outcome and thus also the innovativeness of projects. The status quo they describe—that stakeholders formulate the problem, for which the proposed structure or building constitutes a solution, close to predefined, tried and approved solutions—confines the solution space for many bridge construction projects.

With this approach, innovations in bridge construction in Germany are now hard to implement. As a result, the further development of designs and construction methods is severely curtailed. This hostile climate with regard to innovation is reinforced by other factors.

One major obstacle to innovation is already rooted in the customary approach of allocating the planning phases for a bridge structure among different planners and generally awarding these services to the cheapest bidder. First, it is obvious that the cheapest planning cannot and will not deliver the best (i.e., most innovative, most aesthetically pleasing, and most economical) bridge design. Instead, the focus is on minimizing the cost of the planning service for the engineer, so that the project can still be realized economically for the engineer. Inevitably, this leads to a less innovative, more standardized solution that is as simple as possible in terms of planning effort.

Additionally, the phased awarding of contracts to different planners diminishes the identification of the planner with the object. The motivation to successfully complete a good and innovative design solution and to actually realize it recedes into the background. Instead, the goal of minimizing one's own risks and costs is reinforced. In Germany, execution planning in bridge construction is not usually carried out until after the construction work has been awarded. As a result, project risks are only identified at a very late stage and have a direct negative impact on the construction process and construction costs. The engineer responsible for implementation planning is bound by the construction company and is thus obliged to serve the interests of that company. Innovations in projects are always associated both with greater opportunities and with greater risks than is true for conventional solutions. As a result of the practice of awarding contracts, the risks are more likely to be realized in projects than the opportunities, which is why builders prefer to avoid innovations (= risks).

Another factor preventing innovation in bridge construction is the distribution of responsibility (or liability) in the approval process and the ability to influence the implemented solution. Although the planning engineer is fully liable for his services, the approval authorities, checking engineers, and other experts often impose extensive additional requirements on innovative solutions that are hardly foreseeable or controllable in the course of the project. This reduces the motivation of all the parties involved—clients, engineers, and construction companies—to develop innovations in bridge construction or even to systematically promote them.

There may be many good reasons for the established procedures in bridge design and other publicly financed construction projects, but they do not provide a good basis for innovation. From the point of view of a project manager, the general avoidance of innovation in individual projects is then the only logical and understandable consequence. Viewed globally, however, this is a creeping disaster. General avoidance of innovation leads to a standstill in development and, in the long term, to falling behind in international competition. If innovations cannot be sensibly realized in individual projects, it is imperative that they be effectively promoted from the perspective of the overall system. Two basic approaches are necessary to improve the climate for innovation in bridge construction.

First, new and innovative developments in construction must be better promoted by central construction administrations and implemented in projects. To this end, the project portfolio of large building owners (e.g., railroad companies or the Federal Highways Administration) must be regularly reviewed and specifically filtered for projects in which innovations are to be implemented. Special advisory boards with independent experts (such as DBAG's Bridge Advisory Board) can support this selection process. This also includes a general acceptance of risks and appropriate processes to identify these risks at an early stage, evaluate them and mitigate them in a way that is compatible with the project. In addition, a special budget must be set aside in the project for innovations and innovation support.

Moreover, we also need to foster more research in the seemingly mundane field of bridge construction as a joint endeavor between the construction industry and universities. Despite huge public investment in bridge construction, research spending in this area is vanishingly small. In the area of railroad infrastructure, for example, just 0.02 percent of the federal government's investment funds are currently available for research. Other sectors of the economy are much more research-intensive: for instance, the automotive industry invests about 8.5 percent of its total sales in research and development.

The chapter supports this view by offering a starting point to "inject" innovativeness into construction projects. Involving multiple actors in the problem formulation stage and strengthening the bond between clients and civil engineers complements the approaches outlined above. Moreover, the act of "transforming the problem formulation" into an innovative result is an opportunity to rethink the civil engineer's role in construction projects and draw on the high standard of civil engineering knowledge in Germany.

If we want to have the brightest minds among civil engineers in the future and be able to hold our own in European and global competition, we urgently need to improve the climate for building innovation and its implementation in projects!

Dealing with Materiality: The Role of Engineering Thinking and Material Knowledge for Innovation in Construction

Johanna Ruge/Annette Bögle

Introduction

Today, the construction industry faces multiple challenges, that are both a consequence of external factors such as climate change and urbanization, and the result of internal developments such as the digitalization and internationalization of the sector. There is also a huge pressure for change resulting from new technical requirements and possibilities. Additionally, both society and engineers in particular claim that more innovation in construction is needed (Clegg and Kreiner 2014). In this chapter, we address the role of materiality for the generation of innovation in the construction industry. We argue that to understand and meet the industry's challenges as well as to gain an in-depth understanding of innovation processes in construction, it is essential to deal with the interdependence of innovation and materiality.

In the field of engineering there is ample research on materiality, for instance on specific materials, their behaviors or their influences on important parameters of structures such as load-bearing behavior and serviceability. Such research often aims at better judgements of what could be structurally feasible with certain materials. Moreover, engineers working in engineering offices or manufacturing and construction firms, who are directly engaged in the materialization process, usually possess a distinct material knowledge (Menges et al. 2014), combined with the ability to make informed assessments as to the feasibility of designs, a pre-requisite for their realization. However, in debates about innovation in construction the role of materiality for innovation as well as the perspectives of engineers on this topic are underrepresented. This lack of engineering input can be attributed to two closely related aspects: first, to date there have been few attempts by the engineering sector to invest in a meta-discussion on the role of materiality for innovation in construction projects—structural engineers rarely formulate their perspectives on innovation in construction, and, when they do, these are rarely given serious recognition by other building professionals or the public. This phenomenon is described by Duddeck and Mittelstraß (1999) with the term "speechlessness of engineers." Second, the material knowledge of engineers can be closely related to the notion of tacit knowledge, i.e., to knowledge that is unarticulated and tied to senses, movement skills, physical experiences, intuition or rules of thumb, and is rooted in actions, procedures, routines, commitment, ideals, values, and emotions (Nonaka and von Krogh 2009; Howells 1996), and therefore difficult to communicate. However, academics concerned with the connection between such tacit knowledge and innovation state that tacit knowledge is one of the prerequisites to be able to innovate (von Krogh et al. 2000; Nonaka and von Krogh 2009).

In line with this, we argue that to understand the mechanisms behind innovation processes in construction the perspectives of engineers, especially their material knowledge, need to be considered. Thus, to encourage greater innovation in construction, a direct and on the ground engagement with materiality and its implications, especially for the feasibility and so the realization of designs, is indispensable. In this chapter, we aim to provide a both theoretically and empirically grounded understanding of materiality in construction. Additionally, on a superordinate level, with this chapter we seek to overcome to some extent the speechlessness of engineers with regard to the role of materiality in construction.

To achieve this aim, we use the following methodology: first, we review literature on the meaning and importance of materiality in construction, explaining the influences of materiality as well as the engineer's task in dealing with it. Second, we incorporate views and insights on the role of materiality for innovation in construction by engineers, all of whom have worked on large-scale construction projects where ambitious designs often require special and innovative solutions. The engineers worked at different types of organizations and fulfilled different functions in the projects, for instance as design engineers, execution engineers or verification engineers. In total, we evaluated forty-five qualitative interviews with fifty-four engineers from all six cases of the research project using inductively generated codes. We specifically analyzed segments coded with "materiality" and "feasibility" as a base for the understanding of materiality and its role in construction. Additionally, to examine how engineers deal with materiality, we analyzed segments coded with "working approach" and "tools." Hence, the interviews allowed for an explorative view on the roles of materiality in construction projects and, furthermore, provided insights into engineering thinking. We aimed for triangulation of findings among different respondents, so that only robust excerpts of interviews are reported in this chapter. Thus, aspects concerning materiality named by several engineers are abstracted, while statements by single engineers are cited literally and used as illustrative examples of the findings. All quoted interview segments are anonymized and labeled with a code indicating the case study and the type of organization to which the cited engineer was affiliated in the project, see the chapter on methods on pp. 28–32.

The chapter proceeds as follows: in the next section, we present some basic reflections on the meaning and importance of materiality in construction. This is followed by two sections based on our empirical data. First, we develop a nuanced view of different *dimensions of materiality* relevant in large-scale construction projects as well as of *dimensions of feasibility* material structures have to fulfill. Second, we describe how engineers deal with materiality, focusing on *engineering thinking* and the *material knowledge* of engineers. In the subsequent section, we discuss how engineering thinking and material knowledge play a role in making complex material structures feasible and hence in the generation of innovation in construction projects. In conclusion, we find that in engineering, innovation is often related to stretching the boundaries of feasibility, often material feasibility. For this, large-scale projects provide a special setting, as they create possibilities to generate material knowledge, which enables the stretching of boundaries of feasibility. We further stress that, to foster innovation in construction, both engineers and non-engineers need to be willing to engage in communication about materiality in construction.

Basic Reflections on the Meaning and Importance of Materiality in Construction

Influences of Materiality in Construction
Taken literally, materiality implies that something is composed out of matter: this essentially means that something is subjected to the laws of physics, first and foremost to gravity. For classic construction materials such as stone, steel, and wood, this is so evident that sometimes the question is rather why daring structures don't col-

lapse. In construction materiality in the sense of corporality is important: structures are not made of loose materials, but instead have a specific form which in its corporality is essentially needed to fulfill the structure's function, for instance to provide shelter or bridge a valley. This also relates to an immediacy of materials, which, as Rice (1996) describes, becomes evident in a kind of real presence of the materials used in a structure, "so that people warm to them, want to touch them, feel a sense of the material itself and of the people who made and designed it. ... . It is the honesty and immediacy in the use of the building's principal materials which determine its tactile quality" (pp. 76–78).

Materiality has a significant influence on several important parameters of structures, for instance on load-bearing capacity, serviceability, durability, sustainability, costs, and construction mode and time. In structural engineering, the influences are particularly high, as the structures usually fulfill long-term functions and are large in size, which implies both that the structures in their material configuration are permanent for many years and that dismantling is very labor-intensive. At the same time, a major and very specific aspect of the construction industry is that each structure is a one-off: while to average construction projects this applies at least due to the adaptation to their respective location, large-scale projects are often even more unique, for instance due to their exceptional architecture. This one-off character implies that while materiality has huge impacts on structures, these impacts cannot usually be tested or exactly preconceived for the unique material configuration of a specific structure. This becomes especially evident when considering safety issues. Safety plays a crucial role in construction as failure usually has fatal consequences; Addis (1994) states that "to design a structure it is necessary to imagine every conceivable type of failure and then ensure that each one is prevented by deft use of materials" (p. 14). However, due to the one-off character of every structure, guaranteeing safety is a complex issue: as structures cannot be tested, sufficient safety of the structures is ensured, for instance, by norms providing standardized procedures or recommendations for material property estimations. Since different materials have to be dealt with differently with respect to calculations, verifications, testing, applicable tools, etc., the choice of material influences the way an engineer can approach the design.

In large-scale construction projects, the influences of materiality are further amplified. Most importantly for structural engineering, due to the size and particular functions of these projects' structures, materials are often at their limits: structures are often particularly high, wide, complex, or all of these simultaneously. While this creates challenges, at the same time opportunities for innovations in construction are often related to materiality. For instance, challenges are met by inventing and employing new materials or new manufacturing techniques.

Dealing with Materiality: A Key Task of the Engineer
Perhaps due to their own speechlessness, "what engineers do" is in the public often

simply perceived as ensuring that an architect's design for a building will stand up (Addis 1994, p. 9). However, the main contribution of structural engineers is the structural design. In essence, a structural design is a concept of how loads are carried by the structure. The concept, design, and arrangement of structural elements and joints as well as the dimensioning (i.e., determining the elements' thickness and height), all influence the appearance and aesthetics of the building or structure. As Rice (1996) puts it, engineers work with the basic and fundamental elements of construction: "They work with the content, not with the image" (p. 76).

In the structural design process, materiality plays an important role, as has been highlighted by many practicing engineers: Addis (1994), for instance, points out that material and structure are necessarily intertwined, stating that "you cannot have engineering structure which is not made of a material, nor a material which is not in the form of a structure" (p. 9). Similarly, Harris claims that "as an engineer, it is impossible to dream up a shape of a structure without having some idea of the material of which it is made" (Harris 1961). Thus, in the design process, engineers draw on knowledge on the behavior of materials and structures, both theoretical and based on experimental findings or their own experience (Addis 1994, p. 9). Harris (1961) identifies the knowledge of material as "the foundation of engineering" and specifies it as "knowledge of what they [materials] are made of, how they are made, how they are shaped, how you fit them together, how they stand up to stress, how they break, how they catch fire, how they react to all the various agencies of ruin which are perpetually nibbling at them, how in due course all fall down." This is still relevant today, as the physical laws to which the materials are subjected remain the same. This knowledge is here called *material knowledge* and can be closely linked to the notions of tacit knowledge (Howells 1996; Nonaka and von Krogh 2009), which is knowledge that is unarticulated and tied to senses, movement skills, physical experiences, intuition.

As the materialized structure is the ultimate aim of the structural design process, the process of materialization is an integral and decisive part of every construction project. This integral materialization, as the design researchers Andreasen and Howard (2011) point out, "is what distinguishes engineering design from any other form of designing," and Petroski (1996) describes engineering as the art of the practical, claiming that "engineers realize that they must at some point begin to manufacture or build." Hereby, as the practicing engineer Rice (1996) puts it, it is the task of the engineer to explore "the nature of the materials and using that knowledge to produce a special quality in the way materials are used" (p. 77). Dealing with materiality and its implications can thus be described as one of the key tasks of engineers.

How Materiality Influences Large-Scale Construction Projects

In this section, we aim to further expand the understanding of materiality in construction by drawing on statements of practicing engineers obtained in the qualitative interviews. We first focus on different dimensions in which materiality comes across and second on different dimensions of feasibility, i.e., which requirements material structures must fulfill to be feasible.

Four Dimensions of Materiality

In the interviews, we identified four different dimensions in which materiality becomes relevant in the course of large-scale construction projects, which are summarized in Table 1, see p. 160. The first dimension is *material*, meaning the physical or other properties of a certain material. The interviews demonstrated that, in large-scale projects, the material's physical properties often play a larger role than in standard construction projects. In large-scale projects, the structures span wide, are often subjected to extreme loads, or need to fulfill expressive architectural designs. As two engineers from the Federal Railway Authority stated, materials are often at their limits, or used in an unusual or new context, or new materials are applied. A very detailed knowledge of a material's physical properties and their fluctuations is thus necessary. Additionally, the material used has a considerable influence on what kind of geometry can be achieved with it. For instance, as glass can only bend in specific ways, "not every shape is feasible" (C1_Supp4). Several engineers working at manufacturing firms emphasized that physical properties of new materials are still hard to model with a sufficient amount of certainty, which makes testing of materials necessary. Apart from the physical properties, the engineers highlighted several other influences of this dimension. For instance, the material influences "how the design of a structure can be approached," as each material requires a certain design and validation procedure (C6_Eng1), but it also influences the "costs of a structure or the building process and time" (C4_Eng4). Hence, it is not only necessary to monitor the physical properties directly connected to the structural behavior, but also to consider properties such as validation techniques, costs, or materialization options related to a specific material.

The second dimension of materiality we identified is *wholeness*, meaning the holistic composition of a materialized entity and its behavior. This refers to the interaction between the distinct material parts of a structure resulting in the integral behavior of the structural entity. Several engineers working as design or verification engineers rated knowledge about this dimension of materiality as extremely important for the design of a structure. They explained that "looking at the structure as an integral entity" (C4_Eng3) is essential to design a structure which fulfills "all structural, architectural, and economic requirements" (C4_Oth1). Furthermore, this integral perspective was referred to as the "concept" and starting point of a structural design (C1_Eng1; C3_Eng2; C4_Oth1). While design usually happens at an abstract and schematic level first, it becomes necessary to "concretize the design quickly with pre-calculations, … and make assumptions for missing parameters to be able to make decisions" (C3_Oth2). Thus, this view is also important to check the "general feasibility" of a design (C1_Eng1) and to ensure that there are "no major difficulties or unsolvable problems at later stages" (C3_Oth2). Additionally, it helps to gain an "overall understanding of the behavior of the structure" (C4_Oth1), which can subsequently be "optimized holistically" (C4_Eng3).

As a third dimension of materiality, we identified *texture*, which refers to the ability of a material to make a design tactile by using materials expressing the design's inner nature (see Rice 1996, p. 77). This dimension thus describes the effects a certain material or material structure can have on human perceptions, feelings or senses. As equally stressed by engineers working in engineering offices as well as in contracting and manufacturing firms, this dimension of materiality is of great importance in architecturally ambitious large-scale projects, mostly due to the texture's influence on appearance. However, in some cases the material's haptic qualities—"how the material feels" (C1_Cont1)—were particularly important, as in the case of the white skin of the Elbphilharmonie. Furthermore, as stressed by both verification and manufacturing engineers, especially when high quantities of certain structural elements are needed, it is important not only to manufacture with constant structurally relevant properties, but also with the same quality in texture. To be able to evaluate the texture of the structures, mock-ups with the proposed material were often built, for instance for the white skin in the case of the Elbphilharmonie or for the façade elements of the European Central Bank (C1_Supp5; C2_Eng3).

The fourth dimension of materiality we identified is *detail*, meaning the properties, behavior, and quality of individual material elements and joints. In the process of structural engineering, it becomes necessary to work on specific critical structural elements to make them feasible. Often, these details are evaluated by pre-materializing them, i.e., by producing them before they are needed at the construction site. The benefits of pre-materialization are equally stressed by engineers working at manufacturing firms and design or verification engineers: these include "learning about the materialization process of these details and the problems arising in the process" (e.g., C1_Eng6) or "identifying the need for new machines" (C5_Supp5). This is essential, as the "parameters important in materialization processes are very different to the ones important in design processes" (C1_Supp2). Consequently, as acknowledged by engineers in all functions, the knowledge gained during the pre-materialization can lead to changes in geometry or in the material, but also in the structural design, as new structural requirements can arise. Lastly, pre-materialization enables testing of complex details, the behaviors of which are difficult to foresee, as emphasized by two engineers working at manufacturing firms (C1_Supp1; C1_Supp6). Particularly in large-scale construction, where customized construction elements or new materials are employed, this can be a "safety measure and inspire confidence," both on the part of the engineers, in their own ability to make the detail feasible, but also on the part of the clients and architects, in the successful implementation of the design (C1_Supp6; C5_Supp5).

Description	Physical or other properties of a material	Holistic composition of a complete structure and its behavior	Effects of a material (structure) on human perception, feelings, senses	Properties, behavior, quality, and materialization of single structural element or joint
Example	Tensile strength of a material	Qualitative flow of forces, dynamics of a structure	Material structure conveying safety, warmth, lightness	Detailed structural and execution design of a joint

Table 1: The Four Dimensions of Materiality

Four Dimensions of Feasibility

With respect to materiality and innovation, whether a designed structure is materially feasible at all is a major consideration. As in structural engineering every structure is a one-off, the feasibility of a structural design cannot be tested. Instead, the responsible engineers are asked for a *judgement of feasibility*, before the design can be realized. The interviews illustrate that feasibility can be understood with respect to different dimensions, which are summarized in Table 2.

First and most importantly, feasibility can be understood with respect to the *structural safety* of a finished structure. This relates to the ultimate limit state as well as the serviceability limit state of a structure, which also accounts for aspects such as maximal deflections.

The second dimension of feasibility deals with the question of *buildability*, which means the building process but also all intermediate states of the structure during that process. Several design engineers as well as engineers working in construction firms stressed that this dimension should on no account be underestimated, as buildability—especially in large-scale construction—can inflict more restrictive boundary conditions on the design than the safety of the finished structure.

A third dimension, which is also particularly important in architecturally ambitious projects, is the feasibility with respect to the desired *appearance*, i.e., whether the design can be realized exactly as planned and imagined by the architects and clients, which in certain constructions is related to the level of accuracy that can be achieved.

The fourth dimension of feasibility deals with *acceptance*, i.e., a certain structural design, even if it is structurally stable, buildable, and meets the architect's and client's design requirements, can still be unfeasible due to an unreasonable amount of costs, time, or construction expenditure needed to realize it. For instance, several design and execution engineers stressed that, for a certain design, it is necessary to find a construction firm willing to build it, a client willing to pay for it, and a verification engineer willing to take responsibility. Billington (2014, p. 14) refers to this as the social dimension of technology. This social dimension can shift in the course of the project: while there was harsh critique by the media and public for the exploding costs of the Elbphilharmonie during the building phase, this seemed to lose its significance after the opening.

In addition to these four dimensions of feasibility, multiple interviewees stressed that especially in large-scale construction, where each project is particularly unique, the structures are technically challenging, and new solutions are developed, the judgement if something is feasible is a critical point in the project and of utmost importance. As the engineering office can also be made liable for the judgement, it often concerns the success of the whole project, as "a design which is not realizable can lead to legal issues, delays and raised costs" (C3_Oth2). To avoid this, both engineers working at engineering and architectural offices stressed that it is important to incorporate the structural engineer or construction firm early on in the project, and that the judgement should be made in collaboration between architect and engineer. Additionally, the judgement of feasibility is of great importance to the engineers making the judgement, as "this is what we live off," as one of them stated (C1_Eng5). However, engineers across all roles emphasized that with this judgement also comes a high degree of responsibility, and one of the structural engineers claimed that a mistaken judgement in a large-scale project leading to legal issues can "in the worst case economically ruin an engineering office" (C2_Eng2).

How Engineers Deal with Materiality in Construction Projects

Building on the different dimensions of materiality and feasibility, in this section we focus on how materiality is dealt with by engineers in large-scale projects. We discuss the ways engineers think,

Table 2: The Four Dimensions of Feasibility

Structural Safety	Buildability	Appearance	Acceptance
Ultimate limit state and serviceability limit state of structures	Building process; structural safety of intermediate states	Desired appearance; realization as planned	Costs, time, and construction expenditures; social acceptance

revealing how they approach designs and deal with materiality, as well as describe material knowledge of engineers, explaining its nature and its generation in large scale-projects.

Engineering Thinking

In the interviews, certain characteristics of engineering thinking with respect to materiality and innovation became apparent. With respect to how different practicing engineers think and approach design tasks, we identified three overlapping aspects.

First, there seems to be a general understanding to approach structural design in a *conceptual way*. Several structural engineers emphasized that structural design means developing concepts, one of them stating that "many aspects need to be considered simultaneously by lateral thinking that tries to combine all sides of a problem" (C2_Eng1). One engineer stressed that an "overall understanding of the structural behavior" should be gained before beginning to evaluate the structure (C1_Eng3). In this context, both an engineer working in an engineering office and one working in a manufacturing firm described how this conceptual approach can lead to a "sudden emergence of an idea or solution" (C1_Eng3; C1_Supp4). This aspect of a design arising as a "complete concept" dovetails with findings from Rice, who identifies working in concepts as a characteristic quite common among engineers (Rice 1996, pp. 79–80).

Second, along with this conceptual approach, there is a certain confidence exerted by the structural engineers that the structural design will be feasible at the end, that solutions will be found. This leads to a *"solution-oriented mind-set"* (C1_Eng4), which becomes explicit for instance in an attitude to "always look and enjoy looking for solutions to problems" (C1_Eng3) and to "really try to make things feasible" (C2_Supp2). As one structural engineer stressed, rejecting challenging designs by stating they won't be feasible is not an option for them: "I can't say— that's not possible, that's not possible, and that's not possible—I have to state how it works" (C5_Eng1). Indeed, this engineering attitude to always give an answer to problems is also described by Koen (2009).

Third, engineering thinking is often characterized by a *clear aim*. This clear aim is for instance to make a certain architectural design or a technical challenge feasible, to find a way to achieve a desired outcome. One structural engineer stated that to find a good solution, he needs "an existing and somehow pressing problem" (C1_Eng3). Hence, questions can be, for instance, about how to realize a given design "with respect to specific materials but also specific materialization possibilities" (C5_Eng1). The interviews revealed that these questions are tackled by a "systematic approach" (C6_Eng1): by picturing the desired outcome in its specific materiality, engineers validate it by asking about the significant points of the structure, for instance the specific risks of this structural design that could become apparent in later stages of evaluation or the problems that could arise in the process of building. This replicates the engineer's approach of imagining every conceivable failure of a certain structure described by Addis (1994, p. 14).

These three aspects of engineering thinking—*conceptual approach, solution-oriented mind-set*, and *clear aim*—are closely related to each other and are driven by the same desire of engineers to *stretch the boundaries of feasibility*. In engineering, doing "something new which hasn't been done before" (C4_Eng3) is usually connected to stretching the boundaries of feasibility, given in the form of norms or built examples. The engineer doing something new is therefore operating outside the normal. In the process of stretching the boundaries of feasibility, both engineers working at engineering offices and manufacturing firms noted that it is very important to know first what is technically feasible at the moment, and then to imagine how this boundary of feasibility can be pushed further and subsequently work on this aim (e.g., C1_Eng5; C5_Eng1). Several interviewees commented that innovations were generated precisely when the engineers were working outside the norms. For instance, one of them stated: "We were at the boundaries of feasibility. And this is when you need to check, which innovations could I implement in order to make it feasible?" (C5_Eng1). Several structural and verification engineers agreed that this is what essentially makes a good engineer. This is underlined by the case of the Kochertal Bridge, where a prize for an engineering service was awarded with the justification that "what the engineers did was far outside of the standardized norm procedure" (C6_Oth1). Another structural engineer stressed that engineering thinking is rather the opposite of looking in the literature or norms but begins when you "have to think about a problem for yourself and generate your own solution" (C4_Eng1). And yet another stated, that engineers in earlier times were more innovative because they were not "shielded" by the numerous amount of norms that exist today (C3_Supp3).

Material Knowledge

In addition to the engineering thinking we identified among the interviewees, multiple engineers expressed the importance of a certain implicit knowledge in their work. They referred to this implicit knowledge with different terms: "a feeling" (C1_Eng3; C2_Eng2), "intuition" (C5_Eng6), "deep and first-hand knowledge or experience" (C1_Eng4), or "past mistakes" (C1_Cont4; C1_Supp4). These interviewees specified that this knowledge concerns structural systems, materials and their properties and behaviors, but also construction and materialization processes or overall feasibility and reasonableness of structural systems. In the opinion of most of the engineers interviewed, this material knowledge is derived naturally from experience. Hence, this material knowledge can be characterized as a kind of tacit knowledge: a non-codified, disembodied knowledge, acquired via informal take-up of learned behavior and procedures, but also in processes of subception, meaning learning without awareness (Howells 1996; Nonaka and von Krogh, 2009). This is illustrated by the following interview statement:

If I say, "I don't believe that," then it's usually true, there is a mistake somewhere [in a calculation]. You develop a gut feeling for statics. ... so, you have to have some kind of physical access to the material as well. ... But there is no point in just saying "Yes, that's wrong," they [young engineers] have to learn for themselves: what is a weld seam? How much space does it consume? Where are the obstacles? And then you will learn to design ... (C1_Eng3).

The interviews show how material knowledge is continuously generated in the process of structural design: the four dimensions of materiality—*material, wholeness, texture, and detail*—and the four dimensions of feasibility—*structural safety, buildability, appearance*, and *acceptance*—alternately become important and are considered by the engineers in the design process, as the engineers move back and forth between these different dimensions of materiality and feasibility. Thus, these dimensions are not independent of each other, but rather represent complementary perspectives on a material structure that are all relevant when designing a structure. In this way, a dialog takes place between the engineer and these different perspectives. Schön (2016) has described this in a similar way: he proposes that engineering design is understandable as a reflective conversation with the materials of a situation (p. 172). By moving from concepts to material tests and experiments to pre-materializations, mock-ups, and material samples and relating the knowledge and experience gained back to the concepts of the structure, scrutinizing their implications in multiple iterations—using Schön's words—"reflection in action" (Schön 2016) takes place, and material knowledge is generated in the process.

Large-scale projects provide the setting for this generation of tacit material knowledge in a special way. They often need special solutions at the boundaries of feasibility and the technical feasibility is often more important than costs. Naturally, large-scale projects often require more detailed material knowledge regarding very specific aspects. Hence, this special knowledge has to be acquired during the projects. For this purpose, often project-bound research is conducted, as the feasibility of new designs has to be proven. Hence, materiality again plays a huge role: according to the engineers across all types of organizations, material tests are often the ultimate proof that something works, and is accepted by clients, building authorities, and contractors. New designs as such often lead to material tests, which then produce material knowledge. Knowledge can also be generated by incorporating experts. For design engineers, these can be more specialized engineers, who have experience in the field in question, for instance façade engineering, but also engineers working in construction firms, with experience in materialization processes:

In this project, with respect to the building process of the struts, we were in very close coordination with the steel constructors. We needed the construction firms, that is crucial, because they have a kind of experience, which we only possess to a very limited extent (C2_Eng2).

The interviews further suggest that simply disposing of material knowledge is not enough to produce value in a project; in addition, it must be communicated. However, communication about material knowledge is hard to accomplish: in line with this, engineers across all roles stress the importance of face-to-face communication or even workshops. Here, visual aids such as presentations, plans, BIM, CAD, or other models are used. As one leading engineer in the Wehrhahn Line project explained, communication about materiality and its effects can also produce trust, both of engineers in themselves and of clients and architects in the engineer's abilities (C5_Eng2). In support of this, an engineer at a construction firm underlines that through communication about materiality, a "certain feeling or understanding for the difficulties of materialization processes can be reached at the side of clients or other project partners" (C2_Supp2). Equally important, engineers can gain an understanding of the specificity of their knowledge and the fact that this knowledge is not apparent to everyone they deal with in the context of a project. It is thus perceived as critical by the interviewees that project partners understand the real problems behind a design or the ideas and thoughts behind it (e.g. C1_Eng3). This is underscored by another structural engineer, who mentioned that in contexts where the different perspectives remained alien to each other, friction among the project partners arose (C2_Eng2).

The Role of Engineering Thinking and Material Knowledge for Innovation in Large-Scale Construction Projects

With respect to the generation of innovation in large-scale projects, we particularly wish to discuss and highlight five aspects which became apparent in the empirical analysis. A very important first aspect many interviewees agreed on is that innovation in engineering is closely related to stretching the boundaries of feasibility. In this way, as also became evident, the boundaries of feasibility are often related to the materiality of structures.

Second, particularly in large-scale construction, there is a continuous tension between the dimensions of materiality and the requirements for material structures that become apparent in the different dimensions of feasibility: as designs are often unique and ambitious, large-scale construction projects force engineers to undertake an intensive engagement with materiality in all its different dimensions: the *material, wholeness, texture,* and *detail* have to be investigated in the course of the project, as knowledge about these often does not exist to a sufficient extent in the very unique large-scale projects. At the same time, dealing with the different dimensions of feasibility of material structures in large-scale projects means taking on huge responsibility: the *structural safety, buildability, appearance,* and *acceptance* of a structure have to be ensured in any case, no matter how little is known about the different dimensions of materiality in a particular case. This is of paramount importance, as failures in structural design can have fatal consequences, in the worst-case scenario the loss of human life. As such, more than the design, its materialization encompasses many legal and liability issues. The responsibilities and constraints that come with materialization can be binding with respect to stretching the boundaries of feasibility. On that basis, it is easy to understand why for many engineers stretching of the boundaries of feasibility is seen as equivalent to innovation.

Third, we also observed that large-scale projects seem to provide particularly good settings for stretching the boundaries of feasibility. Through the intensive engagement with the different dimensions of materiality, while keeping in mind all the different dimensions of feasibility, material knowledge is created through "reflection in action" (Schön 2016). This material knowledge plays a fundamental role for stretching feasibility in construction: first, it provides a base for the judgement of feasibility; and second, this judgement of what is technically feasible at the moment was seen by the interviewees as a prerequisite to stretch boundaries of feasibility and innovate. This dovetails with the findings from Rittel and Webber (1973), who noted that the ability to specify a problem, i.e., to know what the parameters, aim, and boundaries of a task are, is tantamount to the ability to envisage possible solutions.

Fourth, we find that engineering thinking, which manifests itself in an ability to think conceptually, to be confident that there is always a solution, and to approach tasks by focusing on a clear aim, facilitates the stretching of boundaries of feasibility for engineers and hence facilitates innovation. The empirical data indicates that in large-scale construction projects, in order to deal with these tensions between materiality and feasibility, often a conceptual and very solution-oriented thinking is triggered, manifested in the engineering mind-set that there is always a solution.

Lastly, to be able to stretch boundaries of feasibility and innovate, the interviewed engineers agreed that communication about materiality is essential. This communication about materiality is also particularly encouraged in large-scale projects due to the tensions between new materialities and the dimensions of feasibility. Due to the involvement of numerous different building experts and actors as well as the project's relevance to the public discourse, engineers are pushed to communicate about their work and the possibilities and constraints with which they operate. At the same time, it is important that other actors try to understand the material aspects of the project, as these aspects are often decisive for relevant parameters such as realizable design, costs and construction time of a project.

The above described mechanisms, i.e., seeing innovation as stretching the boundaries of feasibility, being subjected to tensions between extreme materiality and strict feasibilities, generating material knowledge, employing engineering thinking, and communicating about materiality, all lead to a particular way of dealing with materiality in large-scale construction, which was identified above as one of the key tasks of the engineer. This is a prerequisite for the generation of innovations: it empowers engineers to deliver structural designs while being faced with the responsibilities and constraints that arise due to the necessity for materialization. Furthermore, the way they deal with these issues empowers engineers to stretch boundaries of feasibility and to innovate: equipped with material knowledge and engineering thinking, innovative structural designs can be generated that stretch the boundaries of feasibility. Hence, the structural engineer Schlaich (2000) states that harsh boundary conditions, for instance posed by an exceptional architecture or new requirements, should be seen as a challenge and an opportunity to design a special solution.

Conclusions

With respect to innovation in construction, we can draw two main conclusions. The first is related to the tension inherent to the structural engineer's task between realizing something new and the huge responsibilities that come with it: on the one hand, new material knowledge generated through intensive engagement with materiality can foster new and innovative solutions; on the other hand, the responsibilities and constraints related to materialization can be restrictive with respect to innovations in construction. To be able to understand and judge innovations and subsequently to be able to use innovation strategically, it is therefore necessary to understand the different dimensions of materiality and feasibility inherent in the work of structural engineers. Thus, in essence, a better understanding of the work of engineers within interdisciplinary project contexts and the constraints to which they are subjected and which they are required to overcome with the knowledge of materials can be gained, an understanding that, subsequently, can lead to better collaboration, something that is ultimately vital for innovation in large-scale projects.

The second conclusion relates to the fact that engineers approach and understand the dimensions of materiality and feasibility using engineering thinking and material, tacit knowledge. As we described in the introduction, engineering thinking and material knowledge are the subject of a certain speechlessness of engineers. Engineers, while being technically competent, rarely reflect on materiality on a meta-level, and instead often hold a certain speechlessness with respect to the general nature of their profession but also to the role of materiality within it. As communication about materiality is central to innovation, this speechlessness can also be identified as one of the factors hampering innovation in construction projects. By describing dimensions of materiality and feasibility as well as engineering thinking and material knowledge, we sought to overcome this speechlessness to some extent. However, to increase the level of innovativeness in construction both engineers and non-engineers need to engage in a continuous dialog about materiality.

References

Addis, B. (1994). *The Art of the Structural Engineer.* London.

Andreasen, M. M. and T. J. Howard. (2011). "Is Engineering Design Disappearing from Design Research?" H. Birkhofer, ed. *The Future of Design Methodology.* London.

Billington, D. P. (2014). *Der Turm und die Brücke—Die neue Kunst des Ingenieurbaus.* Berlin.

Clegg, S. and K. Kreiner. (2014). "Fixing Concrete: Inquiries, Responsibilities, Power and Innovation." *Construction Management and Economics* 32.3: pp. 262–278.

Duddeck, H. and J. Mittelstraß. (1999). *Die Sprachlosigkeit der Ingenieure.* Opladen.

Harris, A. (1961). "Architectural Misconceptions of Engineering." *RIBA Journal* 2: pp. 130–136.

Howells, J. (1996). "Tacit Knowledge, Innovation and Technology Transfer." *Technology Analysis & Strategic Management* 8.2: pp. 91–106.

Koen, B. V. (2009). "The Engineering Method and Its Implications for Scientific, Philosophical and Universal Methods." *The Monist* 92.3: pp. 357–386.

von Krogh, G., K. Ichijo, and I. Nonaka. (2000). *Enabling Knowledge Creation How to Unlock the Mystery of Tacit Knowledge and Release the Power of Innovation.* New York.

Menges, S., A. Müller, and M. Oeser. (2014). "Innovationsmanagement für bauausführende Firmen—Entwicklung eines ganzheitlichen Managementansatzes zur Stärkung von Innovations- und Wettbewerbskraft." *Schriftenreihe der Professur Betriebswirtschaftslehre im Bauwesen.*

Nonaka, I. and G. von Krogh. (2009). "Tacit Knowledge and Knowledge Conversion: Controversy and Advancement in Organizational Knowledge Creation Theory." *Organization Science* 20. 3: pp. 635–652.

Petroski, H. (1996). *Invention by Design—How Engineers get from Thought to Thing.* Cambridge, MA.

Rice, P. (1996). *An Engineer Imagines.* London.

Rittel, H. W. and M. M. Webber. (1973). "Dilemmas in a General Theory of Planning." *Policy Sciences* 4: pp. 155–169.

Schlaich, J. (2000). "Der Bauingenieur und die Baukultur." Stiftung Bauwesen, ed. *Der Bauingenieur und seine kulturelle Verantwortung.* Stuttgart.

Schön, D. A. (2016). *The Reflective Practitioner—How Professionals Think in Action.* New York.

A Synthesis of the Arts: The Materialization of Artistic and Architectural Concepts for the Wehrhahn Line

Heike Klussmann

An outstanding group achievement opened in Düsseldorf in February 2016: the Wehrhahn Line, a new subway connection that runs under downtown Düsseldorf over a length of 3.4 kilometers (see also the case study description on p. 40). For Düsseldorf, it was the largest transportation-related construction project since the completion of the Rhine river tunnel in 1993. It all started in 2001 with a two-stage EU-wide competition for an overall concept, which the Darmstadt office netzwerkarchitekten and Heike Klussmann won in collaboration. The project was completed after fifteen years of planning and construction in close cooperation between architects, artists, engineers, and the municipal administration.

At the opening on February 20, 2016 a large number of Düsseldorf residents came and wandered around the new subway stations and the adjoining spaces, like guests at a private view in a set of galleries, each with a subway connection. The national and international press reported: "Düsseldorf has pulled off a unique spatial experiment: Art and architecture set the tone for urban and suburban mobility," wrote the *Süddeutsche Zeitung*. "What makes the design of the Wehrhahn Line new, daring, and possibly pioneering is the holistic approach. Here art was not retrofitted or applied, but incorporated right from the outset," commented the *Frankfurter Allgemeine Zeitung*. "The new metro represents a rare moment when people who never usually interact—city bureau-crats, engineers, architects, and artists—create something bigger than themselves," stated *The Guardian*. And *The New York Times* headlined: "Art and Magic in a German Subway."

In the chapter "Dealing with Materaility: The Role of Engineering Thinking and Material Knowledge for Innovation in Construction," Ruge and Bögle (in this volume) approach the topic of materiality in construction by abstracting statements from numerous different interviewees on the subject to develop a concept of what material-ization essentially constitutes in construction. In this commentary, I wish to complement this account with insights into the Wehrhahn Line project, thus providing a personal reflection of an integral materialization process. I draw on two examples to explain how abstract concepts and terms used in the design eventually came to be materialized. The first example is the overall architectural and artistic concept of the subway line, the Continuum and the Cut.

The Continuum comprises the entire tunnel construction, including the stations along the line, which are essentially regarded as being a "widening out" of the tunnel section. The uni-form wall cladding used in all the station interiors—precast con-crete panels with joints resulting in a 3D drawing—transposes this concept of a spatial continuum into a recognizable and unifying image. It features a bright, relief-like network structure. The small-est graphic unit is a diamond. It is completed and constantly var-ied by the joints between the structural elements, resulting in a spatial drawing. The structure of the Continuum systematically expands and contracts, creating a sense of dynamic space (see Fig-ure 1). Technical regulations had to be met, which required, for example, fire- and vandal-proof panels. Further thought went into how the individual panels should be joined, and how they might intersect with adjacent areas, as well as the economic feasibility of producing such a raft of different formats. Art was not simply per-ceived as an outside layer, but as an integral part of the building.

Figure 1: Wehrhahn Line Düsseldorf,
Continuum Station Space,
© Heike Klussmann and netzwerk-
architekten, Photo: Jörg Hempel

The artistic concept for the Continuum as well as the later project realization reflect the fundamental concept of the Wehrhahn Line—namely, integrating urban space, engineering work, architecture, and art in dialog with one another. The choice of a precast concrete cladding system for the station walls derives from translating the reinforced concrete prefabricated sectional elements used in tunnel construction into another medium. The cladding's geometric structure—based on a stretched and compressed diamond—echoes the long, winding tunnel. At the same time, the cladding's segmentation, which blends with the respective graphics to form a unity, means that individual elements can be replaced or repaired—a core requirement in subway construction. Gerrit Gohlke (2016) writes: "This facade is no minor matter. It is a mysterious masterpiece of materials engineering which, contrary to all the dogmas of Modernism, creates convincing illusions in space. The more acute the view of the wall, and the further your perspective diverges from the normal viewpoint of a passenger facing the track bed while waiting at the platform's edge, the more the spaces appear to warp."

As Ruge and Bögle describe, it is essential to deal with the interdependence of innovation and materiality. In the Wehrhahn Line project, the production of the concrete diamonds rhombi for the Continuum would not have been possible without research into material development and production processes, making it possible to produce panels with extreme geometries that do not require additional structural bracing while achieving a high degree of precision and surface quality. The emphasis was above all especially on smooth surfaces, acute angles, and precise edges. Precast fair-faced concrete sections are generally produced using formwork. This means concrete is poured into prefabricated casings as a hollow form where the casing side is visible and the filled side is to the back of the finished piece. Because this method only makes sense when it is used for a large quantity of identical elements, a different approach was used for the realization of the Continuum.

All of the 6700 individual diamonds of the Continuum were cut from blank slabs and produced with a vacuum filter molding method. The mixture consisted of high-performance concrete, aggregates of nordic white and quartz sand and, for the pigment, 130 grams of black iron oxide per 100 kilograms of raw mixture. It was only possible to produce the light color with complete consistency using a specially developed mixture: cement and aggregates with a precise amount of added pigment. Then, the basic mold (244 x 123 centimeters) was filled with the raw mixture, leveled and homogenized, so that the material was evenly spread throughout.

The homogenized raw slab then went to the concrete slab press (a sixty-five-ton press, the largest in the world) and was pressed—or rather compressed—with a force of 3,000 tons per minute; in the process, up to fifty percent of the water was removed. This was followed by a hydraulic hardening process in optimum climatic conditions over two days. The backs of the highly compacted base slabs were then calibrated and milled on the surface so that flatness tolerances in accordance with DIN V 18500 were achieved. After another storage period to achieve the final hardness, the slabs were cut and reworked. At this point, the diamonds for the Continuum were positioned using a photo-supported detection system to utilize as much of the plates as possible and then a five-axis CNC saw cut the slabs into the individual diamonds. Finally, the edges were profiled and four anchor holes were drilled into the back of each diamond panel. In order to form the edges a special scheme was designed to guarantee that inspection requirements would be met. Classification as "bottom" or "top" fold panels meant that the entire area of the building shell remained accessible and each individual diamond panel could be removed. At the same time, joints required no sealants and the mounting remained invisible. The minimal waste created was 100 percent recycled and reused as aggregate.

The extremely high standards applied not only to the precast concrete sections, but also to the substructure and its installation. One exceptional challenge was the installation of the concrete diamond panels in the areas where the walls curved. Here, the wall panels take the shape of a small-sectioned polygonal line following the ideal line of a circle segment along the station walls. Because the diamond pattern has no vertical joints, support posts were placed on the nodes of the regular polygonal line frame to avoid the diamond tips getting out of alignment. Thus, a high level of precision in the overall construction was achieved through the dimensional accuracy of the panels and joints combined with a minutely adjustable frame.

The second example is the materialization of the artistic concept behind the Pempelforter Straße station located at the northern end of the Wehrhahn Line. The station has two access points, one on the east, the other on the west side. The distribution levels, which lie opposite each other, are connected by a central cut that bites into the Continuum like a seesaw shape. The angles of the ceilings are designed such that both platform and concourse levels enjoy clear sightlines and there is good visibility, thereby optimizing pathways. In the center of the station, beyond the angled cuts into the incised ceilings, there is a rail substation, connected by enclosed bridges to the concourse level.

The artistic concept "Surround" for Pempelforter Straße works with the space's specific geometry and defines the entire area by propelling an imaginary body through the station's architecture as if it were a pinball (see Figure 2). Rebounding off the walls, it shuttles across the room, etching white lines of its path into the walls' virtual black. The movements start from each of the five entrances and are extended into the station until they leave it again. The band structure has a life of its own after breaking with the geometry of the space and as an inverted sculpture cuts across the perimeters of the station's spaces. Anja Schürmann (2016) writes: "When we are confronted with new experiences, we try to relate them to received and accepted knowledge. At Pempelforter Straße, this is

Figure 2: Wehrhahn Line Düsseldorf, Pempelforter Straße, view of the concourse level, © Heike Klussmann, Photo: Jörg Hempel

anything but simple: the bands cannot be divided into centrifugal and centripetal ones, because there is no center, nothing for us to move toward or away from. We cannot even tell here from there; it is virtually impossible to split our field of vision inside the station. There is no perspective foreshortening of near and far, rendering them nearly indistinguishable. This rupture in making movement subterranean is constitutive for 'Surround': working with the geometries of the interstices, the caesuras in the earth, Heike Klussmann has chosen a design that works with the existing architecture, not on or against it."

Guaranteeing the precise continuity of the band structure represented a particular challenge when coordinating the different trades engaged in the project and required close planning coordination cutting across the various trades. The directions of the stripes run against the grid of the surfaces of the wall, ceiling and floor, and therefore give rise to two-color expansion elements on all surfaces. Each of the two-color elements is unique and provides an individual section of the artwork's theme that is not repeated at any other point. The graphic bands were enameled, i.e., first covered with a wet electrostatic coating method and then seared into the enameled wall panels using a two-layer/single-firing technique at a temperature of 840 degrees Celsius. The continuation of the bands across the ceiling was achieved by screen printing on powder-coated ceiling panels. For the floor, water jet technology was used to cut the bands into the concrete stones. The individual pieces were set in precut recesses. The resulting impression is that the material runs seamlessly across the floors, walls, and ceiling.

On the one hand the bare facts of the infrastructure project are 843.6 million euros in construction costs, 3.4 kilometers double-track tunnels with an inner diameter of 8.3 meters, constructed by means of shield tunneling, 22,000 tons of steel, 240,000 cubic meters concrete, 6,700 individually formed panels for the Continuum, ninety-meter-long platforms, thirteen elevators, fifty-nine escalators, all in all six unique underground stations, which are visited by more than 50,000 people a day. On the other hand, the project has taken the limelight for its experimental character, and for being visionary.

In the Wehrhahn Line project design is understood as a multi-perspective process, an artistic process, a design process, a technical process, an engineering process, a scientific process, an experimental process, an invention process, a planning process, an economic process, a political process, a social process, a communication process. Successful materialization is always about interdisciplinary collaboration and interdisciplinary collaboration is always about advancing your own field and your own work by placing it in another context. You need to be prepared to commit to leaving your own comfort zone. The people who were on board the Wehrhahn Line project all showed a willingness to walk that path. It is remarkable that the quality in all the different fields got better and better during the process. The art gained a quite unique presence through or within the strict framework of a transportation building. At the same time, the interdisciplinary cooperation enabled the strict conditions the engineering set to be taken to the very limits of feasibility in terms of space and the materials and technologies used.

References

Gohlke, G. (2016). "Bounce Pass to the Imagination." Landeshauptstadt Düsseldorf, Kulturamt, ed. *Wehrhahn-Linie*. Bielefeld.
Schürmann, A. (2016). "Where Density Begins." Landeshauptstadt Düsseldorf, Kulturamt, ed. *Wehrhahn-Linie*. Bielefeld.

Large-Scale Projects as Arenas for Interaction: Negotiating Professional Cultures of Architects and Engineers

Venetsiya Dimitrova/Monika Grubbauer/
Johanna Ruge/Annette Bögle

Introduction

Design and construction work are ambitious endeavors and the working practices of architects and engineers have received particular attention in academic scholarship. Scholars from the fields of sociology, ethnology, and history, among others, have testified to the profoundly different forms of educational socialization and distinct professional value systems of architects and engineers (e.g., Bucciarelli 2002; Cuff 1991; Henderson 1999; Hossdorf 2003; Stevens 1998). Yet, the production of the built environment is organized in the form of projects in which architects and engineers work together closely on a daily basis. The collaborative and inter-organizational nature of the building industry requires interaction between professionals from different disciplines and is shaped by their collective actions, negotiations, and compromises (Addis 1994; Harty 2005; Yaneva 2005). The starting point of this chapter is this deep-rooted discrepancy between the mono-disciplinary context of socialization in which the respective professional cultures are developed and internalized, and the collaborative context of practice in which these professional cultures are evolving and being enacted.

University education and the activities of professional associations have contributed significantly to the generation of contrasting archetypes, namely of the architect-artist as a lone genius and of the engineer as their rather conservative, cautious, and rational antipode (Cohen et al. 2005; Cuff 1991; Petroski 2011). This crude differentiation has not only informed academic scholarship to a certain extent, but has also greatly shaped the public perception of the two professions and of their working practices. In the eyes of the public, tensions and struggles between architects and engineers are considered an inevitable part of design and construction work, with the consequence that budget and schedule overruns are often associated with the rivalries of architects and engineers (e.g., Sage 2013). At the same time, innovative design solutions of landmark buildings are mostly attributed to celebrity architects alone, whereas their engineering partners often receive less public recognition (McNeill 2005). Both aspects are particularly relevant in the context of costly and prestigious large-scale construction projects.

What has been less discussed in the literature, however, is how distinct professional cultures are negotiated in practice and how this can serve as a source of innovation and the generation of novelty. Large-scale construction projects provide a particularly fruitful research ground for exploring these negotiations. Considering their extreme complexity and the aspiration for atypical and innovative solutions, large-scale building projects potentially intensify the interaction and interdependency between professionals. Professionals are expected to provide economic, risk-free, and well-established solutions while still delivering unique and innovative designs that push the boundaries of what is technologically possible (e.g., Faulconbridge 2010). In this chapter, we are interested in understanding whether and how the embodied and internalized professional cultures and the challenges and demands posed by the project "reality" clash or interfere with one another, and at what point this is productive for generating innovation.

The empirical analysis of this chapter is based on the in-depth analysis of thirty-three interviews with professionals from both the design and execution phase. For our analysis we selected the

four projects that provide a platform for the simultaneous interactions between architects and engineers, namely the two high-
rise structures (the Elbphilharmonie and the new premises of the
European Central Bank, ECB) and the two hybrid infrastructure
projects (Berlin Central Station and the Wehrhahn Subway Line).
Out of the original set of seventy-four codes, we chose seven[1] in
order to grasp how professionals interact and work together, and
retrieved 650 interview fragments as basic material for our analysis. We analyzed the data through an iterative process, with multiple rounds of interpretation informed by concepts garnered from
the literature review as well as multiple steps of re-coding based
on the empirical analysis. Codes that were generated included, for
instance, "shared values," "overlapping," "dream teams," "innovation drivers," "negotiations," "uncompromising," and "co-opera-
tive." By successively narrowing down the categories, we were
able to conceptualize the negotiation processes in the context of
large-scale projects in terms of practices of *maintaining* and *dissolving* professional cultures; these two categories inform the
analytical structure of the empirical section.

The chapter proceeds as follows. In the following second section we discuss the processes of education and socialization that
shape professional cultures in the building industry. By intersect-
ing the seminal scholarship on architectural and engineering professional practices with pertinent literature on the organization
of projects, we propose that large-scale projects can be conceptualized as *arenas* for the interaction of professionals with distinct
disciplinary backgrounds. This provides for valuable insights into
the negotiation of professional cultures in the working practice of
the architects and engineers involved in the four case studies.
These insights are presented in the third section drawing on our
empirical data. In the final section, we summarize our findings
and highlight the relevance of the work for further research on
built environment professionals and the ongoing transformation
of this field of action.

Distinct Professional Cultures in the Construction Industry and Their Negotiation in the Projects' Arenas

The Role of Education and Socialization

A large body of seminal sociological scholarship on professionalism (e.g., Abbott 1988; Evetts 2003; Grey 1994; Larson 1979) has
studied what it is precisely that makes a "professional." The key
aspects commonly referred to include clear jurisdictional bound-

1 "artistic/technical distinctiveness,"
"assertion," "collaboration,"
"comprehension," "reception,"
"self-image," and "working approach"

aries, possession of specialized forms of knowledge, controlled access to professional associations, and autonomous systems of justification and valuation. Furthermore, scholars have emphasized that to become a member of a certain professional field, one needs to internalize the respective shared values, beliefs, motives, and meanings (Cuff 1991; Grubbauer and Steets 2014). The making of professional cultures is, thus, enabled largely through the processes of educational socialization (Evetts 2003, p. 401; Slay and Smith 2010). Numerous sociological, ethnological and historical studies on the practice of built environment professionals have pointed to the fundamentally different education of architects and engineers in terms of aims, values, and epistemologies (e.g., Blau 1984; Bucciarelli 2002; Cuff 1991; Gutman 1988; Henderson 1999; Hossdorf 2003; Stevens 1998). Despite the collaborative nature of the construction industry (see Harty 2005; Schön 1983), the curriculum for the two professional groups is still clearly characterized by a strong mono-disciplinary culture.

Architectural education is centered on the "design studio" that takes place in a narrow disciplinary context (Cuff 1991; Schön 1983). Students internalize and embody the "habitual, customary, or routine" practices specific to the world of architecture by learning how to advance project work in the setting of the "design studio" and to present and defend their design against peers and educators (Cuff 1991, p. 5). Although technical expertise is crucial as it distinguishes architects from mere artists, it nevertheless plays a subordinate role in design processes (Cohen et al. 2005). Rather, designing is associated with the "prime value of creativity" (Blau 1984, p. 58). Claims for the creative design process as the core of the profession have secured architects their professional status in the eyes of the public. Universities have played a central role in this process by "raising the status of creativity and design expertise within society at large, and positioning architects as the construction professionals best placed to deliver such expertise and to thus fulfil their diverse clients' requirements" (Cohen et al. 2005, p. 3).

In engineering schools students develop a strong solution-orientated working approach and are socialized with the desire to make decisions and to give answers (Koen 2009). Students are confronted with the role-model of the engineer as a sharp thinker and inventor able to find a technical solution to any challenge (Langer and Böhrnsen 2014). To equip future professionals with the necessary skills and knowledge, the curriculum in structural engineering focuses mainly on developing expertise in mathematics and the natural sciences, more specifically in mechanics and the material sciences (Billington 2013; Krafczyk 2014). For their designs, engineers have to take into account numerous aspects—besides criteria such as functionality, aesthetics, and economy, they concentrate mainly on structural safety, as failure can have fatal consequences (Coenders 2007; Schlaich et al. 2008). In order to negotiate between multiple criteria, engineers learn to think in models—they consider different scenarios from which they derive their actions (Duddeck 2001; Schulz 2010).

Public Perception versus Working Practice

The different forms of education and socialization have historically contributed to the emergence of distinct and contrasting professional cultures for architects and engineers. Indeed, in the eyes of the public, these professions are viewed very differently. In the public perception of the architectural profession, the myth of the lone genius is surprisingly persistent and has been further reinforced in the figure of the global architect (Grubbauer and Steets 2014)—with celebrity status and strong relations to wealthy and powerful clients, the so-called "global architects" have secured their access to the restricted "natural market" for "great seminal, monumental buildings" (Gutman 1992, p. 40). Their focus is thus mainly on the creative components of their work (Jones 2011; Stevens 1998). In contrast, engineering is often seen as a profession designed to serve (see Alder 1999, cited in Downey and Lucena 2005; Flury 2011), and the engineer perceived as "narrowly focused on technical issues" (Petroski 2012, p. 252). This understanding, however, often leaves the engineers' design contributions, creative methods, and practices invisible to the public (Addis 1994; Koen 2009; Petroski 2012; Rice 1996).

Public perception is thus largely shaped by prevailing archetypes of the two professions, based on the idea that professionals are a group of equivalent individuals with "no variation by skill, by speciality, by training" (Abbott 1988, p. 61). However, there are profound discrepancies between how professionals are perceived by the public and how they work together on a daily basis. First, the two professions of architecture and engineering are not homogeneous and have significant internal variation in terms of tasks, roles, and expertise (Gutman 1988; Pinnington and Morris 2002). Second, the dichotomous view of the image of the architect being responsible for the creative processes and the engineer for the technical matters, is misleading and therefore often criticized by leading practitioners in the field (e.g., Schlaich cited in Flury 2011). And, third, unlike their simulation in the academic context, design and construction processes are in practice collaborative, communication-based, and inter-organizational, presupposing collective actions, negotiations, and compromises (Cuff 1991; Harty 2005; Yaneva 2005).

It becomes clear that the context of socialization in which the respective professional cultures are developed and internalized differs significantly from the context of practice in which these are evolving and being enacted. In the context of the latter, built environment professionals rarely have sole control over the respective tasks and processes. The reality of construction projects is largely shaped by the inevitable and necessary interaction between architects and engineers. Although these belong to two distinct professional cultures that inform their everyday work, architects and engineers still act as individuals, in messy, contingent, and implicit ways. This raises the crucial question of how practitioners balance the demands and expectations placed on them by their inherent professional culture and those set by the context of the project and the need to interact with other professionals. This requires an understanding of how projects are organized and what kinds of interaction they generate.

Projects as Arenas for Negotiating Professional Cultures

The practice and the everyday interactions of architects and engineers have long since been organized in the form of projects, mainly due to the one-off character of the products they create (Lundin and Söderholm 1995). Beyond the building industry, for numerous sectors (cultural, knowledge-based, professional services, high tech among others) "projects" represent the paradigmatic form of organizing work. The temporal, (relatively) short-lived and non-recurring nature of projects (Lundin and Söderholm 1995) is often seen by organizations and firms across sectors as an efficient way of organizing (Sydow et al. 2004). Scholars have emphasized the productive role of projects in the mobilization and coordination of diverse expertise and intellectual capacities, and thus for the integration of specialized and manifold knowledge (Defillippi and Arthur 1998; Gann and Salter 2000; Lindkvist 2004). Although the one-off character of projects is also considered a threat to the dissemination of experiences due to "broken learning and feedback loops" specific to temporal organizations (Gann and Salter 2000, p. 961; Swan et al. 2010), projects are nevertheless believed to facilitate knowledge exchange and generate innovation (Nooteboom 2000; Sydow et al. 2004).

Academics have also addressed questions of organizing work between various professionals, disciplines, and sectors. Considering that different project partners embody different professional profiles, distinct professional cultures and a specific work ethos, a negotiation between the inherent cognitive distance and certain cognitive convergence is required for their everyday interaction (Grabher 2004). Studies have testified to the fact that although cognitive distance can be reduced through a specific organizational repertoire in order to create, accumulate, and sediment knowledge, under certain conditions cognitive distance can be highly productive (Grabher 2004; Nooteboom 2000). Projects have also been conceptualized as "trading zones"[2] (most recently by Lenfle and Söderlund 2018). The term describes the process of coordination of often profoundly diverse cultures, suggesting that overcoming these differences is central to accomplish innovation (Lenfle and Söderlund 2018).

The above insights are pivotal for enhancing our understanding of how members of distinct professional cultures interact, work, and operate in practice. Large-scale construction projects provide a specific working and organizational context for the inevitable everyday interactions between architects and engineers.

2 The term was coined by the historian of science Galison (1997) in his study focusing on scientists and engineers in physics.

Thus, we suggest thinking of large-scale projects as *arenas* for the interaction between professionals and the negotiation of professional cultures. We ask how in these arenas architects and engineers are prompted to question professional boundaries and knowledge, to revise internalized working dynamics and to shift the pre-set division of roles, tasks, and responsibilities. Our focus in the discussion of the empirical insights is on the related negotiation processes and how they are manifested in the enacted practices. Our main argument is that architects and engineers oscillate between the desire to *maintain* and the need to *dissolve* their distinct professional cultures, simultaneously *preserving* and *reducing* their inherent cognitive distance, a process that is highly productive for the making of innovation.

Negotiating Professional Cultures: Practices of Maintaining and Dissolving Professional Cultures

In the following discussion of empirical findings, we inquire into the interaction between architects and engineers by examining the different practices they enact in the project "reality." We suggest that relevant practices of either maintaining or dissolving distinct professional cultures can be found simultaneously. Thus, architects and engineers oscillate between cognitive distance and cognitive convergence, shifting between distinct perceptions of innovation and a shared understanding of value and worth. For the first category of maintaining professional cultures, we show that practitioners mobilize their embodied professional cultures either by acting out archetypes or by productively asserting their professional values against their counterpart. In both cases, this pushes the generation of ambitious and unique solutions. For the second category of dissolving professional cultures, we show how either practices of distancing from conventional archetypes or of mutual invasion of the terrain of the other discipline allow transgression of clearly defined professional boundaries. In both cases, this contributes to the emergence of a mutual understanding of what constitutes innovative solutions and to a joint effort in executing them.

Maintaining Professional Cultures through Practices of Acting Out Archetypes

Considering the high expectations in terms of symbolic and aesthetic value placed on the large-scale projects examined in this book, enacting archetypical practices internalized during traditional architectural education proved highly productive. As described by the interviewed architects working both on infrastructure and iconic projects, creativity and thinking "outside-the-box" were guiding principles in their everyday practice. This approach facilitated their work and aided their desire to generate novel concepts and solutions, and to distinguish themselves from other architectural firms, as the architects of the Wehrhahn Line emphasized. Furthermore, the architects working on the design of the Elbphilharmonie described the need to scrutinize their experiences and re-evaluate their approach, to diverge purposefully from pre-set guidelines and established routines, and to continuously re-think and refine their ideas:

... and I also think that it's important to approach supposedly established rules and knowledge with openness but also with a certain naivety and impartiality, and to question those ... While experiences are important ... at some point they are also a limitation. And then it is good, to somehow leave that aside and take a fresh look at things (C1_Arch1).

Equipped with values and meanings specific to their professional culture, architects act out their embodied archetypes. Not surprisingly, novel ideas and concepts are thus framed in aesthetic and symbolic terms, and innovation is understood with reference to the master value of creativity (Blau 1984). Hence, design quality is not "an inherent quality of the object or building" (Cuff 1991, p. 196), rather it is ascribed by the "taste makers" in the professional community, namely academics, critics, and elite designers (Jones 2011; Kreiner 2020).

In line with the rich scholarship on engineers' professional practice, the majority of the engineers interviewed across phases and across the four case studies testified to the multiple external factors that impact significantly both the outcomes and the work process. Engineers working on the design of infrastructures as well as of iconic edifices emphasized delivering safe structures as their main responsibility, an imperative of their profession. Furthermore, they continuously needed to consider numerous norms, standards, and regulatory frameworks, and to negotiate between diverse and contradictory criteria (e.g., cost, risks). To do so and yet fulfill the high artistic demands imposed by architects, these professionals perceived the need to mobilize a systematic approach, including numerous experiments, simulations, and intensive work with models that had been internalized in the course of their training. Furthermore, being inculcated with a clear understanding of the division of project tasks and responsibilities, engineers working on complex and design-ambitious structures proved eager to assume responsibility for their solutions:

We want to build ... if we have the opportunity to take this forward then we do it. So our goal is to build the whole thing. So we like to take responsibility. That is what such projects require, that one is ready to take responsibility (C1_Eng3).

As a result, structural engineers often took pride in their work, identifying with their designs and solutions, regarding them as "intellectual property" (C5_Eng3). Yet, across the case studies, engineers working on the structural design acknowledged that there are different ways of developing solutions, and that there is more than one right way to solve a problem. Guided by an internalized solution oriented approach that presupposes the making and evaluating of different options, engineers defined innovative solutions as those that "work" and yet potentially challenge existing regulatory frameworks.

Maintaining Professional Cultures through Practices of Asserting

Considering that professionals with distinct cultures are guided by different values and meanings, as well as by different understandings of innovation, their expectations, priorities, and demands in the context of the projects can diverge significantly. Whereas architects set their focus on the making of non-standard and custom design solutions, engineers were required to come up with feasible solutions that need to be "somewhat optimized in terms of cost, construction technique and time schedule" (C3_Supp1). As a result, architects and engineers often needed to negotiate between contradicting priorities and demands, to reconcile on the ground between aesthetic and technical aspects, between symbolic value and the necessary pragmatism to deliver secure structures and ensure economic gain. Considering their distinct professional cultures and the clear differentiation of roles and tasks, architects and engineers remained persistent and stubborn, convinced of their ideas and concepts, especially during the design phase. The interactions between the project partners were often characterized by an ongoing struggle due to the need to continuously convince each other:

> So we tried for at least a year and a half to teach the architect that it is impossible to build a round station with the cut-and-cover method. And if you can make one, no one can pay for it and it would take far too long. I would say that was the first very grave process (C5_Eng2).

The assertion of values and meanings specific to their professional culture was especially evident in the actions and working approach of internationally renowned architects,[3] for whom the high-quality execution of their ambitious and spectacular designs usually plays a central role in obtaining peer recognition and professional legitimation. Thus, project architects, guided by their desire to generate buildings with high symbolic value, often refused to re-think and compromise with their ideas and aesthetic demands, despite technical challenges, potential financial risks, or the lack of understanding of their project partners:

> Well, it really does require our absolute conviction that it can be done. You have a vision, you have an idea and you believe that it can be implemented. And you perhaps need to take a small extra-step in order to prove to the industry that what you have designed is possible. (C1_Arch4).

3 More specifically those commissioned for the Elbphilharmonie, the ECB, and the Berlin Central Station.

The architects' actions of uncompromisingly asserting their position in their inter-action with engineers potentially generated tensions and frictions between the two distinct professional fields that were, however, highly productive for the mak-ing of innovative solutions and products in the context of the projects:

> As an architect, he was the driving force behind this. He always said to us: "You can do it, you have to do it that way," and of course he also pushed us a little fur-ther on and on, as otherwise we would have probably said …: "No, that is actually way too effortful for us" (C1_Supp3).

By securing clear professional boundaries and thus affirming the inherent cogni-tive diversity, the architects, most prominently in the context of the Elbphilharmo-nie, continuously challenged, urged on and motivated their partners to go one step further, to distance themselves from standardized working approaches, to exceed their own scope of capabilities and thus generate innovation.

Dissolving Professional Cultures through Practices of Distancing from Archetypes

By maintaining clear boundaries between their distinct professional cultures, architects and engineers preserved the inherent cognitive distance, which is often revealed through different perceptions of innovation and of how to generate nov-elty in the context of large-scale projects. At the same time, as we found out in the course of our research, professionals often willingly distanced themselves from their established roles and tasks, which suggests certain overlaps between the two professional cultures, namely between a creative and a more technical orien-tation.

Thus, for instance, some architects sought to distance themselves from being simply "artists," focusing exclusively on aesthetics. The architects working on "iconic" as well as on infrastructure projects considered the high-quality execution of their ideas just as important as the design:

> [X] is an office that has a great interest in the execution quality, also in the details. It is not like a grand gesture that is somehow sketched and then it doesn't matter how it is executed … it is also a core interest of the office that they deal a lot and intensively with how elements are joined together, which material is used (C1_Arch1).

Once the design phase had been completed, the responsible architects proved eager to shorten the distance between design office and construction site, to be physically present and thus actively involved in the decision-making concerning the project's materialization. Especially during the execution phase of the two infrastructure projects, the responsible architects considered the more technical aspects, tasks, and responsibilities as an inevitable and even thrilling part of their

4 This could also be attributed to the fact that before the introduction of the Bachelor/Master system in Germany, architects graduated from (technical) universities with the title "Diplom-Ingenieur," comparable to Master of Engineering.

professional domain.[4] The architects in charge of the Wehrhahn Line revealed, in fact, that they perceive themselves not merely as architects but also as engineers:

> *We are not just architects, we are also graduate engineers and we want to invent something and that is actually something that interests and drives us somehow in every project, what is actually the special feature of a project (C5_Arch1).*

Similarly, structural engineers, commissioned for the design phase, testified to the fact that archetypical perceptions of the engineering profession often overshadow the creative and conceptual part of their work. These practitioners revealed their interest in embracing more creative practices—they are open to new ideas and unorthodox concepts, willing to invest resources and effort, and ready to adopt less linear working approaches. Although their work is shaped by regulatory frameworks, they are eager to push these pre-set boundaries. For structural engineers working in the initial design phase, challenging the constraints of established routines and existing norms is not only a prerequisite for the generation of innovation but also a thrilling incentive. Thus, across the case studies in the setting of ambitious and large-scale construction endeavors, these professionals willingly left the comfort zone of standardized procedures, digital programs, and parametric tools, to create new concepts instead of just calculating structures predefined by architects:

> *On the other hand, of course, you also need an engineer who is able and willing to get involved in something like this and to think a bit outside of the box and not [someone who has never] learnt something other than: "How do I calculate a predefined load-bearing element?" … Namely someone who has never actually learnt to get involved in such things and to develop such concepts, structural concepts (C3_Eng2).*

By intentionally distancing themselves from archetypal roles and practices, the architects and engineers working on the large-scale projects showcased here facilitated a process of rapprochement between distinct professional cultures. In the process, professionals from different fields generated together a common perception of buildings as unique items, the making of which cannot be reduced to standardized products, approaches, and procedures, but rather requires high-quality customized design and execution.

Dissolving Professional Cultures through Practices of Mutual Invasion of the Terrain of Others

Besides exceeding their distinct professional culture, architects and engineers commissioned for ambitious, large-scale construction ventures also actively crossed established disciplinary boundaries and entered the domain of tasks and responsibilities of other professionals. This was mainly achieved by acquiring and developing new skills, gaining specialized knowledge and a profound grasp of fields beyond their respective disciplines. As stated by the chief executive of a glass firm commissioned for the Elbphilharmonie, the architect overseeing the execution of the façade "knows by now as much as we do about glass" (C1_Supp3). Not only did professionals expand the scope of their knowledge and skills, but they were also able and willing to assume the tasks and responsibilities of partners across disciplines. Thus, for instance, the architects of the Wehrhahn Line together with one of the artists developed a customized substructure, a task initially within the domain of the appointed subcontractor. In the process, they shifted the pre-defined interfaces between creative and technical tasks, complementing the work of executive engineers throughout the ambitious project.

By consciously and actively "invading" the field of other disciplines, professionals could gain an in-depth grasp of the working approaches of their project partners and thus of the challenges and problems other professionals face on a daily basis; an understanding that was crucial for reducing the inherent cognitive distance:

And as an engineer you need to learn a little bit how architects think and to understand their situation … . That is also what you expect later on from the architect, that he responds to our ideas, that he understands that … (C3_Eng1).

It is simply important to understand the processes and … the physical boundaries of the way in which production currently takes place. Especially when it concerns the interface or when you go to the boundaries of feasibility, it is very important that you understand that. Otherwise you are talking at cross purposes (C1_Arch1).

This shared understanding of the challenges and the respective tasks facilitated architects and engineers in embracing their inherent interdependency, transforming it into an intensive interplay between different professionals that enables the making of innovation. Across case studies and construction phases, architects and engineers perceived design and structure as a unity, and planning and execution as a joint process. As a result, over the entire course of the projects they could work on equal terms, participate actively in a dialog, and complement one another:

The idea didn't come solely from the architects and also not from us. It is really a collaboration and this is how it works: you sit down together, discuss a problem and make suggestions. It is best when everybody prepares at home, brings a couple of suggestions and then it becomes clear in the discussion, when everyone says: "Ah yes, this is the direction you're going" (C3_Eng1).

In this process, project partners opened their field of tasks and responsibilities to the influences of other disciplines and contrasting professional cultures. Subsequently, requirements and parameters imposed by engineers on architects and vice versa were not perceived as restrictions and obstacles, "as something disturbing, but as a possibility" (C1_Eng7), as an opportunity to advance one's own work and go one step further, to "shift the boundaries of feasibility" (C1_Arch1). As stated by the majority of interview partners, irrespective of which projects they were commissioned to work on, innovative ideas and solutions can only be created and actually executed jointly, through intensive and iterative interactions.

Conclusions: Projects as Arenas for Negotiating Professional Cultures

Through their high levels of complexity and the ambitious demands and expectations, large-scale ventures provide a unique context for the inevitable interactions between the two distinct professional groups of architects and engineers. Over the projects' course, practitioners continuously negotiate their professional cultures—negotiation that oscillates between keeping the inherent cognitive distance, product of diverging practices of socialization and of obtaining peer-recognition, and the need to establish cognitive proximity in practice, in order to tackle pertinent challenges. Professionals actively and consciously expand the scope of their skills and knowledge, challenge embodied approaches, professional roles, and practices, to enter the field of their project partners. However, this dissolving of professional boundaries and cultures is merely contingent and short-term within the project—while cognitive distance can be reduced, professional cultures cannot be entirely blurred; their inherent core remains intact (e.g., Nooteboom 2000). By conceptualizing *projects as arenas* for the interactions between built environment professionals, we have explored these strategies of *maintaining* and of *dissolving* professional cultures, as well as how the continuous and coincidental interplay between cognitive dissonance and cognitive convergence shapes and defines the collaborations between architects and engineers. This conceptualization has proven productive for a number of reasons.

First, the conceptualization of projects as arenas allows systematizing how professionals negotiate their roles and strategies and the practices being enacted (see Table 1). We contribute to a differentiated understanding of project-based collaborations between architect and engineers, providing in-depth insights into how construction projects unfold and how different professionals navigate on a daily basis in an inter-organizational and communication-based context (see Harty 2005; Yaneva 2005). By exploring how the cognitive distance between architects and engineers is simultaneously preserved and reduced throughout the project, the chapter moves beyond the usual focus on a singular "community of practice"

Preserving Cognitive Distance	Maintaining distinct professional cultures	"Acting out" Archetypes
		– mobilizing internalized professional practices, values, and meanings
		– connection to innovation: developing and implementing a different understanding of innovation
		Asserting Professional Cultures
		– (especially architects) challenging, urging on and motivating partners to go one step further
		– connection to innovation: generating productive tensions between professional cultures
Reducing Cognitive Distance	Dissolving distinct professional cultures	**Distancing from Archetypes**
		– challenging the constraints of established routines and existing norms
		– connection to innovation: potentially developing a common perception of buildings (and structures) as unique items
		Mutual Invasion of the Terrain of Others
		– undertaking the tasks and responsibilities of other professionals
		– connection to innovation: transforming interdependence in a productive capacity

Table 1: Overview of Architects' and Engineers' Strategies of Negotiation and the Enacted Practices

(Wenger 1999), and on a single profession and its specific firm-based activities (Faulconbridge 2010). Such a cross-sectorial perspective is highly relevant when exploring the production of the built environment (Sage 2013). In the contemporary context, this production is largely arranged in the form of projects that "invite" an ever greater range of professionals (from architecture, planning, engineering but also from academia and public administration), who need to negotiate between different cultures.

Second, by conceptualizing projects as arenas we contribute to a more differentiated understanding of the capacity of project-based collaborations for the making of innovation. The empirical findings testify that external demands and restrictions, as well as the professional cultures of project partners with their specific values and meanings, internalized approaches, skills, and knowledge are not perceived as a threat but rather as an enrichment (see Imrie and Street 2014; Till 2013). The continuous oscillation between preserving and reducing cognitive distance can facilitate "a liberalisation, or opening up, of practice, in ways whereby opportunities for creative engagement may be enhanced" (Imrie and Street 2014, p. 733). Architects and engineers expand their scope of actions and possibilities to tackle challenges in a creative and project-specific manner. As a result, built environment professionals develop a new, shared understanding of innovation that considers both the outcomes in aesthetic terms and the act of materialization. This potentially allows also for shifting the regulatory boundaries of standards and norms. This new and joint understanding of innovation is central for bridging the gap between the two distinct professional cultures.

Furthermore, our contribution has revealed that professional cultures are not only and not even primarily pre-determined and explained through academic socialization, as is usually emphasized (see Cuff 1991). In particular, in the context of large-scale projects, professional cultures are dynamic, evolving, and exposed to continuous influences as the project unfolds. The empirical analysis has shown how professionals consciously shift disciplinary boundaries, "invade" the domain of project partners, acquire and develop new skills and knowledge, and assume the tasks and responsibilities of others. At the same time, architects and engineers seek to understand in detail the requirements and arguments voiced by project partners, and the challenges and restrictions encountered by others. Such in-depth understanding facilitates a re-thinking of one's own professional culture and a willingness to translate external demands and restrictions into new values and meanings. As a result, evolving professional cultures bridge the gap between aesthetic and technical requirements, and subsequently between design and construction that have been traditionally and "progressively bifurcated into two elements ..., each with a ... set of professional roles, interests and knowledges" (Sage and Vitry 2018, p. 8). The in-depth analysis of professionals' interactions contributes to a more holistic understanding of construction activities and building projects that is still underrepresented in academic scholarship (Jacobs and Merriman 2011; Lees 2001).

Finally, by revealing how professional cultures change and evolve through project-based collaborative work, our conceptualization of projects as arenas of negotiation and collaboration provides insights into the ongoing transformation of architects' and engineers' professional practice. Recently, the existing interfaces between professionals have been re-shaped, questioned, and newly arranged through the rise of digital tools and software-based working methods (e.g., BIM). Moreover, the tasks and responsibilities of architects and engineers overlap significantly, due to the emergence and growing dominance of large, interdisciplinary firms (Cayer 2019; Grubbauer and Steets 2014) as well as of new criteria for the making of the built environment such as the requirements for sustainability (Fischer and Guy 2009). This raises pertinent questions about the future of both professions and the organization of their collaborative work in the project context and with regard to the facilitation of innovation in the construction industry. The division of tasks and responsibilities between architects and engineers needs to be negotiated contractually in a new manner that answers more adequately to their specific way of project-based collaboration. The exploration of built environment professionals' project-based collaborations thus makes for a vital topic for future investigation.

References

Abbott, A. (1988). *The System of Professions: An Essay on the Division of Expert Labor.* Chicago.

Addis, B. (1994). *The Art of the Structural Engineer.* London.

Alder, K. (1999). "French Engineers Become Professionals, or, How Meritocracy Made Knowledge Objective." W. Clark, J. Golinski, and S. Shaffer, eds. *The Sciences in Enlightened Europe.* Chicago.

Billington, D. P. (2013). *Der Turm und die Brücke. Die neue Kunst des Ingenieurbaus.* Princeton, New Jersey.

Blau, J. (1984). *Architects and Firms: A Sociological Perspective on Architectural Practice.* Cambridge, MA; London.

Bucciarelli, L. (2002). "Between Thought and Object in Engineering Design." *Design Studies* 23: pp. 219–231.

Cayer, A. (2019). "Shaping an Urban Practice." *Journal of Architectural Education* 73.2: pp. 178-192.

Coenders, J. (2007). "Barriers in Computational Structural Design for the Free Form Design of the Future." *Journal of The International Association for Shell and Spatial Structures* 48.4: pp. 51–62.

Cohen, L., A. Wilkinson, J. Arnold, and R. Finn (2005). "'Remember I'm the Bloody Architect!': Architects, Organizations and Discourses of Profession." *Work, Employment and Society* 19.4: pp. 775–796.

Cuff, D. (1991). *Architecture: The Story of Practice.* Cambridge, MA.

Defillippi, R. and M. Arthur (1998). "Paradox in Project-Based Enterprise: The Case of Film Making." *California Management Review* 40.

Downey, G. L. and J. C. Lucena (2005). "National Identities in Multinational Worlds: Engineers and 'Engineering Cultures'." *International Journal of Continuing Engineering Education and Lifelong Learning* 15: pp. 252–260.

Duddeck, H. (2001). "Modelle der Technik—Wie Ingenieure die Realwelt in Entwurfsmodelle umsetzen." *Akademie-Journal* 1.

Evetts, J. (2003). "The Sociological Analysis of Professionalism: Occupational Change in the Modern World." *International Sociology* 18.2: pp. 395–415.

Faulconbridge, J. (2010). "Global Architects: Learning and Innovation Through Communities and Constellations of Practice." *Environment and Planning A* 42.12: pp. 2842–2858.

Fischer, J. and S. Guy (2009). "Re-Interpreting Regulations: Architects as Inter-
mediaries for Low-Carbon Buildings." *Urban Studies* 46.12: pp. 2577–2594.

Flury, A., ed.(2011). *Kooperation: Zur Zusammenarbeit von Ingenieur und Architekt.*
Basel.

Gann, D. M. and A. J. Salter (2000). "Innovation in Project-Based, Service-Enhanced
Firms: The Construction of Complex Products and Systems." *Research Policy* 29.7:
pp. 955–972.

Grabher, G. (2004). "Learning in Projects, Remembering in Networks?: Communality,
Sociality, and Connectivity in Project Ecologies." *European Urban and Regional
Studies* 11.2: pp. 103–123.

Grey, C. (1994). "Career as a Project of the Self and Labour Process Discipline." *Sociology* 28.2: pp. 479–497.

Grubbauer, M. and S. Steets (2014). "The Making of Architects: Knowledge Production
and Legitimation in Education and Professional Practice." *Architectural Theory
Review* 19.1: pp. 4–9.

Gutman, R. (1988). *Architectural Practice: A Critical View.* New York.

Gutman, R. (1992). "Architects and Power: The Natural Market for Architecture."
Progressive Architecture 73.12: pp. 39–41.

Harty, C. (2005). "Innovation in Construction: A Sociology of Technology Approach."
Building Research & Information 33.6: pp. 512–522.

Henderson, K. (1999). *On Line and on Paper—Visual Representations, Visual Culture,
and Computer Graphics in Design Engineering.* Cambridge, MA.

Hossdorf, H. (2003). *Das Erlebnis Ingenieur zu sein.* Basel.

Imrie, R. and E. Street (2014). "Autonomy and the Socialisation of Architects." *The
Journal of Architecture* 19.5: pp. 723–739.

Jacobs, J. M. and P. Merriman (2011). "Practising Architectures." *Social & Cultural Geography* 12.3: pp. 211–222.

Jones, P. (2011). *The Sociology of Architecture: Constructing Identities.* Liverpool.

Koen, B. V. (2009). "The Engineering Method and Its Implications for Scientific, Philosophical, and Universal Methods." *The Monist* 92.3: pp. 357–386.

Krafczyk, M. (2014). "Risiko und Verantwortung im Kontext modellbasierter Analyse
und Prognose von Ingenieursystemen." L. Hieber and H.-U. Kammeyer, eds. (2014)
Verantwortung von Ingenieurinnen und Ingenieuren. Wiesbaden.

Kreiner, K. (2020). "Pick the Winner, so You Can Then Choose the Reasons: Epistemic
Dissonance in Architectural Competitions." D. Stark, ed. *The Performance Complex: Competition and Competitions in Social Life.* Oxford.

Langer, S. C. and J.-U. Böhrnsen (2014). "Innovationsschübe und die Verantwortung
der Lehrenden in den Ingenieurwissenschaften." L. Hieber and H.-U. Kammeyer,
eds. *Verantwortung von Ingenieurinnen und Ingenieuren.* Wiesbaden.

Larson, M. S. (1979). *The Rise of Professionalism: A Sociological Analysis.* Berkeley;
Los Angeles; London.

Lees, L. (2001). "Towards a Critical Geography of Architecture: The Case of an Ersatz
Colosseum." *Ecumene* 8.1: pp. 51–86.

Lenfle, S. and J. Söderlund (2018). "Large-Scale Innovative Projects as Temporary
Trading Zones: Toward an Interlanguage Theory." *Organization Studies* 40.11:
pp. 1713–1739.

Lindkvist, L. (2004). "Governing Project-Based Firms: Promoting Market-Like Processes
within Hierarchies." *Journal of Management and Governance* 8.1: pp. 3–25.

Lundin, R. A. and A. Söderholm (1995). "A Theory of the Temporary Organization."
Scandinavian Journal of Management 11.4: pp. 437–455.

McNeill, D. (2005). "In Search of the Global Architect: The Case of Norman Foster (and
partners)." *International Journal of Urban and Regional Research* 29.3: pp. 501–515.

Nooteboom, B. (2000). "Learning by Interaction: Absorptive Capacity, Cognitive Distance and Governance." *Journal of Management and Governance* 4.1: pp. 69–92.

Petroski, H. (2012). *An Engineer's Alphabet: Gleanings from the Softer Side of a Profession.* Cambridge.

Pinnington, A. and T. Morris (2002). "Transforming the Architect: Ownership Form and Archetype Change." *Organization Studies* 23.2: pp. 189–210.

Rice, P. (1996). *An Engineer Imagines.* London.

Sage, D. (2013). "'Danger Building Site—Keep Out!?': A Critical Agenda for Geographical Engagement with Contemporary Construction Industries." *Social & Cultural Geography* 14.2: pp. 168–191.

Sage, D. and C. Vitry (2018). "Introduction: Societies under Construction." Sage, D. and C. Vitry, eds. *Societies under Construction: Geographies, Sociologies and Histories of Building.* Cham.

Schlaich, J., T. Fackler, M. Weißbach, V. Schmitt, C. Ommert, S. Marx, and L. Krontal (2008). *Leitfaden Gestalten von Eisenbahnbrücken.* n.p.

Schön, D. (1983). *The Reflective Practitioner: How Professionals Think in Action.* New York.

Schulz, E. D. (2010). *55 Gründe Ingenieur zu werden.* Hamburg.

Slay, H. S. and D. A. Smith (2010). "Professional Identity Construction: Using Narrative to Understand the Negotiation of Professional and Stigmatized Cultural Identities." *Human Relations* 64.1: pp. 85–107.

Stevens, G. (1998). *The Favored Circle: The Social Foundations of Architectural Distinction.* Cambridge, MA.

Swan, J., H. Scarbrough, and S. Newell (2010). "Why Don't (or Do) Organizations Learn from Projects?" *Management Learning* 41.3: pp. 325–344.

Sydow, J., L. Lindkvist, and R. DeFillippi (2004). "Project-Based Organizations, Embeddedness and Repositories of Knowledge: Editorial." *Organization Studies* 25.9: pp. 1475–1489.

Till, J. (2013). *Architecture Depends.* Cambridge, MA.

Wenger, E. (1999). *Communities of Practice: Learning, Meaning, and Identity.* Cambridge.

Yaneva, A. (2005). "Scaling Up and Down: Extraction Trials in Architectural Design." *Social Studies of Science* 35.6: pp. 867–894.

Interacting In and Out of the Box. A Knowledge-Sociological Perspective

Silke Steets

Based on the variations between the very different professional cultures and respective sub-worlds into which architects and engineers are socialized through their education and the inevitable demands of collaboration in large-scale construction projects, Dimitrova et al. (in this volume) ask what potential such differences might have for innovation. Among their most interesting findings is the insight that unconventional and creative solutions to building problems are rarely the work of ingenious architects or engineers. Rather, as their analysis shows, innovations emerge in the interactive in-between zone of *interdisciplinary communicative action*. The aim of my reflections is to take a closer sociological look at this phenomenon and try to explain it.

The sociology of knowledge perspective on experts and professions provides some initial clues. This research strand has long been concerned with how expert knowledge is acquired, how experts apply their knowledge and, not least, how they legitimize the relevance of their knowledge for society (Schnell and Pfadenhauer 2018). Theoretical considerations on the emergence of innovations, however, reach back to Philosophical Anthropology. Arnold Gehlen (2004), for example, interprets the invention of tools as a practical confrontation of wo/man with the challenges of her/his material environment, which—and this is key—presupposes an *experimental*, even *playful* attitude towards the material world. Presumably, the invention of cutting tools is a consequence of the basic human need to solve the problem of cutting. However, he argues, in order to be able to invent a knife, wo/man must detach her/himself from this primary need and first develop an abstract idea of *cutting as an action*. Oriented to this idea, it is then possible—in a process of trial-and-error—to create a tool with which the abstract action of cutting can actually be performed. Applying the work of Alfred Schutz (1945), one can explain the emergence of innovations in action in a very similar way. According to Schutz, our actions in the everyday are guided by the pragmatic interest in solving the problems of this everyday world. However, greater innovations in action only occur when our primary needs are temporarily put to one side and humans emigrate to other temporally limited worlds of meaning, which Schutz (1945) calls "finite provinces of meanings." One of these "provinces of meaning" is fantasy. In fantasy, wo/man can develop ideas playfully and thus freed from the constraints of the everyday, which then in turn guide action in the everyday world as "phantasms," that is, as vague, abstract, and perhaps even crazy ideas. Schutz sees a constant source of innovation in these mechanisms.

Gehlen's and Schutz's models provide excellent explanations of how the creative activities of designing (architects) or solving technical problems (engineers) require—at least temporarily—an experimental, or playful attitude towards the building task, one that is removed from everyday life. In their analysis, Dimitrova et al. observe that both professions—architects as well as engineers—at times try to preserve "cognitive distances" between *their* very solution of building problems and the solution of the respective *other* discipline. But why do innovations in large-scale building projects emerge precisely in the interdisciplinary in-between of communicative actions? To get closer to an explanation, it is worth looking at the sociological extension of Gehlen's and Schutz's models in Peter L. Berger and Thomas Luckmann's (1967) formulation of the "new sociology of knowledge."

The most relevant further development of Berger and Luckmann lies in linking Schutz's idea of the "finite provinces of meaning" as specific cognitive styles of understanding the world with the social differentiation of modern societies. Accordingly, modern societies can be divided into distinguishable "sub-worlds" (Berger and Luckmann 1967, p. 158), each representing a definite sector of knowledge from which its members develop a sector-specific perspective on the world. To take an example: "The chiropractor has a different angle on society than the medical school professor, the poet than the business man, the Jew than the Gentile, and so on" (Berger and Luckmann 1967, p. 103). Sub-worlds of meaning can owe their origin to different social criteria—such as age, gender, class, religious orientation, or even profession—but they are always "carried" by a social group "that ongoingly produces the meanings in question and within which these meanings have objective reality" (Berger and Luckmann 1967). Such a sub-world consists of specific institutions, roles, and forms of knowledge. Dana Cuff (1991), in her famous study *Architecture: The Story of Practice*, has described the contours of the architects' sub-world in impressive detail. It is built on the certainty of a clear role structure (experts vs. laymen, teachers vs. students, architects vs. clients), it consists of institutionalized rituals that have socializing functions (studio, crit, charette) or mark status passages (graduation, admission to the chamber, founding of an office), and it is based on a very specific knowledge—a knowledge about how to handle things and solve problems *as an architect*, but also about which social conditions determine one's own architectural practice. Moreover, Cuff has shown how a student grows into this architectural sub-world. In addition to gaining explicit expert knowledge, the acquisition of habitual, customary, or routine practices plays a key role in the respective education. According to Cuff, these routinely performed activities form a "culture of practice."

It is highly likely that both the knowledge and the habitual practices and routines that constitute expert cultures are changeable and expandable. Nevertheless, the question arises as to how communication *between* different expert cultures is possible at all, when the sub-worlds in modern differentiated societies tend to clearly demarcate themselves from one another in order to emphasize their independence and social relevance. So how are communicative connections made in interdisciplinary projects? According to the study by Dimitrova et al., the first prerequisite is the definition of a common problem or task to be solved *together*, in this case the realization of a complex large-scale building project. It is interesting to note that the project implies an inherent organizational logic, which, for example, has a temporal structure that generates a certain sequence of actions. That is, one cannot build the roof before the basement. This temporality in turn helps to organize the work in its sequences—the project thus becomes an "arena" in which different disciplines must coordinate their different strategies. This coordination then works through a permanent negotiation of the respective cognitive styles on the problems to be solved. Throughout the project, a continuous oscillation between strategies of cognitive distancing and strategies of cognitive converting can be observed.

I would like to add another facet to this very convincing interpretation. From my perspective, not only are different cognitive styles or strategies negotiated in this back and forth of architects and engineers; however, it seems to me that in the very dynamics of interdisciplinary *interaction* lies a further potential for the emergence of innovations. To explain this, we need to broaden the knowledge-sociological perspective once again—now in terms of communication theory.

In sociology, there have been numerous approaches dealing with the social effects of communication and interaction. Georg Simmel (1983) certainly marks the starting point with his concept of "Wechselwirkungen" (interactions). For Simmel "Wechselwirkungen" are the reciprocal modes of orientation of individuals to one another, which can solidify in forms as diverse as competition, gratitude, faithfulness, or sociability. Interestingly, these interactions can give rise to something that transcends their concrete manifestation. Competition, for example, not only leads to an antagonistic contest between competitors for a scarce good; but it can also result in innovations that add value to *society as a whole*. In his most recent communication-based extension of the sociology of knowledge, Hubert Knoblauch (2020) focuses on the idea, already present in Simmel, of a relationally conceived social. Instead of starting from a static relation between ego and world (as Gehlen and Schutz did), he aims to develop a processual concept of communicative action in order to view wo/man's being in the world as based on social relations. As human beings, we have always been interconnected—and, thanks to our bodies, their sensuality and performance in action, these relations can make sense even beyond the use of signs or language. Moreover, these relations are not ontological objects, but are constructed processually through what Knoblauch calls communicative action: for Knoblauch, communicative action is the temporally and spatially performed process by which social reality is constructed. The relationality of communicative action is due to what he calls "reciprocity," which, in turn, is inherent in the bodily performance, affectivity, and sensual experience pertaining between at least two subjects. By virtue of bodily performance, the relation of communicative action between two subjects is, in fact, triadic. By a triadic relation he means that the reciprocity between the two subjects always implies the mutual reference to a (mediating) third—be it the spoken and heard word, the joint execution of the mutual gaze, or a material object onto which a shared interest is directed. This third—which Knoblauch identifies with what Berger and Luckmann (1967) call "objectivation"—is integrated into the relationship by virtue of its reciprocal orientation, attention, and bodily performativity. Due to the body's materiality and its sensuality, it constitutes the basis for the materiality of communicative action. The ways "objectivations" affect subjects' bodies may be unspecific, unclear, or implicit, but nevertheless make sense in a very sensual way.

It is interesting to note that some important facets of the social can be derived from this basic model, which—for the sake of simplicity—I would like to illustrate briefly using the example of the passing game in soccer (cf. Steets 2019). First, in soccer the passing game is based on the ability to assume the roles of others, i.e., to develop an idea of what the other player can do with the ball where I pass it; second, it presupposes a concatenation of motives—I play the ball *in order to* get it to a teammate, s/he accepts the ball because I played it—and third, a soccer player must be able to mirror her/himself in the behavior of others, i.e., be able to read her/his own game from the teammate's point of view. All three dimensions—role taking, motive chaining, and mirroring—are assumed not to be innate subject abilities, but to be formed only through repeated participation in communicative actions.

The "give and go passing game" between architects and engineers in large-scale building projects can be understood in a very similar way. It is true that they act—similar to soccer players, who as goalkeepers, midfielders or strikers bring different skills and perspectives to the game—against the backdrop of their respective professional expert knowledge and their different social position in the game. However, like players on a soccer field, they pursue a common goal: the realization of a complex construction project. And their communicative actions, i.e., mutual interactive references to one another, also lead to an interweaving of perspectives, roles and motives for action—and thus, as a rule, to the ability both to view the project as a whole and to reflect on one's own role within the project context. Similar to soccer players, however, architects and engineers engaged in large-scale building projects must also learn how to deal with and respond to the sometimes unruly practices and idiosyncrasies of their counterparts. Here the construction project functions as the mediating third, an "objectivation," through which the context of action is constituted as an arena. New things emerge in the in-between of interdisciplinary communicative action.

In summary, it seems to me that what promotes innovation is not only a *thinking* in and out of the box, as emphasized in the analysis of Dimitrova et al., but rather, too, an *interacting* in and out of the box. Further research should therefore take a closer look at the very interactions of designing, shaping and negotiating building tasks.

References

Berger, P. L. and T. Luckmann (1967). *The Social Construction of Reality: A Treatise in the Sociology of Knowledge.* London.

Cuff, D. (1991). *Architecture: The Story of Practice.* Cambridge, MA; London.

Gehlen, A. (2004). *Urmensch und Spätkultur.* Gesamtausgabe. Band 5. Frankfurt am Main.

Knoblauch, H. (2020). *The Communicative Construction of Reality.* London; New York.

Schnell, C. and M. Pfadenhauer, eds. (2018). *Handbuch Professionssoziologie.* Wiesbaden.

Schutz, A. (1945). "On Multiple Realities." *Philosophy and Phenonenological Research* 5.4: pp. 533–576.

Simmel, G. (1983). *Schriften zur Soziologie. Eine Auswahl.* Herausgegeben und eingeleitet von Hans-Jürgen Dahme und Otthein Rammstedt. Frankfurt/ Main.

Steets, S. (2019). "Doppelpass." B. Schnettler, R. Tuma, D. vom Lehn, et al., eds. *Kleines Al(e)phabet des Kommunikativen Konstruktivismus.* Wiesbaden.

Yesterday's Tomorrows. The Demolition of City-Hof

Hagen Stier

"The City-Hof is situated close to the Central Station as entrance to the lofty "Kontorhäuser". It contains a three-storey cellar with parking for 400 cars, and petrol pumps, with above a two-storey shopping arcade consisting of 33,300 sq. feet ground area. In the four multi-storeyed buildings there are 233,000 sq. feet available for offices. Reinforced concrete skeleton with visible supports at ground floor level, and above faced with pale "Leca" tiles. Windows of simple design framed with russet-coloured wood. Escalator, numerous service and public lifts. Pressurization plant and transformer. The multi-storeyed buildings of the City-Hof stand 100 feet apart, are 140 feet high and have side wings of 130 and 40 feet respectively" (Grantz 1957, p. 131–32).

What sounds like the laconic wording of a real estate description in fact originates from the pen of Max Grantz, author of the book "Hamburg baut" (English translation from the book's appendix). Published by Hoffmann und Campe in 1957, the small volume contains an impressive cross-section of Hamburg's post war modernist architecture, which had just recently been completed or was yet to be built. Today it belongs into each architecture student's pocket (where it will fit easily due to its size).

The City-Hof ensemble erected by the architect Rudolf Klophaus between 1954 and 1956 comprised the first high-rise office buildings to be built in Hamburg after the end of World War II. Vast parts of the city still lay in ruins and those four shiny high-risers with the contrasting backdrop of Kontorhausviertel's dark red brick facades must have made quite an impact on the inhabitants of Hamburg as well as on visitors arriving by train. With their light ceramic façade tiles they symbolized hope for a bright future.

Little of that promising appearance was left when I first came across Max Grantz's book and developed a growing interest in the City-Hof. The whole ensemble had been covered with gray fibre cement board and those russet-colored wooden window frames had appropriately been exchanged for white plastic.

What remained was the significant and yet very precise urbanistic placement of the four "towers" that in fact acted very much as an entrance or gate, as described by Grantz. Following the shape of the old Johannisbastion (hence the name of the street, Johanniswall) as well as stepping down the natural topography of the river Elbe's "Geestkante," City-Hof was interwoven with the urban fabric of the city in many ways.

After a long and hard-fought battle over the future of the landmarked City-Hof high-risers, they were finally torn down in 2019. The innovative "Leca" tiles described by Grantz had been used as a lost formwork during the building process and therefore had been well preserved underneath the fibre cement cladding all along. For a short period of time the original façade reappeared during the regrettable process of demolition.

The state of partial dismantlement illustrates two things: City-Hof's bright past as well as the potential of a careful restoration as preferred by many.

Reference

Grantz, M. (1957). *Hamburg baut*. Hamburg.

Hagen Stier | Yesterday's Tomorrows. The Demolition of City-Hof

205

Hagen Stier | Yesterday's Tomorrows. The Demolition of City-Hof

207

Hagen Stier | Yesterday's Tomorrows. The Demolition of City-Hof

211

Hagen Stier | Yesterday's Tomorrows. The Demolition of City-Hof

213

Synthesis

How Large-Scale Projects Drive Innovation in the Construction Industry: Concluding Remarks

Joachim Thiel/Venetsiya Dimitrova/
Johanna Ruge

We started our joint research venture, on which this volume builds, with four sub-teams and from four different starting points based on what each sub-team had done in previous research: exploring construction projects as large temporary organizations embedded in longer-term relational contexts (Grabher and Thiel 2015); examining the role of users in innovation processes (e.g., Skiba and Herstatt 2009); looking into knowledge production in (transnational) architectural practice (e.g., Faulconbridge and Grubbauer 2015); or engaging with the materiality of built structures (e.g., Bögle and Garlock 2015). The idea was that the different lenses through which team members looked at construction innovation would provide insights into the crucial determinants of the industry's innovative activity: its project-based nature; the important role of clients or project-owners; the importance of design professions as creators of the built form; the material and technical properties of the actual building. The research team as a whole sought thereby to gain a comprehensive understanding of how innovation processes in construction occur and what effect large-scale ventures have on these processes.

At the end of a three-and-a-half years' thorough conceptual and empirical engagement with large-scale construction projects and innovation, this book has exposed where this journey, that started from different points of departure, provisionally ends. The insights into the six large-scale construction projects showcased here suggest that the idea of starting from different angles has proved extremely fruitful. The multiplicity of aspects that we have scrutinized alone shows how productive the juxtaposition of our different lenses has been. However, when it comes to the substance of the outcome—i.e., to the answer to what the conditions and forces in effect are that drive innovations within large-scale construction projects— the initial tetrad of project, client, designers, and building appears too coarse grained and to focus too little on the interrelated nature of the four starting points in order to structure our findings. We found practices interacting with "cultural frames" (Rammert 2001); ambivalent geographies and temporalities; decisions made at early stages of the project cycle; different facets of materiality; negotiations among antagonistic professional cultures: all those aspects, it seems, shape innovation processes that run through large-scale construction projects. Our findings, hence, corroborate recent pleas for "multiple perspectives" (Orstavik et al. 2015) on innovation in the construction industry instead of identifying specific elements (e.g., drivers or constraints) that are related to innovation activity.

In this concluding chapter, we nevertheless seek to highlight three themes that, we believe, cross-cut the variety of approaches and aspects that the chapters in the core part of this book reveal: (1) the interrelation (and tension) between the breadth of contextual conditions that frame construction projects and innovative activities, on the one hand, and the narrowness of detailed practices and material conditions that make up the actual innovation process, on the other; (2) the role and function of materiality in innovation; (3) the role of paradoxes and tensions in construction projects. These three themes, we would argue, not only exemplify central mechanisms in construction innovation. They also offer points of departure for answering the initial question of our entire venture: how large-scale projects may drive innovations in the construction industry.

Breadth and Narrowness: Large-Scale Projects as Bridges between Context and Detail
We conceived the interrelation between a broad approach to defining innovation and a narrow one to analyzing innovation processes as a programmatic thread of our research. The "analytical space" that unfolds between these poles would allow for multiple perspectives on construction innovation (see Thiel on framing innovation). A comprehensive view of the findings, however, reveals that this space is not only an analytical tool: innovation processes related to construction projects and buildings oscillate between a broad—e.g., relational, temporal, discursive, institutional, geographic—context, and small details: "a diverse range of more-or-less elaborate, human and non-human, processes: discourses, for example, everyday routines, condensation, conversation" (Rose et al. 2010, p. 3).

Engaging with the first pole, i.e., the context-relatedness of learning, knowledge creation, and innovation, has meanwhile become a commonplace in project management research, as is touched upon several times throughout this book (e.g., Engwall 2003; Grabher 2004; Stjerne and Svejenova 2016; Sydow et al. 2004). Also, recent work on innovation in construction emphasizes the "embedded nature" (Havenvid Ingemansson et al. 2019) of innovation activities in construction. The contexts that we have revealed in our findings go beyond the inter-organizational and relational make-up of construction projects. The chapters emphasize discursive and institutional contexts, for instance, that afford sources of legitimizing deviations from routines and provide criteria for assigning added value to novelty (Thiel et al.); they reveal the role of technological change as a contextual variable (Thiel and Grabher); and they highlight the extension of the geographical context out of which knowledge and capabilities can be mobilized (Dreher et al.), cultures of involved professions that shape identities and modes of collaboration and interaction (Dimitrova et al.), as well as how the formulation of the initial task impacts motivation, scope of action, and innovative capacities (Fahnenmüller et al.).

Concomitantly, our findings also point to the seemingly small, yet invaluable steps out of which innovation journeys are made (not only) in construction: for instance, small decisions about how to solve problems that unusual ideas have triggered (Thiel et al.); immediate reactions to problems that surface on the construction site (Thiel and Grabher; Dreher et al.); an intensive engagement with material details (Ruge and Bögle; Dreher et al.; Thiel et al.). Further, Zimmermann's photo series on the pedestrian and cycle bridge in Lyon has a strong focus on mundane practices and the people behind them. These instances chime well with recent work that points out the "hiddenness" (Sage 2017, p. 657) of the material and the practical in organization research, namely the disregard for practical solution-seeking related to material and other problems, and of those individuals who are responsible for solutions (but somehow "speechless," as noted by Duddeck and Mittelstraß (1999) and taken up by Ruge and Bögle). This narrow perspective on the specific professional practices and everyday interactions of different professionals in the project context therefore provides a more differentiated understanding of who makes innovations—shedding light on invisible professionals (e.g., engineers), who are seldom acknowledged in the public realm and, compared to others, less influential in the shaping of discourses (see Dimitrova et al.).

However, our findings show not only that both the broad context and the narrow detail matter for innovation processes. Large projects, it seems, play a mediating or bridging role between these two poles. Large-scale projects allow for an easier mobilization of legitimacy—for instance, from the discursive and institutional environment—or of capabilities—for instance, from far away. The projects then translate mobilized resources into small novel solutions, and enhance the likelihood of these novelties being recognized and taken up in the industry environment, once they have proved feasible in the respective projects. It would be worthwhile to examine this mobilizing and bridging role of large-scale scale projects in construction more thoroughly in future research.

Materiality: Stretching the Boundaries of Feasibility

It is a truism that materiality matters in construction. From the basic laws of physics, on which depends whether buildings collapse or stay up, to the look and feel of a particular material for the building envelope or interior cladding, construction is an activity that essentially engages with materials and materiality. This inherent materiality is also the motivation for Styhre (2017) to argue that research on construction has the capacity to productively contribute to the recent literature on socio-materiality in organization studies, but also in social science more broadly (e.g., Ewenstein and Whyte 2009; Orlikowski 2007, 2010; Sage and Vitry 2018). Needless to say, that materiality is also part of innovation activities in construction in multiple ways. Whenever the material side of construction is concerned, innovation in construction projects parallels a gradual process of materializing a one-off at a specific site.

Several of the chapters in the core part of the book engage with materiality and materialization: most obviously that by Ruge and Bögle, who work out different dimensions of materiality and propose an important distinction between materiality and feasibility. According to the authors, materials accomplish multiple functions. Across the different chapters one function seems particularly evident: materiality creates incentives and occasions, for instance, to formulate design problems (Fahnenmüller et al.) and to search for solutions by testing and experimenting (Ruge and Bögle; Thiel et al.); to travel (Dreher et al.); to communicate and interact (Ruge and Bögle; Dreher et al.). In addition, Dreher et al. stress the connection between materiality and mobility or immobility, respectively. While in line with recent thinking on the different roles of objects in design and construction, e.g., boundary and epistemic objects (e.g., Ewenstein and Whyte 2007, 2009; Tryggestad et al. 2010), our research has more generally tackled the "materiality" of the entire building and of the processes of materialization. These aspects resonate well with literature that conceives of buildings as "socio-material assemblages" (e.g., Guggenheim 2013). Moreover, our approach to materiality includes dimensions—e.g., "material knowledge" (Ruge and Bögle), scale, local boundedness—that have hitherto largely been ignored.

More importantly with regard to the initial question of this project, however, the notion of "feasibility" seems to provide an entry point into how large-scale projects affect innovations related to materiality. Large and ambitious ventures stretch "the boundaries of feasibility" (Ruge and Bögle), by, for instance, initiating engagement with the different dimensions of materiality; creating problems that have to be solved; requesting a broader search space for solutions; activating a solution-oriented mindset. That large-scale projects tend to challenge extant material boundaries of construction and thereby trigger processes of solving previously unknown problems is certainly one important aspect of how these projects may contribute to innovations.

Paradoxes and Tensions: Negotiating Beyond Trade-Offs

All the chapters in the empirical core of this book placed some sort of contradictory aspects center stage that characterized the large-scale projects examined here. Most explicitly, Thiel and Grabher's emphasis on temporal ambiguities shows how large-scale ventures simultaneously incorporate paradox temporal logics (of both a temporary and a permanent organization). Actors involved in large projects are compelled to negotiate between such paradox logics. In the other chapters, paradoxes and tensions exist between the inertia of cultural frames and the will and capacity to change them (Thiel et al.); between distance and proximity or mobility and immobility (Dreher et al.); between strategic problems and design problems as well as early problem formulations and late solution-seeking (Fahnenmüller et al.); between the rigidity of physical restriction and the possibility of stretching boundaries (Ruge and Bögle); between cognitive distance and cognitive proximity in terms of disciplines and professions (Dimitrova et al.).

In the conclusion to their recent collection of chapters on construction innovation Havenvid Ingemansson et al. (2019, p. 285) suggest a "paradox perspective", as a "fruitful lens to further investigate the tensions and contradictions of innovation in construction. ... The central idea is that by addressing such conflicting forces, structures or goals as co-existing and co-evolving, new understandings and theories of why things are as they are and why they may or may not change could materialise." Our discovery of multiple contradictory forces inherent in planning and implementing large-scale buildings, and of the need (and capacity) of involved actors to negotiate contradictions, corroborates such a paradox approach. However, we feel that we have moved on one step further. Emphasizing contradictions, it seems, not only helps understand why things are as they are; it also offers a clue for understanding how innovations come about and how large-scale projects contribute to the emergence of innovation. In a sense, the evidence presented in our six empirical chapters suggests that negotiating between contradictory aspects can also be a source of innovation as it both widens the repertoire of options and forces a search for alternatives (e.g., Stark 2009). In short, large-scale projects impose collaboration across organizational and professional boundaries and at the same time enable professionals to cross these rigid boundaries (Dimitrova et al.; Fahnenmüller et al.). Large-scale construction projects, hence, shape a very specific context that—given its complexity—nurtures contradictory forces and, at the same time, facilitates negotiating contradictions by helping involved actors deal with paradoxes and tensions. In this context, the projects' size and complexity offer an additional, albeit crucial asset. They allow for dealing with contradictory aspects without running into "trade-offs" (Thiel and Grabher)—thereby opening avenues to translate contradictions into productive (and innovative) solutions.

Epilogue

The four sub-teams with which we started our research venture not only represented four different disciplinary backgrounds and perspectives on a joint subject of research. The composition of four sub-projects was overarched by a more fundamental split between the different academic cultures of social science and architecture and engineering research. In her short chapter on the interdisciplinary nature of this research project in the conceptual and methodological part of the book, Grubbauer uses the distinction between reflection-oriented and solution-oriented disciplines to label this basic division.

The empirical results presented in the book's core and the cross-cutting themes outlined in this concluding section confirm that our research primarily followed a reflection-oriented approach. Our work was essentially designed as a social science research program, based on the respective literature and systematically employing a methodological apparatus of social science. However, this program was undertaken collaboratively by social scientists as well as architectural and engineering scholars, who additionally brought in their expertise and therefore rendered empirical results far more robust than they would have been in a monodisciplinary setting. In a sense, through this collaboration we were able to accomplish the ambition of contributing to the literature on socio-materiality in the productive fashion that, among others, Styhre (2017) formulated. We have, too, been able to develop more comprehensive and cross-sectoral understandings of both large-scale construction projects and innovation in construction, but also of how these two are intertwined—by probing into the role of large-scale projects as drivers of innovation generation and innovation diffusion in the construction industry. In future research on construction innovation, a valuable exercise would be to reverse the roles, with an emphasis on solution-orientation that benefits from the reflection-oriented focus of social scientists.

References

Bögle, A. and M. Garlock (2015). "Efficiency + Economy." C. Schittich, ed. *SOM Structural Engineering*. München.
Duddeck, H. and J. Mittelstraß. (1999). *Die Sprachlosigkeit der Ingenieure*. Opladen.

Engwall, M. (2003). "No Project Is an Island: Linking Projects to History and Context." *Research Policy* 32.5: pp. 789–808.

Ewenstein, B. and J. K. Whyte (2007). "Visual Representations as 'Artefacts of Knowing'." *Building Research & Information* 35.1: pp. 81–89.

Ewenstein, B. and J. K. Whyte (2009). "Knowledge Practices in Design: The Role of Visual Representations as 'Epistemic Objects'." *Organization Studies* 30.1: pp. 7–30.

Faulconbridge, J. and M. Grubbauer (2015). "Transnational Building Practices: Knowledge Mobility and the Inescapable Market." *Global Networks* 15.3: pp. 275–287.

Grabher, G. (2004). "Temporary Architectures of Learning: Knowledge Governance in Project Ecologies." *Organization Studies* 25.9: pp. 1491–1514.

Grabher, G. and J. Thiel (2015). "Projects, People, Professions: Trajectories of Learning through a Mega-Event (the London 2012 Case)." *Geoforum* 65: pp. 328–337.

Guggenheim, M. (2013). "Unifying and Decomposing Building Types: How to Analyze the Change of Use of Sacred Buildings." *Qualitative Sociology* 36.4: pp. 445–464.

Havenvid Ingemansson, M., Å. Linné, L. E. Bygballe, and C. Harty (2019). "Tracing the Connectivity of Innovation in Construction Across Time and Space." M. I. Havenvid, Å. Linné, L. E. Bygballe, and C. Harty, eds. *The Connectivity of Innovation in the Construction Industry.* London.

Orlikowski, W. J. (2007). "Sociomaterial Practices: Exploring Technology at Work." *Organization Studies* 28.9: pp. 1435–1448.

Orlikowski, W. J. (2010). "The Sociomateriality of Organisational Life: Considering Technology in Management Research." *Cambridge Journal of Economics* 34.1: pp. 125–141.

Orstavik, F., A. Dainty, and C. Abbott (2015). "Introduction." F. Orstavik, A. Dainty, and C. Abbott, eds. *Construction Innovation.* Chichester.

Rammert, W. (2001). "The Cultural Shaping of Technologies and the Politics of Technodiversity." K. Sörensen and R. Williams, eds. Shaping Technology, *Guiding Policy.* Cheltenham.

Rose, G., M. Degen, and B. Basdas (2010). "More on 'Big Things': Building Events and Feelings." *Transactions of the Institute of British Geographers* 35.3: pp. 334–349.

Sage, D. (2017). "Thinking with Materialities in Construction Management: A Response to Alexander Styhre." *Construction Management and Economics* 35.11–12: pp. 657–662.

Sage, D. and C. Vitry, eds. (2018). *Societies under Construction. Geographies, Sociologies and Histories of Building.* Cham.

Skiba, F. and C. Herstatt (2009). "Users as Sources for Radical Service Innovations: Opportunities from Collaboration with Service Lead Users." *International Journal of Services, Technology and Management* 12.3: pp. 317–337.

Stark, D. (2009). *The Sense of Dissonance. Accounts of Worth in Economic Life.* Princeton; Oxford.

Stjerne, I. S. and S. Svejenova (2016). "Connecting Temporary and Permanent Organizing: Tensions and Boundary Work in Sequential Film Projects." *Organization Studies* 37.12: pp. 1771–1792.

Styhre, A. (2017). "Thinking about Materiality: The Value of a Construction Management and Engineering View." *Construction Management and Economics* 35.1–2: pp. 35–44.

Sydow, J., L. Lindkvist, and R. DeFillippi (2004). "Project-Based Organizations, Embeddedness and Repositories of Knowledge: Editorial." *Organization Studies* 25.9: pp. 1475–1489.

Tryggestad, K., S. Georg, and T. Hernes (2010). "Constructing Buildings and Design Ambitions." *Construction Management and Economics* 28.6: pp. 695–705.

Contributors

Authors

Annette Bögle is professor of structural design and analysis at the HafenCity University of Hamburg (HCU). Her research focuses on lightweight structures, approaches of conceptional design, and methods of designing in structural engineering. She has curated several exhibitions, is a member of international associations, and sits on competition juries.

Maude Brunet is assistant professor at HEC Montréal (Canada) and associate editor of the *International Journal of Project Management*. Her research interests focus on the governance and innovation of megaprojects and public-private partnerships. She has published in several project management and administrative science journals. Maude has fifteen years' experience in project management, including working as a consultant, researcher, and lecturer.

Patrick Cohendet is professor at HEC Montréal in the International Business Department. His research interests include theory of the firm, economics of innovation, economics of knowledge, economics of creativity, and knowledge management. He is co-director of the research group Mosaic at HEC Montréal on the management of innovation and creativity, and co-editor of the academic journal *Management International*.

Venetsiya Dimitrova is a research associate and doctoral student at the research unit History and Theory of the City at HCU. She has a background in architecture, and planning and environmental research. In her research, she focuses on the internationalization of architectural professional practice and knowledge transfer in the construction industry, dealing more specifically with the role and responsibilities of project architects in renowned architectural firms. Her doctoral work has been awarded a scholarship by ProExzellenzia.

Johannes Dreher has worked since 2017 as research associate in the Constructing Innovation project at HCU. Prior to this, he was research associate for the Chair of Urban Development at the Technical University of Munich (TUM), where he was part of an interdisciplinary research project funded by the German Research Foundation (DFG), titled "Star Architecture and its Role in Re-Positioning Small and Medium Sized Cities." Johannes holds a degree in geography from the Goethe-University Frankfurt and has worked as a research analyst at CBRE GmbH in Frankfurt.

Lennart Fahnenmüller is a senior consultant in an accountancy firm in the field of transportation with a specific focus on the passenger rail industry. During the project, he was a research fellow at the Institute for Technology and Innovation Management at Hamburg University of Technology, focusing on the pathway from problem to solution in interdisciplinary contexts.

Gernot Grabher is head of the research unit for urban and regional economics at HCU. Previously he held positions at the Wissenschaftszentrum Berlin (WZB), King's College London, and the University of Bonn, amongst other institutions. Currently he is conducting research on the emerging platform economy, the new experimentalism in urban governance, and the role of uncertainty in creative processes. He has written extensively on project organizations and their embeddedness in wider project ecologies in particular.

Monika Grubbauer is professor of History and Theory of the City at HCU. She is interested in the interdependencies between economic, social, and material processes of urban change. Monika publishes on urban transformation and socio-economic restructuring in different geographical contexts, with particular focus on the role of architecture, planning, and construction.

Heike Klussmann is artist and professor at the Institute of Architecture at the University of Kassel. She heads the transdisciplinary research platform BAU KUNST ERFINDEN that is dedicated to the research and development of new materials at the convergence of art, architecture, and new technologies. She has taught and conducted research at numerous institutions including the Art Center College of Design, Pasadena (USA), and Monash University, Melbourne (Australia).

Steffen Marx is endowed professor of civil engineering at the Technische Universität Dresden. His main research area is bridge design, especially the design and construction technology of high-speed railway bridges. He is founder and partner of Marx Krontal Partner, a consulting company which is mainly active in bridge design. Prior to his appointment as professor, Steffen worked on major projects of Deutsche Bahn for many years.

Werner Rammert has been professor of sociology (faculty Planen-Bauen-Umwelt) at the TU Berlin since 1999, and since 1991 at the Free University Berlin. He is a pioneer of science, technology, and innovation studies who earned his Dr. rer. soc. at Bielefeld University. He has held research positions at the Northwestern University, SOFI Göttingen, TU Vienna, ZiF Bielefeld, and Stanford. He headed the interdisciplinary "Center of Technology and Society" and initiated the DFG Research Programs "Socionics" and "Innovation Society Today."

Johanna Ruge studied structural engineering at the KIT in Karlsruhe and is currently a research associate and doctoral student at HCU. Situated at the interface between design studies and philosophy of engineering, her research focuses on the role and potential of model-use as a method in epistemological design processes and interdisciplinary collaborations. Her work has been awarded the Young Engineers Outstanding Contribution Prize by the IABSE Association, as well as a doctoral scholarship by the Studienstiftung des Deutschen Volkes.

Jonas Söderlund is a professor of strategy at Linköping University, Sweden, and professor II at BI Norwegian Business School. He is presently conducting research on knowledge integration, temporality, and project-based organizing. His work has been published in journals such as *Organization Studies, Research Policy, Management Learning*, and *Human Relations*.

Silke Steets is professor of sociology at FAU Erlangen-Nürnberg. Her research interests include social theory as well as the fields of space, popular culture, religion, contemporary art, materiality, and the city. In her book *Der sinnhafte Aufbau der gebauten Welt* (Suhrkamp, 2015), she develops a knowledge-sociological theory of architecture, which extends Peter L. Berger and Thomas Luckmann's *The Social Construction of Reality* to the built world.

Joachim Thiel is senior lecturer and postdoctoral researcher in urban and regional economics at HCU. He is currently undertaking research on innovation processes in large-scale construction projects and on the governance of smart cities. Prior to his current post, Joachim worked for four years as head of the strategic development unit in the presidential office of HCU.

Photographers

Hagen Stier studied architecture at the University of Fine Arts in Hamburg. Parallel to his work as an architect, he began teaching himself architectural photography early on and has also worked as a commissioned photographer for more than fifteen years. Along with documentations for architectural firms, galleries, and museums, he has developed free artistic photo series that have been both exhibited and published in the specialist press. Hagen Stier lived and worked in New York and Stockholm for several years, before returning to Hamburg where he lives and works as an architect and architectural photographer.

Michael Zimmermann is a structural engineer and photographer. After completing his studies at the University of Stuttgart, he started work at Schlaich Bergermann Partner in 2000. From 2010, he concentrated in particular on their French projects, becoming the managing director of Schlaich Bergermann France in 2015. Michael Zimmermann's passion for photography and his desire to put architecture, engineering buildings, and mainly technical processes into pictures, are a part of every new project. Aside from publications in the field of landscape and architecture photography, his work has been shown at the Pavillon de l'Arsenal, Paris, and the Akademie der Künste, Berlin.